Joshua L. Chamberlian

A LIFE IN LETTERS

In fond memory of NCWM Board Member Jim Scheiner, at whose encouragement this project was undertaken.

Joshua L. Chamberlian

A LIFE IN LETTERS

The
PREVIOUSLY UNPUBLISHED LETTERS
of a GREAT LEADER of the CIVIL WAR

Edited by

THOMAS DESJARDIN

THE NATIONAL
CIVIL WAR
MUSEUM
HARRISBURG, PENNSYLVANIA

First published in Great Britain in 2012 by Osprey Publishing,
Midland House, West Way, Botley, Oxford, OX2 0PH, UK
44-02 23rd Street, Suite 219, Long Island City, NY 11101, USA

E-mail: info@ospreypublishing.com

© 2012 The National Civil War Museum and Thomas Desjardin

Every attempt has been made by the Publisher to secure the appropriate permissions for
material reproduced in this book. If there has been any oversight we will be happy to rectify
the situation and written submission should be made to the Publishers.

The National Civil War Museum and Thomas Desjardin have asserted their right under the
Copyright, Designs and Patents Act, 1988, to be identified as the author of this work.

A CIP catalogue record for this book is available from the British Library.

Print ISBN 978 1 84908 559 5
PDF e-book ISBN 978 1 78096 425 6
EPUB e-book ISBN 978 1 78096 426 3

Page layout by Myriam Bell Design, UK
Index by Mike Parkin
Typeset in Sabon and Magesta Script
Originated by PDQ Media, Bungay, UK
Printed in China through Worldprint Ltd

12 13 14 15 16   10 9 8 7 6 5 4 3 2 1

Osprey Publishing is supporting the Woodland Trust, the UK's leading woodland
conservation charity, by funding the dedication of trees.

www.ospreypublishing.com

Contents

Foreword

With the publication of Michael Shaara's novel *The Killer Angels* in 1975, Joshua Lawrence Chamberlain began his ascent to the stature of a Civil War icon. As colonel of the 20th Maine Volunteer Infantry during the Battle of Gettysburg, Chamberlain commanded the regiment's defense of the left flank of the Army of the Potomac against a determined Confederate attack on Little Round Top during the late afternoon of July 2, 1863. After repelling several spirited Confederate assaults, the 20th Maine ran out of ammunition. One more enemy assault was likely to overrun the position. Undaunted, Chamberlain led a bayonet charge that drove off the attackers and captured many of them. For his courage and leadership, Chamberlain was later awarded the Medal of Honor.

During his three years of service in the Civil War, this former college professor was wounded six times (once almost fatally), had six horses shot under him, was promoted to brevet major general, and commanded the Union detachment that received the official surrender of arms and colors from the Army of Northern Virginia at Appomattox. Until the appearance of *The Killer Angels*, however, only the most dedicated students of the Civil War had heard of Chamberlain. Few visited the 20th Maine monument at Little Round Top, which was hard to find. But all of that began to change after 1975, when author Michael Shaara made Chamberlain one of his main protagonists in *The Killer Angels*. The 20th Maine Monument became one of the most visited sites at Gettysburg National Military Park. Chamberlain's story inspired an interest in the Civil War by documentary filmmaker Ken Burns, whose 1990 television series "The Civil War," which prominently featured Chamberlain, has been viewed by more than 40 million people. The movie and television miniseries "Gettysburg," based on *The Killer Angels*, gave Chamberlain even greater exposure. In the 1990s, a small bronze statuette of Chamberlain, advertised in Civil War magazines, became a best-selling item in the repertory of Civil War generals next only to Robert E. Lee. Several biographies of Chamberlain have appeared in the past thirty years.

Chamberlain is an appealing hero. Although thirty-three years old and married with two children, he left his professorship at Bowdoin College to enlist in the Union army in the summer of 1862. He explained that decision to his beloved wife Fannie in a letter included in this volume. "There are things worth more than life and peace," he wrote to her. "Nationality—the Law of Liberty, public and private honor are worth far more, and if the Rebels think they are fighting for all that men hold dear, as I suppose some of them really think they are, we are fighting for more, we fight for all the *guaranties* of what men should love, for the *protection* and *permanence* and *peace* of what is most dear and sacred to every true heart. That is what I am fighting for at any rate, and I could not live or die in a better cause."

After he had almost died for this cause, shot through both hips leading his brigade at Petersburg on June 18, 1864, he came back for more, even though he had not fully recovered from that wound. When he returned to his brigade at the end of the year, his mother tried to persuade him to change his mind. "Surely you have done & suffered & won laurels enough in this war," she pleaded. He replied that "I am not scared or hurt enough yet to be willing to face the rear when other men are marching to the front." To return was the only course "which honor and manliness prompt." Surviving another potentially serious wound at White Oak Road on March 31, 1865, he fought through the rest of the campaign to Appomattox.

Elected overwhelmingly to four consecutive terms as governor of Maine after the war, Chamberlain then returned to Bowdoin as its president. Despite constant pain and debility from his Petersburg wound, he lived to help plan the fiftieth anniversary commemoration of the Battle of Gettysburg in 1913 and died the following year at the age of eighty-five.

The letters in the first half of this volume cover the years from 1849 to the outbreak of the Civil War, during which Chamberlain was a student at Bowdoin and at Bangor Theological Seminary, and then an instructor and professor at Bowdoin. They are mainly love letters between Lawrence and Fannie (Frances Caroline Adams), whom Chamberlain married in 1855. Several important war letters occupy the second section of the volume, followed by many letters to Chamberlain in 1880 when, as commander of the state militia, he skillfully mediated a potentially ugly armed conflict over a disputed state election.

The originals of all but three of the letters are housed at the National Civil War Museum in Harrisburg, Pennsylvania. They have never before been published or cited by historians or biographers. They provide important new information and insights on Chamberlain of great value to historians of the Civil War era. Their publication is especially welcome during these years of commemoration of the Civil War sesquicentennial. We owe a debt of gratitude to The National Civil War Museum for making them available in this format and to Tom Desjardin for his skillful editing of the collection.

—James McPherson
Autumn 2011

Introduction

The National Civil War Museum is pleased to bring this wealth of material out of its secure home in the Archive stacks and offer it for the edification of Chamberlain enthusiasts, Civil War buffs, and scholars worldwide. It is our belief that this unique collection of letters and documents will provide new insights into one of the Civil War's most compelling historical figures. In addition, it is our hope that it will help spark enthusiasm in a new generation for the unlimited lessons the American Civil War and its complex cast of characters can teach us.

About the Chamberlain Collection

The bulk of the Chamberlain Collection came to the Museum by way of artist Don Troiani, who had acquired it from descendants of the Chamberlain family. Although Joshua Chamberlain has no living direct descendants, his papers and personal items have been donated to various collections by descendants of his sister Sarah (fondly known as "Sae") and by other indirect heirs. Several other Chamberlain documents were collected by the Museum from various sources. All together, the collection totals more than 250 letters, documents, and artifacts directly related to Joshua Lawrence Chamberlain. Although it primarily consists of his personal correspondence with his wife Fannie from before the Civil War through his years as governor of Maine after the war, it also includes his commission to major general of the Maine State Militia, telegrams, official correspondence, and *cartes de visite* of Chamberlain's family members and fellow officers. The artifacts in the collection are comprised of Chamberlain's top hat and hat box from his time as governor and a small baseball bat made of wood from an apple tree at Appomattox.

The letters that appear in this book are unedited, and as such are full of the original quirks of spelling, punctuation, and language of the writers. Chamberlain is referred to as "JLC" in many of the letters.

About the Collection As a Whole

The Museum's holdings include artifacts and documents relating to many significant historical figures as well as the common soldier. Various aspects of this time period also are well represented, such as music, medicine, slavery, agriculture, clothing, weapons, and equipment. In total, the Museum cares for more than 24,000 archival items and 4,000 artifacts, a third of which are currently on display in the galleries. The collection continues to grow thanks to donations from Civil War descendants across the country seeking a safe repository for their family's treasures.

About the Museum

The National Civil War Museum opened in 2001 with a mission of telling the complete story of this most troubled chapter in American history, without bias to North or South. The Museum seeks to present information through a humanistic perspective, focusing on the individuals involved in this conflict and the lives that were affected. Exhibits investigate the causes and ramifications of this war that divided a nation, while presenting both Northern and Southern viewpoints and highlighting military as well as civilian perspectives.

The Museum is an independent 501(c)3 nonprofit organization dedicated to education and preservation of the Civil War, its causes and effects. At 65,000 square feet, The National Civil War Museum is the largest museum in the United States to cover the Civil War in its entirety, telling a story of national importance and international interest. Each year the Museum hosts approximately one hundred educational offerings to visitors of all ages, including living history encampments throughout the summer, lectures, hands-on activities, performances, book signings, and a Civil War Adventure camp. In addition to the visitors and school groups who tour every day, the Museum is dramatically growing its outreach efforts with educational information available on the Internet and through virtual presentations made to schools across the country.

INTRODUCTION

About Harrisburg

The question often has been asked why a national museum dedicated to the Civil War is located in Harrisburg, Pennsylvania. A benefit of this seemingly random choice is that because it is not connected to a specific battlefield or event, the Museum is able to approach the topic with a broad and even-handed perspective. Although Harrisburg does not come to mind as a pivotal city in the conflict, Harrisburg did play a significant role during the Civil War. With four major railroads intersecting this capital city and home to Camp Curtin, the largest mustering camp in the North, Harrisburg served as a major rail hub for men and materials, acting as a lifeline for the Union. The northernmost skirmish of the war was located just across the river at nearby Sporting Hill. Harrisburg was twice the target of invasion by the Confederate Army of Northern Virginia. In 1862, when General Robert E. Lee explained his invasion plans to General John G. Walker, he placed his finger at Harrisburg, Pennsylvania, and said, "That is the objective point of the campaign." In 1863, General Richard Ewell received orders from Lee stating that "Your progress and direction will of course depend on development of circumstances. If Harrisburg comes within your means, capture it." Both attempts to capture the city were turned back, first at Sharpsburg, Maryland, in September 1862 and finally at Gettysburg, Pennsylvania, in July 1863. Lee recalled his scattered army just as the northernmost element near Harrisburg was preparing to take the city. At the end of the war, Harrisburg was the site of a national event. Men of the United States Colored Troops, who had been denied the privilege of marching in a Grand Review in Washington, D.C., were invited to have their own review on the streets of Pennsylvania's capital city.

It is only fitting that a city so crucial to the war effort has become a national center for understanding the culture and history of the American Civil War through the collections and galleries at The National Civil War Museum.

—Janice Mullin
Museum Director
The National Civil War Museum

Dramatis Personae

Ashur and Amelia Adams—Fannie's birth parents, who lived in Boston and Roxbury, Massachusetts. When Fannie was four years old, they sent her to live with and be raised by Ashur's nephew, George.

Charlotte Adams—Fannie's older sister and the only sister who shared the same birth parents. Charlotte was raised by these birth parents in Boston while Fannie was raised in Brunswick, Maine.

Frances Caroline Adams—"Fannie" to all who knew her, she was sent at age four to live with a nephew of her birth father. As a result, she was raised as the Congregational minister's daughter in Brunswick, Maine. She met Lawrence while playing the organ in the church choir when he was a student.

George Adams—A graduate of Bowdoin College and the Bangor Theological Seminary, Reverend Adams was the minister at the Brunswick Congregational Church throughout his adult life. In 1829, his uncle's young daughter Fannie came to live with him. He later adopted another daughter, Anna.

Helen Root Adams—Reverend Adams's third wife. Just six months older than Fannie, her arrival in January 1852 cast the entire family into turmoil.

Sara Ann Folsom Adams—The second wife of Reverend Adams and the woman Fannie considered her mother. Her death in 1850 created great tumult in the Adams household.

4

Grace Dupee "Daisy" Chamberlain (Allen)—Fannie's and Joshua's oldest child. Grace had three daughters, their only grandchildren.

Hannah Chamberlain (Smiley, Keene)—"Cousin Annie," as she was known, was the daughter of Joshua's uncle, Jefferson. She and Joshua had an intimate relationship while he was a student at the Bangor Theological Seminary.

Harold Wyllys Chamberlain—Fannie's and Joshua's oldest child. He did not marry or have children.

Horace, Tom, and John Chamberlain—Lawrence's three brothers. Horace (or "Hod") followed Lawrence to Bowdoin, and John did as well, to both Bowdoin and the Bangor Theological Seminary. Horace became a lawyer in Bangor, Maine, married, and died of tuberculosis in 1861. John married, became a teacher in Castine, Maine, and died also of tuberculosis in 1867. Tom served throughout the Civil War with his oldest brother but became an alcoholic afterward. He married John's widow, failed in his postwar business ventures, and died in 1896.

Joshua L. Chamberlain, Jr. and Sara Dupee Brastow Chamberlain—Parents of Joshua Chamberlain, they lived in Brewer, Maine, for most of their lives.

Joshua Lawrence Chamberlain—Born Lawrence Chamberlain, he added "Joshua" as his first name while in college in deference to his mother. His family continued to refer to him as "Lawrence" for the remainder of his life.

Sarah Brastow Chamberlain (Farrington)—The only sister of the Chamberlain siblings, "Sae," as she was called, was the anchor of the family, sending and receiving frequent letters to and from her brothers.

Anna Davis—An adopted daughter of Reverend and Sara Adams and granddaughter of a Bowdoin Medical School faculty member. She married Amos Atkinson in 1855.

Deborah G. Folsom—Known to the Chamberlains as "Cousin Deb," she was the sister of Sara Ann Folsom Adams and effectively an aunt or older sister to Fannie. The Chamberlain children called her "Aunty."

Timeline

1828 (September 8) Lawrence Joshua Chamberlain was born.

1848 Chamberlain enrolled at Bowdoin College.

1850 (February) Fannie's stepmother Sara Ann Folsom Adams died.

1851 (March 2) During an antislavery sermon preached by the Rev. George
E. Adams, Harriet Beecher Stowe envisioned the plot of a novel
depicting the cruelty of slavery. She rushed home after church and
scribbled down all that she had pictured. (JLC likely was present.)

Joshua met Fannie in the church choir (she played the organ).

Fannie's stepfather George Adams married for a third time (to Helen
Root).

1852 (April–June) Fannie went to New York to study music.

(September 1) Chamberlain graduated from Bowdoin College during
the semicentennial of the opening of the college.

1853 (January) Fannie moved to Milledgeville, Georgia.

1854 Fannie's mother Amelia Adams died.

1855 Fannie's sister Charlotte died.

(December 7) Fannie and Joshua were married.

1856 (October 16) Fannie gave birth to Grace Dupee "Daisy" Chamberlain.

1857 (November 19) Fannie gave birth to a boy three months prematurely.
He died shortly afterward.

1859 Fannie gave birth to Harold Wyllys Chamberlain.

John Chamberlain graduated from Bowdoin.

(May 11) Horace Chamberlain married Mary Ann Wheeler.

1860 (May) Fannie gave birth to Emily Stelle "Mary" Chamberlain.

Fannie's brother George Adams died.

(June) Fannie's father Ashur Adams died.

(September 23) Emily Stelle "Mary" Chamberlain died.

TIMELINE

1861 (December 7) Horace Chamberlain died.

1862 (August) 20th Maine Infantry Regiment formed; JLC appointed lieutenant colonel of the regiment after declining the colonelcy.

(September) The Battle of Antietam

(December) The Battle of Fredericksburg

1863 (May) The Battle of Chancellorsville

(July) The Battle of Gettysburg

1864 (June 18) JLC was badly wounded leading a charge in battle at Petersburg.

1865 (January 16) Fannie gave birth to Gertrude Loraine Chamberlain.

(August 15) Gertrude Loraine Chamberlain died.

(March) Battles of Quaker Road/White Oak Road

(April) The Battle of Five Forks

(April) Surrender at Appomattox

1866 (September 10) John Chamberlain married Delia Jarvis.

(September) Chamberlain was elected governor of Maine by largest margin ever.

"Cousin Deb" Folsom died.

1867 (July 14) Sarah Chamberlain married Charles Farrington.

(August 10) John Chamberlain died.

1870 (December 14) Tom Chamberlain married John's widow Delia Jarvis.

1878 Chamberlain appointed by President Hayes as a U.S. Commissioner to the Universal Exposition in Paris.

1880 (January) The Great Countout Crisis

(August 10) Chamberlain's father died.

1881 Daisy married Horace Gwynn Allen.

1888 (November 5) Chamberlain's mother died.

1893 (December 13) Daisy's daughter Eleanor Allen (JLC's first grandchild) was born.

1896 (August 11) Tom Chamberlain died.

(January 24) Daisy's daughter Beatrice Allen was born.

1898 (December 26) Daisy's daughter Rosamond Allen was born.

1900 Delia Jarvis Chamberlain, John's and Tom's widow, died.

1905 (October 28) Fannie died.

1914 (February 24) Chamberlain died.

CHAPTER ONE

The Early Years

Bangor, Maine, in the early half of the nineteenth century was a bustling and constantly changing place in the world. In the first five or six decades after the American Revolution, it became what was described as "the lumber capital of the world." Tall, straight pine trees from the state's still-virgin inland forests could be brought there on the waters of the Penobscot River and then placed aboard ships along the waterfront or tied in huge bundles under tow behind them for exportation to virtually any port in the world. As the population of the country grew at a rapid pace, the need for sawn lumber grew with it, and dozens of sawmills along the Penobscot rumbled to meet the demand.

Growing up along the banks of the Penobscot, in Bangor or on the eastern shore in Brewer, this thriving international commerce must have provided a world of wonders for a young boy. On any given day, he might watch the poor Irish laborers, driven from their homeland by famine, trying to make a living doing harsh work at the behest of wealthy ship owners and captains who, in a voyage or two, not only could recoup the cost of their ship, but see sights of which a young Maine boy had only dreamed. On returning, both classes of men would bring food, household goods, and, most of all, stories from places as far away as a young imagination could travel.

It was into the midst of this vibrant community in early September 1828, that Joshua L. Chamberlain, Jr., and his wife Sarah brought the first of what

---

1   During his college years, Chamberlain reversed his first and middle names to become Joshua Lawrence Chamberlain. Genealogically, this made him "J. L. Chamberlain, III" but he never used the "third" as part of his name. Despite the change, his family continued to call him "Lawrence," though today he most often is referred to as "Joshua."

would become five children. They named him Lawrence Joshua Chamberlain[1] with the middle for his father and grandfather and the first for Commodore James Lawrence, whose words "don't give up the ship" were remembered in the American navy long after the 1813 naval battle in which he spoke them.

In due course, the Chamberlains provided four siblings for their eldest son: Horace or "Hod" in 1834, Sarah or "Sae," in 1836, John in 1838, and Tom in 1841. The children grew up in a home very much like that of most older New England families, under the guidance of a strong, often strict father and a warm, loving mother. As Congregationalists, the Chamberlain family adhered to a more conservative Christian view that had descended from the Puritans.

Chamberlain's father worked in the timber industry, managing log harvests in order to supplement the resources of the family farm. As a boy, Chamberlain did his share of chores, including haying, planting, wood splitting, and other farm work, and then spent his free time playing in the woods or along the banks of the Penobscot. At various times, when work allowed, the family might enjoy a hiking or sailing adventure.

Among the more formative elements of his childhood, beyond the experiences within his family and community, was a great difficulty that plagued Lawrence into adulthood. In an autobiography written much later in life, he described a particular malady, which he called "One of the miseries of his life." It was a speech impediment that caused him to stammer when trying to speak words that began with the letters p, b, or t. "It was," he later remembered, "at times impossible to get off a word beginning with one of those letters." This was a problem that greatly imposed on his youth and, he later surmised, affected his whole life and character.

As a young boy he was able, more often than not, to overcome the problem when he taught himself a breathing pattern put in action when the letters approached, and he would "sing" his way past them. "But in truth," he remembered,

> "The sleepless anxiety on this score was a serious wear upon the nervous system. It was not much short of agonizing ... This positive disability added to a natural timidity of self-assertion, apt to disclose itself on untimely occasions in that stupidity called bashfulness, had a decided effect on habits both of speech and action, which placed one at a serious disadvantage."

Growing up bashful, timid, and stammering hardly limited him, however. By the time he had grown into a young man, Chamberlain decided that he should attend college. The nearest was Bowdoin College in Brunswick, more than a hundred miles down the Maine coast. Bowdoin was a well-respected institution that counted among its graduates the likes of Nathaniel Hawthorne and Henry Wadsworth Longfellow. To be admitted, however, Chamberlain first had to learn a great deal in order to meet the college's strict entrance requirements. With a persistence that would serve him well in later years, he spent each day studying, from 5:00 a.m. to 10:00 p.m., secluded in the family attic. His only break from the rigorous schedule came when he walked more than a mile over to Bangor to recite his lessons with a local teacher, and then back home to the attic for more study.

In the tumultuous year of 1848, when revolutions rocked much of Europe, Chamberlain entered Bowdoin College as a freshman. During the next four years, the young scholar found himself exposed to myriad new experiences. The rigorous college curriculum in those days involved the study of classics, rhetoric, and theology. Students were required to read and recite numerous foreign languages, and, despite his speech impediment, Chamberlain mastered them all with great effort.

Among his most memorable experiences at Bowdoin must have been a handful of "Saturday Evenings" spent at the home of one of his professors, Dr. Calvin Ellis Stowe, near the campus. Professor Stowe enjoyed having his students over for less formal discussions outside the classroom and on one particular evening announced a special surprise. The professor's wife, Harriet Beecher Stowe, entertained the students by reading a story that she had been writing about slavery in Kentucky. She called it "Life Among the Lowly," and read it in installments to the students during these gatherings. Little did her polite young listeners know at the time that the quaint little story she read aloud and discussed with the students would soon become one of the bestselling books of all time under its new name: *Uncle Tom's Cabin.*

Bowdoin offered a fairly common classical curriculum that included subjects such as rhetoric, philosophy, numerous foreign languages, religion, and literature. As part of his studies, Chamberlain wrote numerous essays while at Bowdoin, including "The Monomaniac," "The Pope," "Despotisms of Modern Europe," "Easter Morning," and "A Chair."

Chamberlain Essay, 9/11/1849

Theme Sophomore
No 10
J. L. Chamberlain

The Monomaniac

It was at an early period in my professional career, that I was called to attend a person with whom I had previously had some acquaintance. The call was a very urgent one, and as the nature of the disease was not stated, I went prepared to relieve her suffering in any form. On entering the house I was immediately conducted to the room of my patient, whose disease from the silent alarm which pervaded the house, I began to consider dangerous. As the door was gently opened and I threw a hasty glance within, judge of my astonishment when my eyes fell on the person of my friend mounted on a table before a mirror, examining very attentively the most prominent part of his physiognomy. Expecting a scene of a totally different nature, I could not fervent a considerable relaxation of the muscles around my mouth. As soon as he became aware of my proximity, he leaped down and grasping my hand, said in an earnest tone "Doctor look at my nose! Don't you see the trouble?" I assured him that I saw nothing at all remarkable in its appearance. "Nothing? said he— Why don't you see that it's glass?" "Hear this!" And he commenced thumping that organ very carefully and precisely. "There! Don't you hear it ring? I tell you my nose is glass!" It was in vain that I tried to reason with him on the probability of the case. He always silenced me with that incontestable proof—the ringing. Besides he affirmed that he could see through it, and asked me how far, its transparency allowed me to look into his head. I brought up the case of a man who once believed that he had a cast-iron nose. My friend ridiculed the idea. "Nonsense!" said he— "A man with a cast-iron nose? Why it is impossible! How could he fasten it on?" And he brought up various arguments to prove the absurdity of the thing. Whenever he could be persuaded to speak of other subjects, he was perfectly reasonable; but his mind was employed on one topic only. His glass nose was a lens which brought all his ideas to a focus between his eyes, and he could see nothing else. He was evidently a monomaniac. Suddenly assuming an air of confidential mysteriousness he discovered to me an article of the most extraordinary appearance. I was at a loss as to

11

to its purpose, but whispered he with a look which enjoined secrecy, "there! I have to put that on my nose when I eat or go out of the room; for if I should break it, what would become of me?" Do you suppose you can do anything for me?" Seeing that he was offended because I did not recognize his misfortune, I thought it best to agree with him, and made the remark "I see through it." "I see through it?" echoed he—"so do I. But can you cure it?" An idea came into my head, and I answered, "I can, if you will submit to an operation somewhat disagreeable." "O yes!" said he, and we appointed a day. Bidding him be careful, I left. The plan I had adopted was to assent to all his ridiculous fancies, and by a mere farce, relieve his mind from the goblin that haunted it. On the day appointed, having prepared an array of the most formidable instruments, I called on my patient. I found him on his bed in all the pallor and stiffness of death. There was however one life-like feature. That place on his countenance usually occupied by a nose, was not surmounted by a bag of cotton of still more remarkable dimensions. It was labeled "this side up with care," and outside of all, was a wooden frame fitted to his nasal appendage in such a manner as to prevent the approach of anything within some ten inches. Such a proboscis was never to be seen in all the nasal creation. It resembles a dromedary in a cage. As I surveyed this strange scene dumb with astonishment, his eye caught mine in a look of the most unutterable agony. I could endure no longer. Dropping at once my surgical instruments, and the dignity of a physician, I sunk to the floor in convulsions of laughter. My roars aroused the sufferer. The upper half of his body slowly assumed an erect position—the nose-cage dropped off, and he surveyed me with a stare of mingled anger and surprise. "Doctor, said he, I am a dead man." His solemnity was intolerable. However regaining my self possession, I tried to assure him that in a half hour he should be a well man. While he was preparing for the operation, his accident was related to me. Last before my arrival, in attempting to cross the room, his foot caught in the carpet and he was precipitated on to his most delicate frontispiece—the nose and the cotton bag were thrust down his throat. All attempts to revive him were fruitless; at least in his own opinion. He affirmed that he was a dead man, and requested to be laid on the bed in the shape in which I had found him. It is needless to describe the operation. Suffice it to say that persuading him that I was in solemn earnest, I achieved a cure the most wonderfully by the parade of my instruments and taking a little blood from the diseased organ. His recovery was more rapid than even the progress of his disease and he now assures me that the glass nose was a solemn reality; and that my skill had restored it—an idea which will probably never relinquish.

May 11th 1849
J. L. Chamberlain

The subject of this writing was probably suggested by reading the story of the "Turned Head" and the "Diary of a late Physician"; but the fact that I read that, ten years ago will save me from the charge of plagiarism.

Chamberlain Essay, "Despotisms of Modern Europe," 3/3/1852
Four years after monarchies across Europe put down attempts to liberalize their governments in 1848, the "Year of Revolutions," the issue of human rights and democracy were still prevalent among political thinkers. This is evident in this essay from Chamberlain's senior year at Bowdoin.

The Despotisms of Modern Europe
In this day of enlarged benevolence and enlightened policy, we might hope to see no more of despotisms. We might hope that Europe had already lain long enough under the scourge we might hope that the time had come when insulting burdens should be taken off from men's shoulders and souls.

But it is not difficult to see that, although the diffusion of intelligence had brought men to understand and assert their rights, the tendency of things is to greater concentration of power, and the aim and course of those who are at present in authority is to absolutism. Instead of being the representative of the nation, in trusted with its obligations, and invested with its rights, the sovereign becomes the oppressor. The people have no voice, privilege after privilege is taken way—burden is laid upon burden. It is a principle of despotism to crush every free expression, to obstruct every ray of light and truth, to impede the advance of science and of art; and in fact to oppose every thing which can raise the subjects of their tyranny in the sale of intelligence and morality, for it is, no doubt, a truth in nature, that in proportion as men are enlightened they desire to be free: but it is not true that the same proportion they deserve to be free. We hold that every man who has not violated the laws of nature is fit to be free. We hear it said now and then even in this land that for Europe in its present condition absolute monarchies are just the thing. But what has brought Europe to its present condition? If it was, in the days of the old republics, capable of supporting and enjoying free forms of government, and now in these latter years of monarchy has lost its birth right what but monarchy itself has thus laid it low? What else but that absolutism that feeds on the life of its subjects, tends to keep it down? And because it is fallen shall it not rise? Are right and wrong, then, transient and relative, or are they independent and immutable? If despotism has brought Europe to this when will despotism make it better able and worthy to be free? If absolute monarchy is the ultimate perfection of human government, then there is something strangely absurd in man's nature. But we believe that if men were born to be free, despotism is not the right school to fit them to enjoy so great a blessing. We believe that Europe is worthy to be free now—that if the fetters which have bound her, and the burden which as crushed her, be at once taken off she may take her appropriate station in the progress of light and liberty over the world.

March 3rd 1852
J. L. Chamberlain

Chamberlain Essay, "A Chair" (nd)
The purpose of this essay is unclear. If written as a class assignment, it appears too romantic. If it was written as a romantic gesture, then it seems not romantic enough.

If anything could tempt a restless (and roving) spirit to repose it would indeed be so sweet and graceful an allurement as you were pleased to send me with your love. It is not always that one has two such delightful ideas so beautifully blended as <u>rest and love</u>; for I suppose the very idea of love is care—a care which never slumbers yet you never would grow weary of it or seems to wake me. And one does not often get so delicate a symbol of these two blessed blended things as your fairy chair rocked by love. A chair 2 yr love! How suggestive! You would have me, I fondly think, rest in spirit in that chair which unseen angels spirit would have me in it far away though the dreary pain to the blessed hands that sealed and send it all in love and to the beautiful home of those fingers etc. fingers that fashioned it or indeed you would have me imagine that your love so gracious offered was sitting in that chair beside me fondly musing and wishing it had but a visible hand or human tongue to soothe and comfort me. A chair! How (needful) and how universal! In the glowing hours of joy, or in the heavy night of gloom and anguish how welcome a chair! All over the world you need it—if you are alone—or if the dearest are also the nearest, you need it too. I may say too how endearing and endeared we love a chair because the dear form that has vanished from the earth once used to sit in it—because it is hallowed by many a smile and kiss a tear and many a prayer breathed over it. We love it because they have loved it only a love has passed into the heavens! Would be that they—she that gone and she that sent—were only see how dear in and beautiful a they was that fairy chair. Oh and be that they where hands that wonder came were bending over me smiling to see how dear a thin was that fairy chair.

Chamberlain Essay, "Easter Morning" (nd)

Easter morning.

It is the Easter morning. Why this joy? Why these flowers? We come into our sacred places,—into our Houses of Worship—to give special thanks; — as if something as come for us, —Which in itself means morning; we duplicate our words; put together things drawn from far, into one glad consummation.

This word Easter is not a Bible word; —the word there used is Pascha, a Hebrew word, meaning a passing over, as in sparing mercy. So this is associated with the memory of the passing by of the angel of death, the smiting of the first-born. But in the association of this with the offices of Christ in the minds of his followers, a new meaning seems to have been given; and in conveying this to our minds our translators render this word "pascha", in the one time it stood for this meaning, by our English Easter. The word is a survival of the old mythology of the German races, of which our Anglo-Saxon speech hold many a remembrance, —the goddess Easter being the divinity of Spring, and festivities appropriate to that season being held in the month of April. It does not appear that the early Christians observed a sad festival at this season, but the idea of Christ at the Paschal lamb, led to the association of the Passover with his worship. But our festival also connects itself with the world-wide thought of the "east" as the bringer of light out of darkness, the triumph of life over death, as shown in the legends and myths of all peoples capable of spiritual thought, or even of thoughtful observation of the vicissitudes of nature and of man. The changes of night and day, the waxing and waning of the moon, the long passage of the sun through its tropic journey,—the reign of darkness and suspended life,—all symbolized the deep experiences of man. The earth passing through its seasons of darkness and death, then with the returning sun coming forth in newness, and brightness, testified to a continuity of life, — showing that it was not overcome of death, but that it overcame death. This was the ground of deep-born myths, — simple, trusting faiths,—celebrating in festivals their central thought; and it was natural that the revelation of Christ should fasten on these in this consummate illustration, this sublime evidence, that there is also a continuity of life for the soul,—passing also through its darkness and sorrow, but to come forth again in newness of life, under God's smile. So let no one think slightingly of this Easter custom as being "drawn from" or allied to, old heathen customs; for these speak the cry of the great human soul.

To us this Easter means also something coming out of the east,—from the gates of the dawn. It means the light that rose for men when our lord, being in his sojourn here a man also,—rose from the grave,—so proving that he was the Lord, having power over that darkest power of death, and revealing to man that he too, had a belonging, a dignity, a deathlessness, only tremblingly dreamed before.

Why was this so precious a truth,—the fact that Christ rose from the dead,—that the Apostle Paul makes it the very ground-work of the Christian evidences, the great theme of his preaching, the dearest thought to which he clung?

There are two aspects of the one answer, I think, which warrant this conclusion. 1st. That this proved Christ's divinity, by his triumph over death. 2nd. That it proved also the divinity of man,—the strong nature within him capable of lifting the material to some higher sphere, and in its yet rarer workings asserting its likeness and title to the divine. Surely here is cause for rejoicing,—reason for our worship of the returning dawn.

That Christ died for man is one great truth; that so he made the supreme self-renunciation, which if apprehended and applied by man, helps him to gain the mastery for the good over the evil in him,—of the spiritual over the sensual life, and attain the guerdon, or boon, of forgiveness and salvation. His dying for man, however, I look upon as most real in the self-renunciation of his life, more than in the physical fact of his death on the cross. In this way, other, too, have died for man. More clearly so, more distinctly effectual for this end, more agonizing in mere physical suffering,—this dying for others such as I have seen, and such as the nobility of manhood has shown all through human history, in self-denial and sacrifice for others' sake, in the struggle and martyrdom for the "deliverance from evil".

How can such mere dying of the body "take away the sins of the world"? It was the dying in his life,—the killing out of the evil among the possibilities of our nature, (Meaning by this "evil" the desire and power to hurt what is divine in the creation,) this dying which holds us so strongly and strangely to the earth, for the sake of something which is our true living; this renunciation and triumph which our Savior showed in his life, up to the supreme earthly testimony of "obedience unto death" this, which by it's example, it's deep spiritual power to touch our hearts, to clarify our minds and consciences, to "possess" our souls; — that is what, if we follow him, saves us from our sins.

We should think this the one great truth.

But now this Easter morning,—what does it commemorate? What does it bring of joy? The resurrection, we say, and immortality. Christ's rising from the dead,—the reanimation of his body, to live forty days more; to walk in phantasmal form such that his dearest friends, walking with him to Emmaus did not know him; passing over long spaces and throw locked doors, like a bream of lightning; then suddenly vanishing away in a bright ethereal cloud. What kind of resurrection of the body was that? And what proof of immortality was that? If that was the same body, it was much transformed. some new notion of identity must be accepted, if this is the immortality of the body which is thus foreshown. Is it immortality that this material body shall be reabsorbed into the invisible, impalpable, imponderable ether? This all may be, for aught we can prove: and this may be foreshadowed by the resurrection and ascension, so strange, so beyond experience and comprehension. Or did it typify in humble form a far, august, diviner truth,—that we hold in our nature even her, an image of God which is not laid down in the grave, which dwelling within our bodies rules and masters them during life, if not perverted and betrayed by evil will,—and which Christ shows can master them even in death; can lift out of the grave, and put in motion again while it will; that this risen body is the

17

inner body still animating the visible one for littler longer just to show to those who could not otherwise understand, that there is a spiritual body; a body dwelling within this, sometimes transfiguring it for a supreme moment; capable of rising out of it, and of raising it up for a brief space; and for a demonstration of a sphere of earthly possibilities whose laws are little known; capable of preserving its identity through passages of existence of which we cannot look from one boundary to another.

I have no difficulty in understanding that things were done in those marvelous days, in the stress of bringing this disclosure to quick consummation, which transcend our ordinary ways and so-called "laws". Call this miracle, if you please, and say, without reason, that "hence it cannot be true": but what is miracle but seeing for a moment through a veil which for ordinary sense and mood hangs thick and dark? Christ rose to show us that death has no power over those like him,—over us, if we are like him. And he showed this in a form which his followers believed to be his own, though somehow sublimed. He means they should so understand it,— that it was his own body, and not another. It was the same, yet not in our ways the same. Some of his nearest, could receive this without coarse, material demonstration. Even as he said to the loved Mary, "Touch me not; for I am not yet ascended", tho' she doubtless had the right to touch him better than the doubting Thomas; but because he would not have her thoughts drawn back earthward by earthly love, but fixed ever upward where he now belonged, and where too, she was going.

This is the beauty of this Easter thought, and of the Christ-though:— that it does not leave our hearts sorrowing for any thing. It touches with a pitying yet loving angel's hand this dearness of the present body to those who love; because it is the mask of the sweeter body, lying close, soon to replace it with identity intensified, glorified. This is that inner body Christ showed to the loving on the mount of transfiguration,—the body seen in great moment by those who draw us to them by heroic action or stirring power of utterance,—seen, too, in the inner revelations of the faces of those we love.

We need not wait for the resurrection. We may walk in this body even here. We may be inwardly transfigured. Light may shine around all the places of the soul. This domino over death can now begin. Mastery over evil, over darkness, over pain, over loneliness and sorrow,—this Easter morning,—this Christ-smile,—these earthly flowers breathing tones wafted from all the worlds,—will show us the way.

Chamberlain graduated from Bowdoin in 1852, after what could rightfully be called a successful college career. During his college years, he had won several awards in both composition and oratory, despite his challenges with stammering. He was a member of Phi Beta Kappa, the academic honor society, and of Alpha Delta Phi, a fraternity. He also joined the Pecunian Society, a literary society with Federalist leanings. Also during his college years, he would meet a young lady who captured his attention.

CHAPTER TWO

Joshua and Fannie

A mong Chamberlain's many Bowdoin experiences, those that in time
had the greatest impact on his life were the hours he spent conducting
the local church choir, though it was not the music that made the hours
*memorable for him. It was during this time that he first met the pastor's young
adopted daughter, Frances Caroline Adams, a distant cousin of John Quincy
Adams. "Fannie,"[1] as she was called by friends, played the organ for the choir
and in a short time became Chamberlain's first love. As the years passed, their
love grew and talk of marriage became a regularity.*

*Fannie was born in 1825 in Boston to Ashur Adams and his wife Amelia.
At the time of her birth, Ashur was already forty-eight years old while Amelia,
his third wife, was thirty-nine. Fannie was the youngest of six children, and
eight years had passed since the birth of her nearest sibling. For reasons
never entirely made clear, the couple chose to send Fannie to live with Ashur's
nephew, George Adams, then the minister at the Congregational Church in
Brunswick, Maine, and his wife, the former Sara Ann Folsom. While she
stayed in contact with her birth family in Boston, Fannie grew to love her new
"parents" deeply.*

*The Adams household included Mrs. Adams's sister Deborah, with whom
Fannie was very close, calling her "Cousin Deb" throughout her life. Letters
between Fannie and her Boston family indicate that she was happy in
Brunswick and harbored no deep resentment toward her birth parents for
sending her away.*

---

1 In letters, friends and family used both spellings, either "Fannie" or "Fanny."

The remainder of the letters show a growing love affair between Fannie and Lawrence that eventually resulted in their marriage, but not before years of separation strained their bond.

~~~~

Deb and Fannie to Mother and Charlotte, 1/19/1839

January 19th 1839

Dear Mother

I suppose you think I have done very wrong in neglecting to write to you for so long a time, however I will as usual begin with my excuse; I thought by waiting a little while I might have more to say, and you know I dislike to write so much, but I do not know as waiting done much good. I have lately been learning The Captive Knight[2] which father likes very much, and we often sing it together; I have learned several other tunes in the choir. I am not studying much of anything now but Latin and Arithmetic and Spelling; I am trying to get through Smith's arithmetic by spring, and cousin Deborah is to give me a handsome present if I do. I intend to take up French soon, and geography in the spring. I expect Charlotte has got a great way before me in French. I got safely home and am very well indeed, and so are the rest of the folks. I cannot think of anything more to say now, so I will lay by my pen till another time.

Monday evening

I have just finished my Latin lesson for tomorrow so I will write a few lines. Has Mary made many dresses yet? The other day I went into Mrs. Welds to invite Miss Emeline, and Doctor Eugene to drink tea with us; they said they would be happy to come; but cousin Mary said she thought Doctor Eugene would be happier to come if Charlotte had been here, quite a compliment for her. Give my love to dear little Sarah and tell her I am very glad she added something to my letter, I want to see her and all of you very much. We have had a mild winter thus far and but little snow. We have a juvenile antislavery society in this place to which I belong, but I suppose you would

---

2 A song from the poem by Felicia Dorothea Browne Hemans. Officially, "The Captive Knight, the words Mrs. Hemans the Music by her sister, and both respectfully dedicated to Sir Walter Scott." Harriett M. Owen wrote the music.

not be much interested in hearing about that as you are not very zealous in the cause. I wonder if Charlotte would not make a needle book in the shape of a baker, with white peppermints for cakes, for the fair; they are very pretty. Give my love to all, and return good for evil, that is, answer my letter quicker than I answered yours. You see I have complied with your request to write without effort or study, and now as I have told you all the news I bid you good bye. From your affectionate daughter Frances C. Adams.

Postscript: We have had a tremendous freshet here which carried away seven bridges on the Androscoggin, and a number of mills; there was about twenty-five thousand dollars lost in logs in one night by one man. In Hallowell and Augusta the water was so deep in the streets that the people sailed about in boats; and I believe there was a great deal of damage done in New York.

Dear Charlotte, Frances seems to think if I add my might to her labored epistle it will pass off quite respectably—If it were not so long a time since she came I should tell you how glad we were to see her home again how much we thought she had improved etc etc. I have felt desirous to know how you liked her upon better acquaintance—I was very much obliged to you for the worsted they were just what I worked—if there was any opportunity to send from Boston I should invite you to purchase for me another supply. E. Cleveland returned yesterday from Boston who went on two weeks since to pass a few months with her sister, but probably could not endure so long a separation from the Doct. I should think by this time she might think her chance a slim one with him. For those thousand flower seeds you sent me you have a thousand thanks, I think if you will come on next summer I will show you a finer pasture than you saw the last. The fence is moved to this side of the garden which has cut short the promenade of the cow and will keep her from many a dainty bit. You of course thought I had for other [… letter torn …] promise to send you a copy of the mathematical puzzle but I have borne it in mind continually, but when there has been an opportunity to send to your town the book has not been in my possession. I shall add another, to which you must sent me a solution, for it is beyond my powers of riddling and all the nucleus. My best love to Mary and Catherine and all who enquire. All are well and send much love—yours affectionately

D. G. Folsom

Charlotte to Fannie, 1/3/1848
Fannie's sister Charlotte wrote to scold her for not writing often enough and described the family's New Year's celebration.

[Top] Mr. Fish, is engaged! How will the poor man continue to remember his wife's name? You perceive by the date that this is rather old news, but the author having been inflicted with Lyspepsico Influenza, it didn't get sent.

[Side] Ma says "give my love to Fanny, and tell her I feel very anxious about her." I suppose it is because you show such a bad disposition in not coming for us, nor thinking any about us, nor writing to us, nor nothing. You perceive that I have not asked you a single question about your health, or any thing else—so I shall be sure to have them all answered.

Roxbury, Jan 3rd, 1848
Dear Frances,

   No—not dear Frances—I'll take that back.
Frances Adams, you ugly tyke! I was going to wish you a happy New Year, but I won't—I anathematize you.—
   May your hair turn grey,
   And your teeth decay,
   And your nose point up to the sky;
   May you lose all your beauty,
   And Jack Frost pinch your toes,
   And be ever more froze till you die!
      There! What do you think of that?

But don't tremble so—it's only a conditional anathema; if you repent of your delinquencies, and sit down immediately, and write me a good long letter, none of these things that I have spoken, shall come upon you. And now before I proceed any further, I wish to enlighten you, as to your amount of indebtedness, for this communication. I am not writing to you because you deserve such a favor; far from it—but I feel just like writing, to night, and I wouldn't write to any body else in the world, not even a heathen on such a paper as this; these are my reasons, I hope they are satisfactory. You ought to have been here New Years day, to witness the delight of our "olive plants", at the opening of their budgets. Long before "Phosphor brought the dawn", (as Ma would say) we were all duly be-waked, and be-wished; and after responding to their good wishes, went to sleep again, as in duty bound. But soon, peals of laughter and yells of delight, drove sleep from our eyes for that day—I rose and descended to the scene of action—Mary was seated on the floor, laughing, as Mary can laugh, at a ridiculous sugar Santa Claus, seated on a band; Sarah's gift to Mary Kate: to aunt Mary, her chief pet, she gave a little pewter candlestick, about 4 inches high with a brilliant red candle in it. "I thought darling," said Sarah, "That I would give you something useful—and I heard you wishing for some candles the other day, so I bought you one, according to me means." Those stockings! They must have been miraculously enlarged to contain such quantities of "plunder"; books, worsted caps, hair ribbons, gimcracks for the neck, paper, cards, fancy wafers, boxes, "tin", great papers of candy and sugar things, from Aunt Mary, "et cetara, et cetara as our friend Leconte hath it; or had it rather, poor old object!"

But the best of all were the gifts from "Mother". She always makes each of them a new year's present, if she possibly can. Julia unrolled a nice white paper, and a beautiful gold pencil greeted her astonished eyes—a gold pencil! The thing above all others that she most wished to have, but hardly dared hope for, how her little black buttons of eyes glittered with joy! Mary Kate unearthed a "perfect love" of a silver comb! She shook her ambrosia curls and grinned powerfully. But the best fun was to see Sarah: all trembling with excitement, she unrolled paper after paper, till she came to a tiny green box; a very ominous looking little box indeed, with a jeweler's card upon it. She hardly dared open it; but "nothing venture, nothing have"—it wasn't large enough to contain any very terrible wild best—so at length she peeped; and there all hidden in pink cotton, was there very prettiest little gold ring that you ever did see—with a little topaz in it too! "Hurrah! Ooooo! Eeeee! Why mother! Why mother!" shouted Sarah, laughing and jumping and blushing all over. "I didn't expect it, I didn't expect it, mother—and it just fits my finger too; how did you know how big my fingers was? Oh! A good mother you are!" in the bottom of the box was a little note, containing good advice for the new year, and Kate and Julia had each one.

But what most excited my envy (I hope you won't think me greedy as well as envious) were three ponderous bags, larger than that Brunswick mail bag, containing provisions enough to last through the Mexican War. Apples, mints, raisins, grapes, dates, from "Aunt Mary"— she is great on our "creature comfits"! If you had ten of those bags, you would have thought the owners had "much goods laid up for many years". "Aunt Mary" herself had a beautiful bag, from Catherine, and the rest of us came off rather "second best"— however, we abounded in marks, convenient gifts! What quantities are manufactured annually, from the little two inch "remember me" to the gigantic foot and a half, with a figure of David wrought in gold thread, with steel beads for eyes, and the whole 103 Psalm for a motto. Julia worked "Gandpa" a cross and a crown, with the motto "No cross on earth no crown in heaven."

But "uncle George" had a pig!—malicious insinuation! Though Sarah stoutly denied any evil intent in presenting it, she bought it she said, because it was the only thing that suited her exhausted purse, and she thought it might make him laugh! That was all she hoped for her gift—poor Sarah! She came softly up in the grey of morning, and put it in a little box by his door, a hone hound candy pig of a dull yellow tint— she told him she would have bought a red one but they were three cents. Beside the pig, and various articles of home manufacturing, she presented two shawl pins to her friends, made of a darning needles, with a little glass bird at the top, very pretty, and what was of still more consequence, considering her limited "means", very cheap. But I mustn't forget Mary Kate's gift from "Jimmy". The "Opal for 1848", a large and splendid book, flittering in red morocco and gilding, with her names on the back. "Jimmy's" are very convenient—don't you think so?—

Now I don't know but all this talk about play things is very uninteresting to you, and upon the whole, I don't care if it is—I am writing to please myself, as I told you.

We were looking over some old letter the other day, and among the rest there was one from cousin Eliza written about the time of your "father's" marriage. Cousin E, and I, I don't know who else, went from our house in Boston, to Andover, to meet cousin George, and she describes their journey, and tells how he stood at the door to welcome them and "was just preparing to call them all manner of fools if they hadn't come". The wedding, she thought, would not be so remarkable a thing to her uncle and aunt, as it was to "little Mary Brown" — "Oh why! Said she, Why! Miss Adams, did you see Mr. George Adams married? Where did he get the woman?"!

There were some verses describing little Henry's feelings at the sight of the hearse, almost in his own words—very pretty, they were, I wish I had room to write them here—but I'll show them to you some time. There was another letter from cousin George, when he first went to Brunswick—giving his first impressions, at length, with some queer little message from "Fanny" to her Boston father and mother, to the effect that she was growing good, fast, and if they wished to see her, they must come to Brunswick, etc. Subsequently, there was a letter from Fanny's own self, folded square, with a sort of a "cocked up", "ye see how large a letter I have written unto you with mine own hand," appearance; containing accounts of proficiency on various knowledge, the practice of "calisthenics, or orthodox dancing" etc. etc.

But I must cease reminiscences, for Ma with a broom in her hand is giving me a practical reading of the episcopal burial service, "dust to dust". It's morning now, though it was evening, a fortnight ago, when the major part of this epistle was indited.

Yours conditionally,
Charlotte

[along the side of the page] My love to all my good friends—I wish them a happy new year, most sincerely: and if any body wishes to make me a new year's present, I would suggest a goose quill. Marry sends her love to you, and wants to hear from you, and considers herself very benevolent in so doing.

Fannie to Charlotte, 1/18/1849

Brunswick. Jan. 18. 1849

Dear Charlotte,
I am very much obliged to you for taking so much pains to accommodate my unworthy self; when you mentioned the "tight boot" and the "swollen foot" I felt a kind of twinge in the region where my conscience used to be; I imagined you trolling about Boston streets, tired to death, and I actually had quite a severe pain in my left pedestal, (I hope by the way that it will

"turn out" to be your left foot that ached) in sympathy with yours. When I wrote you, Mother had been quite well and strong for her, for a long time, with the exception of a slight cold; but for a few days past, she has not seemed as well: Father wishes her very much to go to Bangor with him next week, but she dreads a journey in this cold weather. We have been our own "Catherine" this long while, and Mother will do more than I think she had better.[3] Perhaps you will think that there is a grammatical error in that former part of that last sentence, but I assure you, it is no such thing—I am sure it takes decidedly "we" and even more than all of "we" to begin to constitute one "Catherine." You can easily believe that if you remember what a nice girl she was. As to the long-mooted question of the tippet; I do not fancy the fitch-slain much; there is a skin called "American Sable" that I have heard makes very pretty "hand-cuffs" etc; it is light brown—not exactly brown either, but the color of real sable; with black or dark stripes in it; and I think I should much prefer that. Next to the American Sable if you do not find that, I like some sort of grey fur; nothing very dark. I do not know what a "Victorine" is exactly, but I "had in mind" an affair with a flat collar, and as long ends as would be expedient! I guess upon the whole, it was a Victorine only I did not know it. There is a widow-woman (of course a woman) here, who has "learned the trade" and worked at it all her life, and she will make them for me very nicely.

If it takes a little more money, I will send it to you as soon as I get some more, which ought to be pretty soon. I do not know of another chance for sending, but perhaps you had better send by express, for I am rather suffering for a warmer "skin" and it will take some time to get it made up. Don't forget that letter—all our loves to the folks—and good night

Yours affectionately—but hastily.
Fanny

P.S. if I have misspelt any of my words don't notice it if you can help it—for I believe it is morally impossible for me to learn to spell—it's really curious—my utter inability on that score—it is a kind of mental defect I believe.

3 Catherine was Fannie's half-sister. They shared a father.

Fannie to Father, 6/20/1851

Fannie described a wedding to her stepfather, Rev. Adams, relaying all of the social details.

Brunswick. June 20. 1851

My dear Father,

Poor cousin Deborah has been sick several days with headache and ague, and has hardly been able to sit up at all; yesterday afternoon I went in to her room and she told me that you wished to have a letter mailed that day, and directed to Cleaveland [Street], that you might find it there on your arrival; but as it was, it seemed impossible for me to write then; for what with piano-lessons that could not be postponed and Harriet Stanwood to see to, who was sewing for me; getting ready for the wedding at six o'clock, and various other cares and responsibilities too numerous to mention. I had just as much to do as it was possible to accomplish.

John Pennell[4] was polite enough to come purposely for me, and bring me home again after ten o'clock at night; we had a very pleasant but quiet wedding, I expressed to the best of my ability, your regrets with regard to it. Jane and Mr. Reeves were exceedingly disappointed that you were not there. Jane said that she always expected that you would marry her, a great deal more than she ever expected to be married; it was so much of an Irishism, that it amused me very much, but I presume it was a conscious one.

I told Mr. Reeves that I was going to write you today, and that I should tell you all about him; he seemed quite anxious to know what I should say, but I rather left him in suspense: he seems very intelligent and bright and pleasant; he is very gentlemanly, and John Pennell avers that he is "quite a scholar". "Mr. Kellogg, ladies and gentlemen" officiated;[5] he was rather doleful, rather prolix and rather flowery; his prayer was in part to this effect: "O Lord thou knowest that these young people are setting out in life with bright anticipations, but that they are all doomed to disappointment; and thou knowest that they have had a dreadful time of it, and almost wish they hadn't enlisted, and so forth: "truly encouraging"! Thinks I, "the parties especially concerned must be gifted bountifully with hopefulness and

---

4 John Pennell became a shipmaster.

5 Elijah Kellogg (Bowdoin, Class of 1840) was a pastor in Harpswell and Topsham, towns on either side of Brunswick.

courage, if they can stand that." Mrs. Wingate insists upon it, that you will go to Europe before you get back; I tell her I rather guess you would make it in your way to come and bid us good bye at least.

We had a fire again last night; cousin D thinks that effect is always bound to follow your going away. She says I had better find out where it was and let you know, but I tell her that it will be safe to tell you that it was the "dry house" (Mrs. Humphrey's) or it always is, and besides it was in that direction.

We were delighted to receive such a cheerful, bright letter from you the other night; it really did us good; and we are so glad that you are having so fine a time, and probably deriving so much advantage from your journey. Which Mrs. P. is the "remarkably quiet, sensible, considerate woman"? Mrs. Palmer or Mrs. Phillips? Louisa Leland's "Nabob" is a sort of cousin of Sarah William's; she considers him some of the salt of the earth.

How terribly tantalizing it was in you, Father, to say in your letter, after describing the good times you were having and the good people you were seeing, "Love to Fanny—how I wish she could be here." We read your letter just at night, or dusk; our lonely time—when we want to see you most, and I for one could not help contrasting our forlorn condition with your seeming exhilaration of spirits. That beautiful "hundred dollars!!" how refreshing the very sight of the words was! "down east" means Bangor. I suppose—doesn't it?

Try and find time to tell us soon Father, exactly what you mean when you say that your journey promises to be of great service to you in more ways than one. Cousin Deborah just came in an uttered somewhat to this effect. That she hopes you will not view the Albany stars through "the Spaniard's glasses!"

We have nothing new and interesting to tell you, everything is nearly motionless but vegetation apropos of vegetation—our garden excites universal admiration; Hunney's pride is flattered occasionally by hearing it pronounced the prettiest garden in town. Give a great deal of love to Dr. Delamater, and Elizabeth, their being here and our pleasure in their society seems like a strange but pleasant dram; how long ago it was!! I wish I could see them. Shall you not see Jeremy? Do write me a long letter soon, good bye,

From you affectionate daughter,
Fanny

Dear brother Baron's letter came yesterday. I wrote him this morning, that a letter in the course of two weeks will find you in Albany also that I thought it not improbable you would preach in August a few Sabbaths in Chelsea—a letter from Anna said she had been sick two or three days and was very homesick after you left. Thought she should go to N.B. on tomorrow Saturday, she had found it impossible to get away—Henry Lord she had not see—Joseph but once when she first when on—the Doct. she had not seen or heard from since the interview at Mrs. George's she thinks her patience will not hold out much longer he will receive a letter of dismissal from her quite soon. I tell her when that letter is sent she shall receive my warmest congratulations—Mrs. Cobbs letter has come with a certificate attached, which that Church wish filled out and sent back when she is admitted here—Had the letter better remain until your return or hand it to Mr. Packard to be acted upon? Fanny amuses herself three times a day by catching a box of squash bugs and scalding them.

Hope Elizabeth Delamaker has not forgotten all about her friends in Maine my regards to her if you please and the Doctor—Love to Jamie if you see him Fanny has told you how much refreshed we were by your letter

Yours etc. D. G. Folsom

Fanny forgot when she began her letter I should be well before she was through. Hope you will take time to write those letters to Friday evening and Sabbath school I think they will be very gratifying—I did not attend the meetings at Topsham most of the audience was from Brunswick, there were so very few in all that Brunswick people said it was about as full as our Friday eve meeting—Miss Bailey walked over she was outrageous that the people there should so neglect their privileges wished you had been there to give them a browsing.

I have not heard of a complaining sound in such regard to your absence. Pleasant St. Captains are very much pleased at your independence. Mrs. Mitchel remarked last Sabbath she was very glad you were gone she could see you had failed very much the last year—did not ask her whether in body or mind. You must expect some lessons in humility.

Fannie to Chamberlain (JLC), 9/14/1851
Fannie wrote about her confusion over their relationship and how she missed Lawrence. They met in 1850, were engaged in 1852, and married in 1855.

Brunswick Sept. 14. 1851
Sabbath P. M.

O! My friend how glad would I be if I would come to you now bringing you peace and joy; but I fear that what I could say would hardly comfort you, for I am anything but calm myself—if I could only tell you why and what my feelings are, I would gladly do it, feeling <u>sure</u> that I should get the deepest sympathy and consolation from you.

It is a long time since you went away; and I have not heard one word from you. Are you happy? and why and how? What are you doing? and of what are you thinking? Ah! I have wished several times since you left me, that I had one more assurance from your lips that you had never ever thought—lightly of me in all my disregard of worldly rules and feelings; not that I did not <u>know</u> just what you would feel and think and say about it; I knew also that it was a foolish, unreasonable wish but for all that I wanted to go to you again and ask you about it.

You see what a very <u>child</u> I am; but I know that you see it kindly. Miss Folsom spoke to me the other day, of some things which she was pleased to call "gross improprieties"! it was not, to be sure, until I had asked her about what she had said to Anna.

I really scorned the way in which she looked at things; but was half grieved, half indignant at what she said; —I saw intuitively that it was needless to try to have her understand how different all things were to me from what they were in her eyes;—it is of no use—I cannot make myself a slave to her rules of thinking and feeling—and yet I do not wish, I am sure I do not, to trouble her in anything.

<u>Do</u> tell me, will you not, what she said to you in the entry, the morning you left? She intimates that there was much more than what you told me. <u>Do</u> tell me, no matter what is was; I want very much to know about it for special reasons. Do not be reserved with me; I am not so <u>in reality</u> with you, don't you that I am not?

O! pity me that I am so <u>imaginative</u>! It is a strange way to speak I know but <u>you</u> understand me. My untutored imagination keeps me continually in a wild tunnel of thoughts and feelings and I know not where to turn for rest and support. I wish I could tell you just what a strange life mine is; but there are no words for just that which I would most gladly say to you.

What a strange thing absence is! And what an effect the mere existence of an absent friend has upon one! O! This world is full of mysteries and the greatest of them all are those that are never spoken of. Why is it that when I am with you, even as I am now, I cannot talk? Surely it is not that I have nothing to say; you are sure of that.

Wednesday morn.

This is one of those glorious Autumn days almost oppressive with its beauty; I am spending it in my little chamber alone; but I do not feel as I would— not but that I am cheerful enough but there is everything around me to make me worldly; and I cannot throw off the influence of those around me even though I do not see them. O! that story that you told me the other night! I am glad that I can share your sorrow with you, but ah! it makes me so sad when I think of it! What a world is this!

When you come you must not forget that you are to help me, and I shall go to you with all my troubles, and selfishly make you troubled too, may I? There is a mystery about our acquaintance (no, that is not the word) what shall I call it? Tell me; but I do not know exactly what your feelings are with regard to me, and I am in a sort of maze; are you surprised that I am? Tell me freely. I feel that perhaps I am committing myself; and that is not exactly what I mean either; but it seems to me that you must know just what I mean although I cannot express it.

If you could but know how fully I trust you; and how true it is that I have not only every degree but all kinds of confidence in you; it seems to me that I cannot tell it in words but that I must find some more subtle medium. I know that you would not in any sense or in any way trifle with me for one moment. Do not, do not think strangely of me for anything that I say; in looking back a little ways I see that I have expressed myself ambiguously and that I may have given you a wrong impression; but if there is anything that you do not understand, I will explain it all to you.

I must not write longer now for my eyes are very painful and then I know that you will not be much comforted by such a letter as this. Forgive me for not writing a better and a different one: for really it is not under my control and I cannot now write differently. You will write me very soon, will you not? Be sure to answer everything in this. Poor little Lucy Owen has lost her father. He died quite suddenly Sunday night: his funeral is this afternoon.

I have a new song to sing to you if I ever get rid of this hoarseness which has troubled me so much lately: It is full of witching minor strains, and has been ringing so sweetly in my ears for days, but perhaps you will not like it much; it needs to be sung better than I can ever sing it with my weak and undisciplined voice. I shall expect an answer very soon, do not disappoint me, for I want to know how you feel about everything that I have said to you; write freely—unreservedly.

Do not fear lest I should misunderstand you; however incoherently you may write.

With the best wishes for your happiness
Yours truly
Fannie

~~~

JLC to Fannie, nd/1851
Chamberlain wrote that his Bowdoin classmates had unanimously chosen him to give a special oration at commencement at the end of his Junior year, but that he did not wish to do so.

Tuesday morn. I do not know dear Fannie, but I shall have to send you this letter without any message to Miss Virginia. I am not very well nowadays and I assure you it goes hard with me to get up anything on this occasion, (though I think I am in general quite easy in such things); but if my dear lady who thus honors me with her notice will condescend to write a bit of a note to give me some sort of a clue to her I will endeavor to reply in any language I am master of—from the Syro-chaldaic or Babylonish Aramaian up to the minute eloquence of two kindred souls. If she prefers, however, to wait until some sudden streak of sanity permits me the free exercise of any faculties, I will do my best to sustain the character that I fear my mischief of a w___ has been gilding over her old homely comfort with. I am in a bad perplexity lately darling. The case is this. My class have unanimously elected me to speak at the commencement exercises this summer as a representative/together with one other of the class. I did not want to speak this year—I would much prefer to speak next, when you can be here and when I shall be so much better fitted every way for a public performance like that. I declined on the spot and have resigned formally; but they will not listen to any refusal on my part, and I don't know what I shall do. I am sure I shall do nothing even to sustain my present reputation. Tell me, would you try to do your best or persist in being excused? Will my darling have time to write me a little note pretty soon? Much love from many friends and from one.

Monday morn.

I don't know, dear Fannie, but my letter may seem to despairing so I thought before I sent it I will just say something to comfort poor Fannie. I cannot possible collect any pleasant ideas except those that are connected with you dearest, so you may well excuse me if I only speak right to my own Fannie herself. It may seem foolish in me to tell you again that I love my darling more and more every day—but that is becoming so much more true every day that it is really new. You would like me to tell you if I could, what a solemn joy runs through this old body of mine sometimes when I hear of some friends or other who is going to be names and am thus led to think of somebody and something. Yes it actually comes along the nerves and arteries going me a bound, an impulse that generally results (but doesn't expend itself) in some strange ejaculation that everybody wouldn't exactly understand. However it is a solemn joy half tears—half smiles; for I think how great a thing it is to live a life and how great a responsibility it is to cherish in your bosom, in this rough and dangerous world, a dear, frail, tender one whose life is your own; so that the strongest soul being thus bound onto another must feel all the lightest winds and the slightest ills that might touch his other life.

Fannie to JLC, 1/1/1852
Fannie wrote to reassure Lawrence about her feelings toward him and about the change brought by the arrival of her new stepmother to her home in Brunswick. Reverend Adams met his second wife, Helen M. Root, during a trip to Chicago. She was only six months older than Fannie.

Brunswick, Jan 1, 1852.

O! Lawrence, what a letter I found yesterday when I came home! It grieved me so to think how you were feeling when you wrote it—and I was not near you to help and soothe you as you know I would have done.

I am sitting now at the same window where we sat together all that night. How could you think that I would shrink from you ever! you who seem so holy, so pure and noble to me—how could I even if you did press my finger to your dear lips? O! there was nothing even there, that you could have done that would not have seemed beautiful and right to me. Ah! those nights! so full of terrible beauty; will they never come again? how strange they will seem to me "in the coming time"!

O! dear Lawrence I would know you more and I would have you know me as you never have known me. My soul longs to speak to yours as it never has spoken. Believe me, only believe me as I fear you do not now; I know that I am not natural, and I am not rational, and there are no words to say to you all that I feel and think—but I will tell you more, and you will forgive all that is wrong in me. Friday eve. the great change that I have talked to you of has come at last upon our home. How strange it all seems! I was alone a few moments this afternoon—I was thinking of Mother—how she had passed away so silently—how blessed and holy her memory is! Dear Mother! if I could only have gone to see her for a little while and told her how lonely and sorrowful I felt! I don't know why it was, but I felt the shadow of coming ill: I so longed to go to you dear Lawrence, or have you come to me; but then I am afraid I should have troubled you with my terrible gloom. I thought of your dear holy love for me, and it seemed as if that were enough to live upon. O! sometimes I feel that I am not what I was once, when I was younger but O! Lawrence take me as I am; I am sure that I have as deep feeling as ever, and though the mysteries of life have been unfolded gradually to me, they have not made me less trusting or earnest.

I rest in you as I never have rested before—you know it, do you not? and I would be everything to you; I would nestle closely in your arms forever and love you and cling to you and be your "bird": dear, precious heart! I am not worthy of such a boon. Let me think of you as cheerful and happy this winter, and do not do not let me trouble you in any way. I am not worthy to trouble such as you. How kind you were to me in Boston; you did not know how kind you were, did you? If I was naughty you forgave it didn't you? for you knew how nervous I was, and I didn't really mean to be naughty. I mean to paint this winter, a little at least, and you will feel interested in it won't you? I wish you could be with me while I am painting. I want to feel, and I know I may, that whatever I may be and do, will be a great deal to you. It seems to me that I would have no real reason for trying to be anything or do anything, if it were not for you Lawrence, but then what will it all matter to you if you are going so soon to leave me? it can never cheer and bless your life—and what will it all be but bitterness, if it fail of that?

What are you doing and how are you looking this sad and lonely Sabbath evening? Look not so sorrowfully, for I am coming to you now, soulfully—twice my arms about you and lean my weary head upon your loving and protecting breast. Do you not see me? do you not feel that I am with you? I will not, cannot leave you until you smile happily. You will write me very soon, will you not? I have been expecting a letter from you, but I have not waited for it, for you would have received this long ago, if Father had not desired my attendance upon callers; he having made a special appointment for calls from "the parish" upon their new "pastor's wife"; we have had the house thronged ever since we returned on Wednesday; and Father has wished me to devote myself entirely to visitors and of course I would not object if it would help him in any way. but oh! it is a weariness! I do hope it will be over soon. All blessings be upon you dear one be hopeful and happy; happy in me; if I am capable of making you happy. Good night,

Your Fannie

~~~~~~~

Fannie to JLC, 1/nd/1852

In this love letter, Fannie mentioned scandalous comments by a Mr. Upham about the two of them living together in Boston. Thomas C. Upham was a professor of philosophy at Bowdoin who lived near the Adams's home along with his son George Barnard Upham (Bowdoin, Class of 1846), a thirty-year-old physician.

Brunswick Sun eve.

Dear Lawrence,

What a sweet, sweet letter you did write me! but it made me cry so, and you were not with me to kiss the tears away. You said so beautifully and so truly that we were but two in this great, wide world; I know it, yes I more than know it. I feel it; and that is one reason why I cling to you so wildly. O! how constantly I have thought of you today; I missed you so! I wanted you to take care of me too, for I have not been well. If you had been near me with your strong but gentle, loving hand, and that blessing smile, so full of generous devotion and tender sympathy, how could I have thought of pain? But I am selfish in thinking so of myself, when perhaps you are sick and suffering. I have feared it for I thought that if you had been well, you would perhaps have written me something in answer to the letter I sent you a week ago. If there were only some talisman to bring your face before me tonight, so that I might see what your spirit needed most, I am sure that I could comfort and bless you; but now I feel so sadly because I cannot tell precisely what shade of feeling is just now passing over you: is there no way, alas! in which you can tell your Fannie? Yes Lawrence I could have said to you truly, "do not be troubled for it is not so as you have feared," I can love you as much as I ever could, and you know that I love you, I see in you a soul that I cannot help loving; so noble pure and high. love me, love me still, and do not be troubled about me in any way. Do you ever realize how singular my position is? we are talked of and wondered about, and people have mostly made up their minds that we are "certainly engaged," I was rather troubled for a little while the other day to hear that some comments had been made upon me, in consequence of Mr. Upham's report that I was staying (permanently) at a hotel in Boston with you; on second thought, I felt that it was too absurd for me to be troubled about for a moment; I have not heard the whole story yet. I will direct this note to Bangor as I notice yours is mailed there; my other letter was directed to Brewer; which is right? O! I am sitting now <u>alone</u>, where we have so often and long sat together; if you were only here! I am lonely for you tonight, and long for one caress in your sheltering arms. Can you not come to me for one moment? one! Tell me Lawrence what is the happiness of which you speak where you say that you "can conceive a happiness which this world will never let you feel?" Tell me what it is I have just received your darling letter; (for it is Monday morning now) and "Caty" has just been in with three kind welcome letters and <u>one</u> of is more than "kind" and more than "welcome"! Which one thinks you Lawrence I am speaking of? There is something so noble and beautiful in man's love for woman, so weak as she is and born for suffering and tears, and it is so great a thing to see him so tenderly "comforting the frailer spirit, bound his servitor for aye"! There is such mysterious, wonderful, thrilling poetry in it! I am glad that I am a woman, now that I have such a one as <u>you</u> to love me, although I know that "the life of a woman is full of woe". Lawrence why is it that our love for each other owes not suffice to make us happy? it ought to be so. O! I am so relieved and so happy to have you write cheerfully and trustingly as you do now; you would always be happy if you knew <u>how</u> I longed to have you so. I gave your little message to Miss Folsom, and she said with some feeling that she <u>had not forgotten you</u>, and that she wished you were here.

I think she has a great regard for you. I am sometimes sorry that face of yours and of mine does not give me one kind look; no though I gaze at it so beseechingly, it never, never turns its eyes towards me for one moment. Why is it? Does it love to look at me as you do? I want another picture that will look into my eyes sometimes, but I must stop now or I cannot send this tonight. Good night.

Your affectionate Fannie

Fannie to JLC, 2/9/1852

Brunswick. Feb. 9. 1852
Mon. A. M. eleven o'clock

Perhaps dear Lawrence you would like to get a few lines, if nothing more from your "Fannie" before you come to see her. Your last darling letter deserves a longer and better answer than I can give this morning for this must be ready for the next mail, and I have just finished my part in domestic affairs, so that I would not commence before. O! How relieved and delighted I was to hear from you! You can perhaps imagine how anxious and troubled I was while I was waiting for your letter, which did not arrive until last Wednesday or Thursday; several times I determined to write again, fearing that by some possibility you had not heard from me; but then I thought that perhaps you had been called away from home, or perhaps, though I would hardly allow myself to think of it for a moment, perhaps you were sick and then some one else might read what I wrote for you alone; and oh! How I shrank from that! I might of considered, write you in such a way that anyone might read it, but then I knew that such a letter were only distress you—you would hardly realize why I was writing in such a way. But ok! When Caty did bring me your noble, dear, heart-warm words, I could have dance for very joy of soul.

There are some things Lawrence, that I want to talk with you about when you come, but I'm afraid that I shall not dare to say everything to you: you will never think strangely of anything I may say to you, will you dear Lawrence? but you have so much delicacy in what you say to me, that

I hardly like to talk with you as I might perhaps. The last words that you wrote me were so bright and cheerful that I can only think of you now as happy; you are so, and you will be so will you not, my dear one? I missed you so yesterday! you do not know how much, and then I wanted to write to you in the evening, but my eyes were not fit for use. Why is it that you seem so much nearer to me Sabbath night than at almost any other time? it seems to me as I sat alone in the parlor when everyone else in the house sleeping, that you were certainly by my side with your arms around me, your noble, true and loving heart beating close to my own, and for and with my own. I know that you were there. When shall I see you? will you come Thursday or Saturday? If you have a picture of your dear mother or sister, bring it with you, I want to see them so much! I do hope after all that I shall have another letter from you although I hardly expect it. Good by for a little

Your Fannie

[Written in opposite direction over front page]
Cousin D. says that she has done with "the weeks" now, and is counting <u>the days</u> until you return. How good you were not to scold me about that key; I know I was very naughty. now you will want it so much

[Written in opposite direction over back page]
You say you could not show your mother "that letter" Oh! you have not shown her any of my letter, have you? do not show any of them to her if you have not. I cannot bear the thought of it. I do not show my father <u>yours</u> and I'm sure it would be very ungrateful in you.

Fannie to JLC, 4/22/1852
Four months after her adoptive father brought home a new bride, Fannie began to capitalize on the benefits of her new stepmother. Helen's brother, George Frederick Root, was a noted musician and composer, and Fannie got a chance to study with him in New York. Root wrote well-known songs such as "Battle Cry of Freedom" and was inducted into the Songwriters Hall of Fame in 1970.

New York. April. 22. 1852

Dear Lawrence why did I not receive that darling letter from you this afternoon that I was expecting? I know that I had no right to expect it, but then that matters not you know, in such a case.

I will not tell you what you will probably hear through Father—about my journey and arrival here: but I must tell you darling, how I missed your dear, dear, hand when my head was aching so, that terrible, terrible night in the steamboat.

O! I was so sick, and so weak, and I felt so alone, for you were not there. Are you studying and writing dear, with nothing to molest you or hinder you? I hope that you are free from care, and well. Do not be troubled about your Fannie, for I feel all will be well with her. I think that I shall succeed with my music for Mr. Root says that I learn very rapidly, and that I shall improve very perceptibly while I am here. Shall you not be glad for me dear? O! if you were only here with me, I should be so happy! will you not come by and by? do come.

Why is it Lawrence that you do not write me? are you waiting for me? It seems so strange to have you so silent: you who speak to me so much and so often! O! if I could only know that you are happy tonight, and that there is a bright and glowing future beckoning you on, a future where we shall be happy in each other, dear Lawrence—tell me, are you not hopeful tonight? you will be, darling when I am longing for you to be so.

How do you come on with your writing now, when this little plague of a Fannie is away from you? When you are writing, think that I am helping you, and that I am looking over with all the sympathy and love that my heart of hearts bears for you. Do not believe that you can do nothing, I know that you can do much—anything that you wish; believe it Lawrence, for I think that Fannie knows something about you, does she not dear?

O! when I think of you, you seem so high and pure and noble to me, so far above other men; it is so Lawrence, you know it is do, do you not?

O! this great city! What a lonely place it is! How it sets me dreaming to walk the streets crowded with multitudes of human beings rushing on after something fondly hoped for, but alas! seldom realized. what a great, wonderful mystery is this life of ours! and we are to solve it together Lawrence! O! how strange and great this seems to me.

Only think how quietly our fear had passed away from us—I cannot understand how it is that we have so nearly forgotten it. My eyes are paining me so terribly, that I must not use them any longer, so I must leave this blank paper that troubles you so;—I am sorry for it.

> <u>Good night</u> Lawrence, and be happy in
> your dear
> Fannie

I <u>know</u> that I shall have one of your dear letters tomorrow.
When you write be sure to direct to 95 Clinton place. Perhaps care of George F. Root.

⁓⁓

Fannie to JLC, 5/4/1852

New York May 4. 1852

O those beautiful, beautiful holy flowers, my dear Lawrence! How sweetly they came to me! so full of fragrance and innocence and I know how you sent them to me, indeed I do; I know and feel how full of love they came. Your blessed letter came yesterday afternoon. Dear one! how sad you have been for me! And I not near to soothe and comfort you when you were ill! I shall never dare to leave you again Dear, shall I? So we must not, can not be away from each other three or four years, we cannot indeed, <u>can</u> we darling? You will think perhaps, that I am not reasoning much when I say so, and I am not indeed. I am only feeling. I wish that it did not require so long a time for letters to get to you and to me.

O! I am so glad that you have one of my pictures and that you love it so; I shall have something to paint for now, I wish that you were here to go with me to see some beautiful pictures that there are ere; you <u>will</u> come will you not when Jenny Lind comes at any rate? for you must hear her and <u>with me</u> too. What was it Cousin D. alluded to? when she wrote me the other day she alluded to a remark of Helen's the evening after I left, and said that you were going to tell me of it; don't forget it when you write again.

I am indeed glad that you have made a kind, true friend in Cousin D. she thinks that I do not appreciate you fully! She knows nothing about it, and how can she imagine that she does? for I never talked freely with her about you for one moment.

I am well dear, with the exception of a cold which oppresses me somewhat; and makes me rather hoarse. My music I hope is coming on a little and I shall improve more. Perceptibly by and by. You would leave me a little if you were here to notice my jovialness for a dear little boy of Mr. Roots about two years old. I sit by him and kiss him every night when he is asleep; before I go to my rest and fold my own wings maybe darling you would be jealous of these kisses especially when you considered that I never favored you in the same way you know full well how I hate little children. I never mean—now you need not laugh you rogue! Just opposite my chamber window there is a little room which seems sometimes as I naughtily look down into it to hold about as much happiness as this world ever vouchsafes to us poor dwellers in it—there are two beings there seemingly existing only for each other; and as they stand near the window the frailer form leaning against the stronger and seeming to twine so lovingly about it, I sometimes think how happy we might be in just such a little parlor, and then I fall to dream in dreaming. But then there is a little baby there. Naughty little thing! and its poor little mother looks so pale and drooping! O! I'm sorry, I'm sorry. If you see Caty, tell her I am going to answer her kind letter soon; but I am very much in turreted and find it very hard to write as I can never by any possibility be alone. I have ten thousand things to say to you my own nobleman, but I let this little suffice for this time or I shall miss my chance of sending to the office.

Your own Fannie dear Lawrence

Fannie to JLC, 5/12/1852

New York. May 12. 1852

My own dear blessed Lawrence when I returned from an exhibition of the pupils of the blind institution this afternoon I found a short letter from cousin Deborah in which she told me something about the effect which my last letter had upon you O! darling it has broken my heart to hear it! how can I write? I cannot even think! It was about five o'clock when I received the letter and it is about nine now, but I have been lying upon my bed weeping such tears of agony as I cannot tell you of, ever since. O! if I could only see you now dear, dear Lawrence you would forgive me for making you disappointed and unhappy. Cousin D. would perhaps think it not best for me to tell you this, but I cannot, cannot help it. O! what a bitter, bitter thought it was to me, that that note which I wrote so happily, and sent to you so cheeringly (although it was a poor, little one and not worth anything in itself) should have come to you so differently. I thought it would bring one little, bright ray of sunshine into your dear, lonely heart, but Ah! it did not even that! O! I am disappointed too, and grieved and sorry. Well I can never hope much from my poor, miserable letters again. I knew dear Lawrence that those few, poor words were no answer to the blessed, blessed letter that I had taken into my heart of hearts and wept such tears over there, but there it was all I could do then; and your last letter did not come to me until a day or two after I sent mine. I wish that I could only know how you are tonight, and how you will feel about what I am saying to you now dear! I beg of you not to let anything that I say to you trouble you in any way for one moment; I could never, never be happy again if I thought that I was constantly liable to cause your noble, loving spirit any unhappiness. There! There! dear, darling Lawrence let all those troubles pass and fade away—smile now, smile tenderly and joyfully upon your poor, poor little Fannie or her heart will break. O! if you knew how soothingly, lullingly I am murmuring there—there—to you, you would be happy and hopeful, indeed you would.

O! if I were not so broken down by grief tonight! I wanted to say so many things to you. for several bright, beautiful days past, I have been so happy, so fully of our deal love! and I have been thinking to you how I could joy and rejoice in your great love; I thought that I knew that you were happy with me in this blessed Springtime. O! Lawrence I did want to have such a long talk with you dear, about my present plans and undertaking. I thank you darling more than I can tell for talking to me about these things so freely as you did in your last. I am sorry that you feel as you do about what I am doing now but I cannot think about it tonight, if I can sleep I shall be better able in the morning to say what I would about it. good night dear Lawrence, O! be happy tonight for the sake of your own Fannie. If you would only bathe my aching head for me a little while until I could sleep resting upon your bosom! but no, I must bear all alone tonight; forgive me for all, all, dearest one. Goodnight again, and I know that the angels will watch over you, and it maybe over poor Fannie too. Friday morn. I was not able dear Lawrence to write to you as I hoped yesterday, my eyes were in such a terrible state from my crying, that I could not use them and I could not even bear the light until the latter part of the day; and then

[… letter ends …]

⟶

Fannie to JLC, 5/21/1852

New-York. May 21. 1852

I have but one moment to speak one word to my dear Lawrence tonight; I cannot write to him, but I will very soon. I want to beg of him to come on to New-York and see me, and hear Jenny Lind with me. Why oh why will he not? I would give anything to have him, make any sacrifice if he would only come.

Remember dearest, how little more I can see of you for a long, long time; O it will seem like ages to me. Father did not seem to favor my going to Bangor this summer, and if he continues unwilling, and I go away in September O! when shall I ever see or hear anything beautiful with you! You did not tell me your reason for not coming, and I know that you can overcome it for this once Dear Lawrence. I was bitterly disappointed when your precious, last letter came, to find that you felt you could not come, and I have been thinking about it today and tonight until I felt that I must have you come, for I do want to see you my own dear one, more than I can tell. I have not seen anything beautiful here yet, for I could not bear any beauty alone, and if you were only with me, it would be so much to us. Do not be afraid my darling, that I shall grow worldly and "soulless" here in the city; for it is all nothing to me, but if you were here with me, then everything might be beautiful. If you only knew, if you could only know, how I think of you every moment, you would never fear my being "estranged" from you. God bless you for your boundless, noble, unworldly love for me my dear, dear Lawrence, O! I do love you, I do love you and cling to you so, blessed, holy heart!

But I must say good night, good night to you dear Lawrence and this must go to you early in the morning, or you will not receive it in season. O! yes, yes you will come and see your Fannie, wont you? do not refuse her, when she begs you so hard. Jenny Lind will sing again after Monday night, they say, it is uncertain when, but perhaps Wednesday or Thursday night but if I cannot be certain about it in the morning early, before my letter goes, I will send you word by telegraph, if there would be time for you to come. I shall be looking for you and expecting you, and oh! how bitterly disappointed I shall be, if I do not see you.

From your own, own Fannie

dear Lawrence

Sat. morn. the papers do not tell when the other concert is to be or whether there is to be one at all; but someone says, "probably Friday night." I shall send you word by telegraph as soon as I find out about it. Do come; if you do not hear her, you will always be so sorry; remember, her voice will never be heard again.

Fannie

Fannie to JLC, 5/27/1852

New York. May 27. 1852

Why my darling, darling Lawrence how sweetly and joyfully you did speak to your little Fannie yesterday P.M. when your letter, or rather, my letter came. O! you cannot tell how happy it made me to have you seem just as you did! it was just what I needed in the strain in which I was living just then. The tears of joy fairly sprang to my eyes; how did you know dear, that I wanted you to come to me then just as you did? tell me Lawrence, tell me.

I want to play with you tonight dear, for the influence of all that sunny letter, comes shining back upon me now while I am answering it. But oh! forgive me for feeling so, and don't feel badly about it, when I confess to you that I hardly dare write playfully now, since that poor little letter of mine that was written playfully too, had much an effect upon you. Why, oh! why was it? it is all a sad, painful mystery to me, and I am afraid that I shall never get over my feeling about it entirely. But I must not, must not think about it now, although it seems almost impossible to drive it from my mind. You knew didn't you , that Gardner wrote me as he threatened? it was very kind and friendly in him to do it, and I am going to write a little note to him, may I dear? and thank him for it. I'll show you his letter and you will see how delicate and kind he was; remember me particularly to him won't you. That day when I received your letter, for or five came at the same time; I was out when the postman came, and when I returned I found them all put up for me around the clock, so that I might readily see them; you know very well which one I received first; but it was the last-written letter of yours that dear one, that made me so happy, and I was not looking for another from you, so I read Gardiner's next. O! how much good it did me, how it softened that terrible, terrible letter which I could hardly have borne. Dear Lawrence, you did say some things there, that were too much for me; if I could only have wept on your bosom! but I was alone, all alone. It was strange, very strange, but it was so sad for me to read that letter last, I would not realize but that it was written last, and all my reasoning could not avail to comfort me much.

O! Lawrence, Lawrence, if you only had not said that some things I said to you seemed "revolting" to you! You did not, could not know how deeply, terribly that would wound me, or you would never, never have said those words; if you were only here now, and I could be in my own resting place, you would tell me all about it, would you not?

But I will try not to think about that again, and you will never, never feel so about anything I say to you again, will you? I only wish that you were coming to see me tonight dear, for I have a room to myself now, for a little while, with a piano in it, and it is quite pleasant. I have practiced five hours today, and I do hope that I am improving; don't you Lawrence? won't you be glad with me dear that I have accomplished so much today? You do not know how your Fannie is clinging to your strength tonight, and how her heart yearns towards you, so tenderly, so lovingly!

By the way dear, what do you mean by saying so voguishly that I have been keeping some secrets from you? O! I have not; I have not intentionally, knowingly kept one secret from you Lawrence, don't you know I have not? tell me, tell me darling what you mean. O take me, take me in your arms tonight, fold me clasp me to your warm and noble heart, where my own, own dear home is, for I believe you that it beats for me alone, all unworthy and erring as I am. Bless you again and again for that sweet, happy letter; O I am so glad to see you so playful, so joyful! Darling, how funny that was about Charlotte Johnson! how old did she think I was? a hundred? she had better be careful or she will make herself out to be two centuries old at least; for she was "a young lady" when I was a little girl, I remember. do you want to know how old I am really dear? I don't know that I ever told you, but you probably know; well then I am twenty-six I believe, although I cannot possibly realize it at all for I feel like such a very child, and only think of it, Anna will be twenty-three in two or three weeks; it is possible? (Tell me you rogue, what you mean by those "two secrets" kept from you, for I have just read your darling letter again.) O! but dear Lawrence I don't want to talk in this trifling way any longer now, for I want to tell you what makes me very sad and troubled sometimes. I only hope that these blinding tears that have been coming, will not trouble me while I talk to you now about it. Dear Lawrence tell me, tell me frankly if you are ever troubled to think that I am older than you and if we were not married for four years, or perhaps longer, how sad it seems to me to think that I shall have lost the bloom and freshness of girlhood; when I would come to you with the charm that youth only has. {28th} Perhaps there is some pride mingled with my feeling about it, but I cannot help fearing lest you should be disappointed in me then, for dearest there will not be so much there to attract you I am afraid. You know that I shall have probably everything to wear upon me and weigh heavily upon me for these several years coming now, it must needs be so, wherever I may be, and I do not love to think that I shall come to you then with nothing for you to be proud of, or delight in; O! if I could have given myself to you several years ago, when I was prettier and younger and fresher; and O! if you had only been the first to love me!

I wish that I had never had any admiration but what you could feel for your little Fannie; don't think me vain Dear, in intimating that I have had some little admiration, for it is very strange to me that I could have been so. You call me your "beautiful one," dear Lawrence, you will not, can not call me so then, and then if you are disappointed in me, you will not let me know it, and the thought of that grieves me more. Only to think of your making a sacrifice for the sake of your obligation to me! I cannot, cannot bear the thought of it, I would rather die than have you do it. I have been so afraid lest you might not have considered these things enough. And then even if you should never feel as I fear, others would look upon it in that light, and you could not feel the pride in me that I wish you might feel; forgive me if I am wrong, but I cannot bear these things. What if your dear mother should ever feel so! O! how grateful I am to her, for feeling so kindly to me, and thinking so well of me; I hope that she will never have cause to change towards me. Give my love to her, dear Lawrence but do not show this letter, for it is sacred to you alone; be careful of it then. You remember some other things that we have talked about in relation to this matter, don't you dear? Well—it troubles me to think about them too. O! if you were only here with me now, I could talk to freely with you about it, but it is hard to write all I would say, on several accounts. And now dear, I am sorry that you are not quite satisfied with what I am trying to do now; don't you know that I could never stay at home when you were gone, during all these years? things will probably be growing more and more sad to me, changes more and more frequent; and you already perhaps begin to know abut a thousandth part of what I suffer at home almost every day of my life. Dear Lawrence I must be away from Father (I can say it to <u>you</u>) even if I starve; and I must depend entirely upon my own exertions, I can never consent to be dependant upon him one moment longer, while I live; Then how can I take care of myself so well as my teaching music? and how can I do that to advantage, unless I have I have the instruction for which I am striving now? It makes me very sad to think that perhaps you do not enter into all my feelings about this; but you will now, won't you, my own Lawrence? I feel as if all my future course were so uncertain; I know not what you are going to do, or whether I am going to feel myself able to bear being alone, away from you, so long, <u>so long</u>! All these things trouble me, only I am sure, sure of one thing an that is that my own, dear, darling Lawrence loves me, and that I love him. Did you receive a few, hasty lines from me a short time ago? O! I am so sorry! but Jenny Lind does not sing again. Cannot you come and see me dear? how long is your vacation? be sure and tell me.

[Written on the left side of the first page]
You do not tell me whether Sarah or the rest of them said anything about "the picture" or did they think it so ugly, that you don't like to tell me about it? Sarah, must come and see me when I go home without fair, but I cannot tell you dear quite yet, when I can come down to Bangor, if at all.

[Written on the left and right sides of the last page]
How very funny that order of exercises was! O! dear I am so sorry that my name should be there with those other things.

I shall not be able to write you so long a letter very soon again Dear, because I am losing all my practicing and I shall be blamed for it. I cannot tell you why now. Blessings for you from your Fannie.

Fannie to JLC (nd)

It was impossible for me to be alone or free from annoyance a single moment. O! if I could only have a room to myself it would be such a comfort! but to try to write you as I wanted to write, with three persons watching me and talking, laughing, singing and drumming upon the piano every other moment coming to me with some foolish remark or question! I could not endure it then, nervous as I was. And then, O! that dear bright, happy letter that came to me in the afternoon! I feared to open it, lest it should tell me something more of your suffering or sadness—but O! when it brought such soothing balm to my grieving spirit, I rejoice in all your successes concert, organ, exhibition part and all. And now dear Lawrence I had a favor, a kindness to ask of you; for I know that if I put it on that score, and not on that of your gratification, I shall be more likely to succeed. You know that Jenny Lind is to be here next week, (you can learn all about it from the papers) now do, do come on to New York and hear her with me; do, do, DO come. You will never have another chance of hearing her, for these are her last concerts and I shall be so sorry to know that I have ever seen or heard that vision of music and loveliness, when you cannot sympathize with me in it all. I know that she will all be to you, just what she was and is to me, unlike anything else on earth. You must come, it will be so sweet to know her together. O! she is such a beautiful poem to me; and you darling must read her with me. You will just have finished your work for this term in Brunswick, and just for once you can come, you know.

Darling, please, please—I'm putting up my naughty lips to you now, to be kissed—just as I used to do; give me one now dear, and then say "yes". I think there are three concerts on Tuesday, Friday and the next Monday night after. Next Tuesday, it is. When do you go home? You haven't told me about your exhibition part when I wished so much to know about it; but you will tell me all about that you know, when you come; and then I have a good deal to tell you about my undertaking: so I won't write any longer now, but send this right away, that you may be sure to get it in season. Is not your noble Hossuth to be here next week too? you will know all about that. O dear! how can I write a letter that your dear mother (and mine) may see! don't tell anybody that I said that, you rogue! Dearest one good-bye; who is it who loves you so, but your own little (wif–) Fannie

O! I must not forget to tell you [wc] from some things cousin D said. I feared that she had seen or heard some of my letters to you. O! tell me that it is not so, for I have worried so about it, that I can imagine all sorts of things. I am afraid that she would not like it at all if she knew that I had written you what I have concerning what she wrote me. do as you think best about letting her know of it; but forgive me for begging you not to let her see everything in this letter, or hear it either. don't think me foolish, but I was so troubled at the thought of it.

Fannie to JLC, 6/24/1852

New York June 24, 1852

Perhaps my own darling is thinking that his "little girl" is very silent all this long time, and he would love to get a letter from her so much! but then he is trusting her with all his great heart and he knows how she is dreaming— dreaming of <u>him</u> day and night, and night and day. O! how dearly you did write me, my own, in your last precious letter; you did not want me to be grateful to you once, but how could I help it my soul's friend, when you said those things to me so delicately? Why Lawrence, if you were already my own husband, I could not come to you more nearly, more unreasonably and ask of you to help me in <u>any</u> and <u>every</u> way. I have so much to say to my darling this morning, that I can hardly say one word. He won't be troubled because I write a short <u>note</u> will he? when I have so <u>very much</u> to interrupt me. I have a new teacher dear since I wrote you, a German; and he gives me <u>so</u> much, and so hard exercises to learn and gives me no encouragement for learning anything of him unless I work very hard indeed, for the little time remaining to me here: he gives me three lessons a week—and oh! I am so anxious to profit by his instruction! <u>You</u> know just how and why I feel about it. If I could only practice regularly six hours a day, I might accomplish something, but I only succeed in doing that <u>sometimes</u> there are so many unavoidable interruptions. O! I am so full of joy when you write so happily! You may tease me you naughty man just as much as you please but then never fear but that I shall pay it all back with interest <u>one of these days</u>, when you "two rooms" come. There is one thing I know of, that <u>somebody</u> doesn't do well; I am sure he can't draw <u>shoes</u> worth a cent! I wouldn't recognize them at all, I was determined that I wouldn't! I wouldn't even think of shoes! You asked me darling in your last letter save one, to tell you about my way of getting along with my expenses and so forth; I am glad dear to have you say just what you did, and I will tell you something about it gladly; for Fannie does love to come to him in everything, and she cannot bear to have any kind of trouble that from a feeling of delicacy she cannot mention to her dearest Lawrence. I have been obliged to write to Father for money since I have been here, when I could not bear to do it; for although I felt certain that he was only lending it to me, yet I knew that he hadn't much faith in my success and ability to refund him by and by. O! I am so worried and anxious all the time, and I am sure I am as economical as possible, but then there are so many expenses here that I cannot avoid, and I have been to great disadvantage in many ways, in taking my time from my music in order to do things myself to save expense. O! it is terrible now to be so cramped! I know that Father does what he can to help me and he is very kind, but then so you know darling that I have such a nervous horror of notes, ever since that one had such a terrible effect. I have been waiting on account of that feeling until I could write you a long letter, but I could not wait any longer. O! he will be glad to receive this note from his own, own Fannie won't he? I beg of you darling not to show any of this letter to anyone. Good-bye dear

Forever your own,
Fannie

JLC to Fannie, 7/26/1852

My dear Fannie:
I shall not leave here until Monday next for Brunswick and I want you to wait for me if you please in Portland till the Bangor boat gets in. Your father in Brunswick wrote me that he should not be at home, and the house is shut up. So that you will be spared the decision of that painful question about staying there. Unless you prefer not to wait for me I will go to the U. States Hotel for you, or if the cars for Bruns[wick]. leave at about 6 or 7 perhaps I shall only have time to get to the depot.

I will go and ask some of the students when the cars leave for Bruns.

I find that I can get to Portland at 4 and take the cars at 5 for Brunswick so I want to meet you at that time in that train which comes from Boston so as to get to Portland at 5. I should think it would leave at about one o'clock—perhaps 12. I will meet you there if you please in that train on Monday next. I cannot be absent more than a week that time, as a meeting occurs here August 9th where I must be present, being secretary and an important member. So we can go back to Boston Friday or Saturday and I will come down in the Bangor boat, for a little while unless you will come with me to Bangor from Brunswick. My health is very poor—I am scarcely able to sit up today. Our anniversary exercises closed yesterday.

Hoping and anxious to see you as ever
July 26th Lawrence

Fannie to JLC, 9/22/1852

Brunswick. Sept. 22 1852

My own dear Lawrence
Your Fannie has been thinking of you ever since you bade her good bye that sad dark night in Portland; and she dreamed about you all last night, only she cannot tell exactly what she dreamed, it seems all so shadowy and dim. You were with her though, with all that endearing tenderness that you love to show towards her.

I never can tell you dear, how desolate, <u>desolate</u> my poor little chamber seemed with I came back to it from Portland; I looked for you and listened for your dear footsteps until I felt that it was all of no avail, for you were really far, far away, and I could not see you—I cannot tell how I missed you. Dr. Bacon was sick so that I did not return home until Friday afternoon, and now I must go again next week, for he was unable to finish then. I hope you are well my dear Lawrence; you <u>will</u> not over-exert yourself in any way, will you? for you know you have promised me solemnly that you will be careful of your health, for my sake.

I was so glad darling that you told me your various troubles in pecuniary affairs; you <u>did</u> know that I would understand all your feelings, however peculiar they might be, and that you <u>might</u> come to your little girl for sympathy and even for strength in it all, did you not, my dearest <u>friend</u>? Now my dear, don't ever let me hear you use that word "penuriousness" again as long as you live; I will not have it breathed in the same world with <u>you</u>, my noble-souled.

Do not my dearest make any sacrifices <u>now</u> for me, for you will have enough of them I fear, when that blessed day comes, when I shall have to call upon you for everything; don't be afraid though Lawrence, for I don't believe I will make it hard for the dear one I am going to live for; I hope my husband won't ever scold at his poor little Dora? though, "what do you sink o'sings"? Last eve I heard that a Mr. Wolf of Florida was going to write me or coming to see me soon about going with him to Florida; what would you say dear, if he offers sufficient inducements? You know the climate is splendid there, and probably my health would be better there (shouldn't you think so?) than in most other places, where I would be likely to go. I cannot go west, for Fannie D's case weighs very strongly with me there; she was exceedingly robust and perfectly healthy, but came home from Kentucky with fever and ague, and is now <u>very</u> sick, dangerously it is feared; not able to rise from her bed, and will probably never recover from the effects of his illness, even if she lives to get about again. I have not heard one word from Miss H. of course she has not heard from Pennsylvania; and probably Mr. Huntington is away from home; in that case he will be likely to secure a teacher now, even if he has not already. I will see what Mr. Wolf says, and then tell you immediately, and you will arrange it so that you may get the letter if you are away from home, in season to tell me what you think about it. I feel pretty hopeful now dear Lawrence, only I can't bear to be <u>seeming</u> to leave you so, and go so far away. You send your dear love to our Cousin D. but I cannot give it to her with my lips, for she is far away from us now; she left B. the day before I returned from Portland; Amice said she could not control her feelings in the last, when she was at the cars, but wept like a child—poor Cousin Deborah. I am sorry for her! I am trying dear, to be as energetic as possible, so that I may be prepared to go whenever it is best. I have written to Caty and to my sister Charlotte since I have returned wasn't that right? I am trying in addition to everything else to keep up my practicing regularly everyday, even if it is every so little; only I do so miss your pleased and approving smile! O! this is so beautiful, <u>beautiful</u> a day, that you <u>ought</u> to be here with me in my <u>dear</u>, little chamber, <u>I cannot bear it all alone</u>. Do not say dear Lawrence that you "too, would be <u>noble</u> and <u>generous</u>" to me, if it was yours that you had to give; you are <u>now</u> noble and generous to me, and I feel it more deeply than I can express; and I cannot bear that you should feel a care for me now dearest, in addition to all other cares; so you will not let these things trouble you will you darling? for I feel sure that I shall do well. Good bye my dear Lawrence for a little while and remember that I am always your grateful, affectionate little

Fannie

~~~~~

Fannie to JLC, 9/6/1852
Fannie wrote this letter to Chamberlain five days after commencement at which he graduated from Bowdoin.

In Father's study. Sabbath eve
Sept. 6th 1852. 5 ½ O'clock

I have been to church all day dearest Lawrence, but somehow my thoughts would wander far away from the sermon and everything around me, to one who seemed as pure and good and exalted as anything there. It was not wrong dear, I am sure it was not; and I only wish you could know just <u>how</u> you seemed to me; you were indeed a sermon to me, calling my thoughts to all that was high and beautiful and unearthly. There was a kind of religion in it, a religion in which I cannot help believing and I know in my soul that such a state of mind must be right and good.

I have been thinking Lawrence how many many things there are, which cannot be expressed in words; it is not only that words are inadequate <u>fully</u> to express our thoughts and feelings, but there are thoughts and strange states of feelings which simply <u>do not suggest words</u> by which we can tell them to each other. It seems to me my soul's friend, that when we can be together always, there will be such a growing bond of union between us, that we shall know all these things of each other by a kind of magnetic influence, is it not a strangely beautiful thought darling?

Cary and I had along talk last night, mostly about you and Scott, and since then I have been feeling so happy, thinking about your pure way of looking at all things: I don't know why I should feel it so much more now than at almost any other time, but perhaps it is owing partly to the way in which we talked of you. I am sorry you and Carrie never had that talk about Southgate; I think she would have felt better if you had.

O! I want to see you tonight my own dear Lawrence, and I know not whether to think of you as at your own dear home among so many dear ones who love you so proudly, or as away from them all, perhaps among strangers. O! if I might be sure that you are well and happy; for I cannot bear to feel that you may be ill and sad and lonely, when your little girl who loves you so cannot be near to soothe and bless you. O! I am so lonely tonight and there is such a terrible gloom settled down so heavily upon me; what shall I do, dear Lawrence? I want to come to you and weep on your true, loving breast; the only place for me, with my wild and terrible soul, in the whole great, cold world. I hardly dare come to you either, lest I should add to your own sadness, for I fear that my dear one is sorrowing too, tonight.

I sat today in Church in the same place where I sat that glorious night when we went there together, when you pressed that <u>first</u>, holy kiss upon my brow—do you remember dear how sorry you were for me, when I grieved and cried so bitterly? I can never, never tell you <u>how</u> you seemed to me then—so like a pure and blessed guardian angel! Why did you love me so dearly? Why dear? What was I—a poor, sorrowing lonely child wanderer in a strange, strange world—that you should come to me bringing me that deep and wonderful soul full of unutterable love? Tonight I am so full of thoughts and feelings, that I am overwhelmed by them—weighed down to the earth— all the past and all the future in their mighty presence seem to be with me; and I cannot help feeling dear Lawrence that you are with me in it all: tell me; you are now watching the sky in that dear little room, and sending your heart's warmest blessings to your dear absent Fannie? But I must not write longer now Lawrence, for I must try to get quiet, and I fear that it makes me more nervous to write, even if it is to you my comforter and rest. I shall have a letter tomorrow shall I not dear? and that will soothe and cheer your own

Fannie.

⁓

Fannie to JLC, 9/30/1852

Brunswick. Thursday eve
Sept. 30.52

My darling Lawrence I'm so sorry that my last letter wasn't a better one, but then dear, it <u>could not</u> have been "wanting in tenderness" when my heart was so full of tenderness for you all the while I was writing. How <u>blessedly</u>

you did write me in those dear letters! and how you can always cheer me if I am ever so drooping and sad. Don't be troubled my dearest at anything in the letter which I wrote Sunday eve. for I don't feel so sad and depressed now—forgive me for coming to you so, when I ought to have been cheering you only—but then I couldn't help it, I couldn't bear it without you. By the way Lawrence darling, you did not guess rightly about the first letter that you wrote me; I did like it, and it was kind and just as it should be. I wanted you to tell your little Fannie just what you did about all your troubles—yes all of them dear, and you will again will you not my own one? The ring darling I love dearly, and I had to sleep in it, for I couldn't bear to have it away from me so long as all night would have been; it is a beautiful, rich, ring, dear, and I want you to feel satisfied with it and fancy it. I was grieved too, that we could not have been alone when you put it upon my finger. I am so very sorry dear Lawrence that I could not send this letter yesterday, but it was impossible to do it. I can't stop to explain to you why, now. O! I have written dear to the Rev. Mr. Green, New Jersey, near Trenton about a situation in his Seminary, shall probably hear in a day or two. Not one word as of yet from Pens. Anna goes to Miss very soon. Why my own dear Lawrence couldn't expect his "little wifie" to say everything she wished to say to him in one letter, could he? darling mustn't expect impossibilities you know mind you dear, I'm not scolding, I only mean to make a little remark to him. I have never had one such terrible time since I came from Portland, as I used to have when you were here with me to help me bear them; I could not endure them without my dear, blessed protector and comforter, and that must be the reason that they have not come upon me. I long, long for you darling! why, why can I not see you tonight? You will visit me in my dreams will you not dear, dear Lawrence? I am grieved that you are not better in health; you will take care of yourself won't you? my own, noble Lawrence. Those were dear letters that you wrote my Father and mother; thank you love for sending them to me, for I wanted to see them. O! Mary Wheeler! Mary Wheeler! What a naughty girl you are to talk so terribly! I'm ashamed of you! You ask me when I received your first letter; it came to my hand Sat. night was mailed in the morn. How did it come so quickly? As to writing to that office in N.Y. I supposed it would not be best, would it dear until we hear from some of these other places? what do you think I don't care to ask father about it somehow. I had a letter last night from a friend in N. York; and she enclosed one from a friend of her's in Columbus, Georgia to whom she had written in my behalf; he thought if I would only come out to Geo.

I would find no difficulty in securing a good place, but he knew of no one in particular just now; however he had spoken about it to the Rev Dr. somebody there and he was looking out for me. (Friday A.M.) You wouldn't like for me to go there would you dear? even if something fine offered; I hardly think that the climate there would do for me, it is very different from Florida you know. I seem to prefer going farther south than N.Y. for I am quite sure that I should get better in many respects if I would escape a winter or two, and I have an idea that New Jersey is scarcely preferable to this part of the country, is it dear? Father is kind to me now; more quiet than he was, but then I do not feel <u>safe</u> a single moment while I am here; so I shall be glad when I can go away. I don't think I shall ever be here again, unless it be for a very short time do you think I shall dear Lawrence? Good bye—be happy and well dear for your little wife loves you.

Fannie to JLC, 10/10/1852
A love letter in which Fannie explained that her new "stepmother" had been opening her letters from JLC. She also mentioned that her teeth and eyes were bothering her.

Brunswick, Sunday A.M. Oct. 10.1852
My dearest Lawrence

I received your last two letters on Friday eve. in Portland, from whence I returned yesterday afternoon. I missed you there dear, O! how much! and it seemed very sad to be there without you. How good and kind and indulgent you were toward me when we were together there did you know it? When I came home and felt that there was no one for me to come to, and thought how like a stranger I was now in my own home, and how changed, terribly changed everything here was it was hard indeed for me to bring myself to come into the house, so I stayed over at the depot a long time, part of the time talking with Miss Hinkley—she thinks very highly of you dear; so of course I do not think <u>ill</u> of her; isn't that all natural? I want to tell you Lawrence dear what a very strange child I am; I mean that I am a <u>queer</u> child, I won't say "strange" for I believe you do not like the word, does you darling? well, as I was saying, I'll tell you just as if you did not know it all before. When I received those letters dear in Portland, they had been taken from their envelopes, and put into new ones directed by Father; and I could not satisfactorily account for that, unless Helen in her great anxiety to her concerning "a place" for me had proposed to Father to look at "his little girl's" letters, just to see what news there was concerning that important matter. You know H. seems to consider me in the light of "aged twelve" and it would all have been perfectly proper. But when I found all those words sacred to <u>you</u> and <u>me</u> alone had been exposed to other eyes even for a moment, I lost all the enjoyment of them, for I found myself involuntarily imagining how they would have seemed to Father, and wondering whether he might possibly and luckily have misunderstood <u>some things</u> at least. You don't know how just this little thing worried and depressed me; and then I felt so badly as I was approaching home, or <u>Brunswick</u> for I felt that It was no <u>home</u> for me. But I want to tell you dear Lawrence how funny it was that just after I had opened the door feeling so terribly depressed, the least little circumstance should have such an effect upon me. Our good, pleasant Mary hearing the door, came to the stairs, her innocent face beaming with pleasure, exclaiming, "O! ye are welcome, ye are welcome Miss Fanny! and how is Mr. Chamberlain indeed? Oh! I'm very glad dear, ye are very welcome!" bless the poor girl! the house really seemed less desolate after such a greeting; and besides she almost cheated me into the idea that I had been with you, when she asked for you so earnestly, and I didn't undeceive her. There was no one else in the house but when Father came, he seemed so glad to see me, and put his arms around me and kissed me so affectionately, that my heart gave a spring and I began to feel confirmatively happy but then I think I could guess what would make me happier still dearest Lawrence can you? O! there is such a wonderful beautiful rain today, and I am sitting alone in the dining room by the table near the parlor door, do you see me dear? I did not dare venture out in the rain with such sensitive teeth for they will not get over the effect of being operated upon, for some time, I fear. I am glad darling that your health is improving, now be careful of yourself, do dear. I don't know what to think about that school Agency, but I don't like the deer of the thing much better than you do. How we do agree about <u>almost</u> everything don't we Lawrence and I think it's omicrons and "a forerunner" only not such a one as you are you otel rogue! I declare I'm afraid half to death of you already and there is unknowing what I shall be one of these days if you know what that means. I ought to tell you that when I first saw father I asked him what he thought of the "Agency" and when he answered that he knew nothing of it I asked him if he didn't see what you had written to Mr. Wilcox, but he said that all he saw was the direction of such a letter; so I suppose my suspicions were all groundless after all. I will not write you so much this time dear but will send my letter tomorrow, for I have a great deal to do with my eyes and they are troubling me very much of late. I have a great many letters to write but I do not understand how I am to accomplish them. You are a treasure to me dear Lawrence in every way and I feel it more than I can tell you; you are all I have to lean upon and I am leaning pretty heavily if you did but know it. I thought dear that those letters to my father and mother were beautiful, but then perhaps you think very little of my taste and judgment, well I'll remember that with regard to the copy of Milton darling Mr. Barrett brought it in for me to see and I think it is very fine, but then I have not seen many different styles of binding. He got a fine book upon painting for me, but it was not the book we sent for, I think he will send again so that I may take my choice what if the naughty child should cry for both would you whip her? with how big stick? Cousin D is in New Jersey. (NJ here) direction is care of Mr. A. Brower. 18 Franlkin Terrace Hoboken Good bye again darling for a little while. Give my love to your dear mother and father and Sarah and tell whom you love. Your affectionate little W——

Tell me Lawrence if any of my letters lately have not been marked "paid", sometimes when I have not had a stamp at hand I have requested them to charge to Father, tell me. Yes dear I do want to get a letter every Sat. eve. I've been reading about Dora in David Copperfield and I keep forgetting that I'm not your little "child-wife" I do feel so just like another Dora what does you "sink" about it I wonder!

I am enjoying your letters now dear after all. When shall you hope to hear from the advertisement? There are no engravings in the copy of Milton but the type is beautiful I think, and the binding is in the antique style—very fine.

O! I am so glad that you love Cousin Deborah, and then she thinks so much of you! perhaps some day we may be able to show our gratitude to her, for all her kindness to us, who knows what may happen! There is one thing about it she never need feel "alone in the world" while she has such a noble friend as you, my dear Lawrence, I am sure of that! I have been dreaming so often about you of late, and I have been with you, O! so many times to see your dear mother—and sometimes she seemed to love me but I always loved her, and she appeared to fill a place in my heart that only a mother can fill; for she did seem like a mother to me, and she will be one, after all, won't she dear Lawrence? Tues. June 8. I am going to write a note to cousin D, and enclose it with this; so you will give it to her alone for me and no one else need know that she received it. for it will be for her eyes <u>alone</u>. Tell her so, if you please dear Lawrence. O! I am anxious and troubled about you today. I wish that I could know just how you are <u>now</u> this very moment. Bless you dearest again and again! do not despond; you will be, you <u>are</u> everything that I wish you to be, believe me, I know that is saying much but it is <u>true</u>. Your own

Fannie

Fannie to JLC, 10/24/1852

Brunswick. Oct. 24th 1852

Oh how good and kind my blessed, dear—husband? is to his Fannie! what are you <u>so</u> good and generous and noble <u>for</u> dear? I am sure I don't deserve it all, but then I am pretty grateful after all, do you know it my dearest Lawrence? Come and let me kiss those dear, pure, precious lips, (just under where the fine moustache was, did you say?) and thank you from my heart for <u>all</u>, especially now dear, for what you enclosed in your last letter; only I'm <u>so</u>, so afraid that you made some sacrifice in sending it to me. I wish Lawrence that I could only tell you the whole story and then you could begin to imagine <u>how much</u> it was to me then. You know, dear, that I was going to buy me a "winter bonnet" as a present from you with <u>that</u> (you remember about it don't you darling?) but now I supposed I must take it to go to Roxbury with; for if things continue as they are now, father will not help me about it. Things seem to be coming to some terrible crisis here <u>at home</u>? now. Father and I have been having some very painful talks within a day or two and I have been distressed to death; only dear I can endure now when I have your blessed heart, strong and noble as it is, to lean upon what I never could have borne without you, <u>never</u>; I should have gone crazy or sunk in despair. We had been talking yesterday afternoon when your letter came; and father had been terribly excited and unreasonable and unaccountable. I thought he must be insane; but how I sprang up from it all, and almost danced in fur and joy when you came to me so <u>daringly</u>; so full of sunshine and hope and light. How did you know just what to say just <u>then</u>? it was wonderful, wonderful! And then again at night dear, when I went to my own little chamber full of grief, with my eyes swollen with weeping, and read your precious letter again through my tears, you would hardly believe how soon they were dried; and instead of tears I know there must have been sparkles of joy in the poor little eyes that you love (for you told me you loved them darling, didn't you?) blast every hope of happiness I have in the world and I should give up all, in utter despair. I have felt it more of late since I have had such terrible troubles at home. Lawrence tell me O! tell me if the fault is altogether with me, in my temper, my disposition and feelings; if it is dear, tell me so, and I will take it kindly whatever you say to me; I shall know that you say it with love and tenderness, and that you will treat your poor grieved little girl, who had thrown herself helplessly upon you, with gentleness and care. If I had more of the loving tenderness that I am sure I have in my heart, I could not be reproached more severely— I could not have more of these (to me) mysterious and unaccountable troubles. What does it mean? I can believe nothing now, everything is uncertain and obscure. (You know what I mean by that, dear, nothing connected with you.) You are indeed my only, only hope and refuge; O! let me be sure that I can never, never cause your dear heart any unhappiness in those days fast coming when we shall be one. Do you ever fear my Lawrence lest we should ever live over again those trying times we have had? tell me, tell me, as you love me dear. There dear I won't talk so any more, it is of no use to say anything more about it now, but I will tell you how delighted I was with your suggestion in the letter before your last in regard to what your father told you about securing a place as secretary and so forth. O! Lawrence, Lawrence dear, do, do "say so early enough." O! it would be so glorious! I cannot cannot give it up. O! I should go with you you know you said so darling, and I would be such a good girl, I know I would. Why is it not practicable dear? you father knows and if he thinks so, I don't believe there would be any doubt about it, don't give up the idea, but talk to your little wife some more about it. she loves to hear about it. Now don't laugh at her, and call her a "silly child" What shall I do if I fail after all of securing a place for this fall? Did I tell you that I had another letter from New Jersey? it was very curious, but they expressed great disappointment at my declining their offer, and hoped to be able to prevent sufficient inducements in the Spring as their school increased. But I don't believe that would offer me salary enough even there do you? Charles Gilman has I believe written to a friend of his in Kentucky, but I do not imagine there would be any place in a school there at this season, so late as it is—there might be a situation in a family. What do you think dear about that? I've always had a kind of horror of going into a family but it is somewhat better than nothing, and perhaps might prove in some cases even better than anything else for me; I might have more time to myself, and receive as much compensation besides: but then if they pretended to treat me differently from what I have been accustomed to, I would never brook it for one instant; would you have me bear it dear? How very strange it is that my last letter was so much delayed; it was put into the office on Mon. afternoon. I carried it my own self; and you did not receive it until—Friday? I am sorry dear to disappoint you by not sending this before, but I could not help it. You ask me what I do evenings, and where I go; "what societies, parties, lovers, remarks, praises, etc." I meet with in these days. You are a rogue and you know it, and I've a great mind not to tell you for your comfort, that I never go anywhere, and that as to those aforementioned particulars, I know of and have to do with nothing of the kind. I have grown faded and homely and I have no lovers now; don't you pity me dear? I want to tell you darling what a new affliction I have; did I ever tell you how I had suffered from chilblains? Well I have been so very lame with them for several days that I have not been able to wear my shoe and my foot pains me very much, especially in the night. I have every various trouble don't I dear? I don't believe but that you were cheating me when you told me what Gardner said about me, for I know he doesn't like me, he doesn't act as if he did, what do you mean rogue by telling me such a story but good bye my dear Lawrence I must not write any longer now.   Fannie

Oct. 29

And so my dearest Lawrence opened his letter to ask his little girl if she was always loving (I didn't mean to repeat it, it's pretty natural though isn't it dear?) well as I was saying, to ask her if she was "always loving him" yes dear noble heart, she does always love him and her own heart is so full of gratitude to him, O! she cannot tell him anything about it, perhaps she may show him someday. I like you Lawrence to hear; (do you like me?) I like your large, free, gentlemanly way of doing things, and I couldn't love you as I do if it were not for that. It makes me honor you so and respect you so, never fear dear lest you should not always have "your wife's respect" (you remember you asked me about it in your last letter) for that she never can fail to give you—full and free too, while you are the generous, manly soul, you are now. And then dear one I will tell you now that I never fear or "doubt or regret or hesitate" when I think how wholly your lot is to be mine. I am sorry that you felt as you did about it for I know and feel that you are capable of much and I know that you will be all that I wish you to be, and that all you will strive after. I do not fear my darling, on that score; but I do fear lest you should injure your health by too constant application. Do not study too hard, and Oh be careful and remember your promise to me. I have been thinking of you, dear, every moment almost, although it is so long since I began this letter, but our house has been full of people all the week and I've been obliged to devote myself wholly to others and have not been able to be alone one minute so that I could write to you, I mean it literally too. I have been hoping of late that we might be certain dear that we should never, <u>never</u> again suffer as we have sometimes when we have been together. You know what I refer to Lawrence don't you? When we have been so grieved at each other, and that too when there was no reason for it. O! if I thought we could ever be so unhappy together again it would …

A little while since the bells were tolling for Webster[6] Mary came up to me with a very earnest, solemn face and said, "there's a death bell! O! there's a death bell Miss Fannie" I wish you could have heard her, it fairly made me shudder; A death Bell! what a fearful, solemn word! I suppose it was more striking to me, coming as it did from Mary with her wild, superstitious thoughts and feelings. She sends her love to "Mr. Chamberlain the good boy! nice boy!" Father and Helen send their love to you, dear.

Fannie to JLC, 11/14/1852

Brunswick. Nov. 14th 1852

Bless your dear, precious heart, my Lawrence, for the beautiful, beautiful things you sent me. The moccasins, dear, I put upon service immediately and Oh! they are so nice for my poor, lame foot! What a rogue you were to send them so mysteriously. As to the picture, I don't think little Sallie will get it again very soon. you can have another taken at anytime you know, for her. It is a great comfort to have something more than a profile—something that at least will <u>almost</u> look at you, although I would be glad if the kind, blessing eyes I have seen would glance into mine full of sympathy once in

---

6   Former U.S. Senator and Secretary of State Daniel Webster died October 24, 1852.

a while. I hope they will really though and oftener than that, someday. I watched anxiously for your letter last eve. for I was sadly in need of it. Thank you dear for your heartfelt pity for my sorrows, but dear Lawrence I am afraid that I fail of expressing to you all my feelings in the matter. I know that my words are miserably powerless at all times; and then there is such an insurmountable difficulty in writing about anything which takes such terrible hold upon your feelings for while we are feeling most there is no ability to write and so we are obliged to wait until the paroxysm is over and then there is often a reaction and an entirely different state of mind comes on. Oh if I might only <u>tell</u> you about it, with your sheltering arms gently wound around me, then you might perhaps know what it all is to me; but I cannot write it.

Forgive me dear, I'm not complaining of your dear, kind letter, but I was a little disappointed when you merely said as you did, that "adversity was the school of true greatness". I could not help feeling that I had entirely failed in conveying to your mind any idea of the state of mind I was in, and of the certain terrible and lasting effect these things were having upon my whole nature. Father tells me I have been deteriorating, and I feel it to be too true. Last eve. as I looked out at the window upon a scene of beauty which once would have filled my whole soul with pure and high and glorious poetry, I turned away from it all, almost with disgust; for I was full of bitterness and wretchedness, and then burst into a passion of agonizing tears, when I thought how sadly I was changed. Oh if I am to lose all that I have reverenced in my own nature, all that kept me above the common groveling herd of coarse and merely worldly, earthly minds, then I must give up in despair. What does it mean? Father said the other day, that he had no expectation of my ever having any other home, and that he was the only or almost the only friend I had in the world. What does it, what can it mean, Lawrence? What does not certainly, imply any recognition of your love for me. I could not ask him what he meant, but tell me dear, if you gave him any idea with regard to your interest in me, when you talked with him, I am in such a morbid state of mind that everything distracts me, and the former part of what he said, haunts me like a prophecy; I cannot throw it off. Dear Lawrence you do not consider, do you? that this is a tremendous crisis in my life; my whole future depends upon it; would to God that I knew what do do! I told father that I must go away forever; that was the only thing that could be done. He seemed very much distressed, and said it would be a very dreadful thing to him to have me leave him—estrange and feeling that I had been unkindly treated, after all the many years that he had made an idol of me and watched over me with prayers and tenderest anxiety; and that it would break him down completely, but that he should try to consider it as a first and righteous punishment for his having set his affections and hopes so much upon me and been so bound up in me as no person ever was in another. O! if we had not knelt together by the death-bed of my blessed, sainted mother (Oh I cannot write her name reverently enough) if we had not gone through so much together, I could bear it better. When he went away last eve. poor man sent Helen to ask me to come to him for a moment and then putting his arms round me and kissing me, he enquired in such a grieved and tender voice, why I could not just have come to bid him good bye. Speaking of my leaving him, he says, that I am throwing away my best friend; that no one is the world can have such associations with me as he has. But it is of no use for me to try to write to you about it in this way—you can realize something of the terrible conflict of my feelings can you not dear? do only tell me that you do sympathize with me in this, although you remember that you did not last summer. Think how father and my deep attachment to him, is interwoven.

~~~

Fannie to JLC, 11/21/1852

Brunswick Nov. 21.1852

dear, your two most welcomed letters came safe to my two hands yesterday afternoon; I am sorry you have not been feeling well—I was in hopes you would become permanently better, when you had had time to recover from the ill effects of Brunswick hours—they being rather long and late if you remember.

It was indeed a great comfort to read the letters but then reading them only made me long the more ardently to talk with you and to get rid for a time of the miserable, unsatisfactory media of pen, ink, and paper. You were writing me dear just at the same moment that I was writing you.—I seated at cousin D's little work-table (you recollect it?) in the corner of the north parlor, above, all the people having gone to meeting; you in your pleasant room at the seminary I suppose. But ah! I cannot see you sitting there, for I never saw the room, never was in the building that you are to make your home for so long a time, and where you are laboring to earnestly and wearily. I wish I could have gone into the seminary with you Lawrence. When I was in Bangor I had a letter from cousin D a night or two since, and she speaks of having received "such a sweet letter from C" it really gladdened her heart I am sure. It's a cheap way of gladdening a heart isn't it dear? If I thought there was one heart to be made glad by any poor letters from any poor little girl, I think I'd have her write once in a while; but the trouble is, I don't know of anybody who loves her well enough; do you?

I do not want to plague him, but I must tell him that I do not see how he can give up that beautiful plan he has written me so much about, so very easily. To be sure he owns that he has some doubts about whatever he brings up as objections, and says "but I do not know about that" to a great may things connected with granted that you would be or might be only an "undersecretary"? and then with regard to "your proposed domestic arrangements" as you call them, why would there be anything impracticable there? You would certainly have some salary and we could easily make it enough for us two. You know it is much easier living in Europe almost anywhere, then here. You see dear, I'm making all the plans, in good faith too. but seriously Lawrence, I do not see why you might not get such a situation as well as anyone else who will get if you do not. You need not fear lest I should be a burden to you dear. for I would not: I would only help you and take care of you.

My dearest Lawrence would scold me if I told him what I was just thinking of; so I wouldn't dare to tell him how I couldn't help thinking of poor little Dora—how she used to sit for hour after hour, close by somebody she loved, while he was writing, helping him in her sweet, affectionate little ways. Only dear I would not be like Dora because you don't want me to be; and besides I am sure (and so are you) that I am capable of a thousand times more than she ever was. It is evening now, pretty late too, for I was disappointed in not being able to write you before tonight; for Helen was trying to play sometime and made such sad work of it that I could not possibly write; the terrible discords distracted me so. Nothing encourages me so much as the regards my music as her wretched obtuse way of reading the notes (in playing I mean) for you know she considers herself quite an oracle in the science. I'm not saying this ill-naturedly you know dear, only candidly. O! dear me! how I have been longing to see you tonight dear; I've been so sad and lonely; and when Helen sat on father's knee and seemed so happy with him, think I, "well! I rather think I know of somebody who wouldn't be very sorry to have his bird perched upon his knee tonight and tightly around her too" and upon the whole darling, I rather imagined myself wishing pretty strongly that it could be so. What does you sink o'sings? I want to tell you Lawrence of something new I have in mind just now: a friend of mine in NJ not the lover, but only a lady had just written me concerning a place she can procure for me in Penn. I'm waiting now to hear again from her. The salary will be rather small, but it is better than nothing, and there will be some one to look out for me and felt an interest in me there for a sister of this good kind friend of mine, has promised her to do everything in her power for me if I'll only come. I should really be very happy at your home this winter dear, and I can picture our many pleasant scenes there; but I must be doing something in another way you know as long as this debt to father (more especially Helen) is upon me. I have been thinking how Sarah and I might practice our music together, and how I might help Johnny in his drawing, and teach him what I know of painting in oils; and then I could hardly help imagining myself running down to the door from the dear little room, just to meet a certain Lawrence I was of, when he should chance to come over to see his little girl for a short time.

I have been delaying to send this letter so that I might write more, but I must send it now as it is. Fare thee well dearest. A beautiful Thanksgiving to you. And who does he guess I talked myself to sleep with last night, I wonder! Tell him Fannie

~~~~~

JLC to Fannie, 12/22/1852

Bangor Dec. 22 1852

My own dear Fannie,

Most gladly would I see you again for your sake and for my own; and I can feel but too deeply and too keenly the pain of this parting without meeting. But I cannot go to Boston my dear one even to see you, however strongly my own heart draws me (with) and however sweetly and sadly you may plead. I love you my precious one with all my soul and strength—my love is with you always hoping and seeking to bless you and to shelter you if it can. I am not well dear—do not be anxious but I think I am scarcely able even if other things were free to go anywhere now. And then dear Fannie to see you only to part from you—it would certainly be too much for me. I knew your dear letter would come last evening, I was waiting for it. Bless you for all your rich love to me—poor boy; but not so very poor How it lives in my heart even when all else seems dead and cold. How bright like a blessed home-fire it burns and glows and warms! Dear Fannie do you know how my heart "leans over" toward you at the very sight of your name and how the soft sweet dream glides through all the paths and chambers of my soul, making sleep oh, how beautiful! May God bless you my precious one and overshadow you with his peace. I cannot write very well tonight I am so ill just for a little while you know that is all but I had a heart full of things to say to you as you are going away—a thousand blessings to speak to you I only am trying to write so that you may hear from me once more before you leave. How many prayers go with you my own prayers daily and hourly and almost every moment for you my Fannie. Do not let this world be all Fannie—it is little worth and unsatisfactory—and even, dearest, we must not make each other supreme above the higher worship of our Father above. He may see it to be necessary to remind us by a terrible lesson of his superior might to our affections by such a lesson as I shrink from naming to you—only sometimes I fear that the lesson may be needed and let us love such other in him. Take my words to heart Fannie, they are full of a great truth. Oh, how many things would I say to you now—not the vain and meaningless phrases of common farewell but things that belong to the souls which God has given us. Go my noble girl with the seal of my dearest love imprinted on your brow—even where the first kiss was imprinted sown in tears; go dear one bravely and full of love and hope. There is brightness for us somewhere—let us make it ours. I am patient, yet full of earnestness, sorrowing sometimes yet always rejoicing; but what ever betides me one pure steady glow ever warms my soul and grows and grows till it will warm us both sometime and then will glow and grow still. Fannie you know how I love you.

What more can I say than you know already? I should like to write a word to your father and mother but cannot now. My love to them. You will not let me wait very long to hear from you.

A thousand blessings and the constant prayers of my most earnest soul for you my Fannie.

Good night
Lawrence

JLC to Fannie, 12/26/1852

Bangor Theol Sem. Dec. 26th 1852

My own Fannie

I have been very lonely for you tonight. My thoughts have been with you all day—I was wondering where you might be today and I was sorry that I could not know. I was sad this evening without you but I did find some comfort in the dear picture (doesn't look much like you after all; but it <u>is</u> you) I have not been well for a week past and am quite down today and dear it did send a sweet peace and rest over my heart to kiss the dearest face in all the world—and then as I lay on the sofa I fell asleep with wet eyes. But it was a feverish sleep and I awoke from it all the more wearied for the sleep and feeling quite unwell. I was going to write you the first part of the eve but (though my heart was warm and full and winning over to you) I put it off till after my sleep I am sorry; for I cannot write now as I would then. Does she remember last Christmas day? Does she? What a little, little time it has been—it don't seem half so long to me, as these three months of our separation do. How I do love to think of my Fannie when we were in Boston and perhaps it is not wrong for me to be glad that I was kind to her and tender of her as I could be. Dear, dear, darling! Bless her!

January 2nd 1853 Evening

Dearest one somewhere, I hope, in the great world loving me still and thinking of me; I too love her and think of her. I have been to hear Prof. Hitchcock preach this evening and oh! how often and how deeply was I reminded of those other times I have heard him, so happily; and so happily because "my own" dear little "honeysuckle girl" was close to her own "heart" that was strong and warm then. And so dear it is strong and warm now stronger than it was then—stronger, larger, but not warmer perhaps; because you know it was pretty warm then—rather too much so sometimes I'm afraid. I went with my cousin Annie, dear (the dear is for you) and I suppose you won't be jealous—she won't even let me kiss her now as she used to though I want to kiss her sometimes just to keep me steady, but you with your experience wouldn't think that a very remarkable quietus to my warm blood. So I have to get along without any kiss at all, only somebody's picture I kiss time and again every single day and night too. You see I love a girl "away down south" somewhere and I am afraid some rich planter will try to get her away from me to be his wife and so poor I will be all alone in the wide world. Well, it will be a very wide world then and the little nook of it that I shall fill will be none the sadder and none the wiser for that but then if she is self-sacrificing enough not to be won away from her first love (?) he will try to take as good care of her as I can, and then to find pretty soon a little home for her, and some little "gold__" ear-rings)! there! "You wouldn't think I would!" I suppose. Well, dearest, another year is gone—a year how eventful to us! Still in that regard perhaps the year before that was somewhat more eventful to us what do you think? Can it be—it was two years ago now that the sweet strange girl gave me the honeysuckles and I lifted the dear creature to reach the prairie roses—two years! Blessed years! ye have gathered for me fairer flowers and richer fruits than all the other years. Holy years! I will remember you and cherish you forever. You see, Fannie love, I always date my love from the honeysuckle time—so you may know how I may be "won" if you ever have occasion to instruct anybody in winning me. But then Fannie maybe there is coming a time when even the dear honeysuckles will seem dim and dull compared to its beauty and its holy calm. How sweetly our little horse will ride over the storms and billows. How stoutly and proudly cold I bear up against the blasts and steer the home so fondly freighted and shrink not from the cold and sleety storm, if only the one dear, precious one were there to be sheltered! Well there will be storms enough and occasion enough to bear up! And then the other times will come too sometimes and two poor ones worn and wearied will rest how, I guess I'll not say. May it be a happy new year to you my precious one, wherever you may be.

Tuesday Evening January 4th 1853
My dearest Fannie, I do think there is not one other in all the world who could ever have been to me, by any possibility, what you are. Every dear little personal habit is so original and (after all my terrible scoldings) so winning to me that in that way of looking at it you take stronger hold of me than any other and then too I do believe those cheeks are a little softer and the lips a little sweeter than the face a little dearer than any that even lay in a man's bosom. I have been thinking of my wild terrible soul—life two years ago—your marvelous songs were gushing through my heart all that winter, I did not quite know what it meant, though I used to ask myself if I loved you then even. I was bewildered, unreal, disordered. You know that poor Fanny and Mary saw me very often (I do not so much say I saw them) but

somehow or other my soul would burst out as you have seen it in those old paroxysms of sorrow and I would talk scarcely knowing what I said, though not by any means thinking of "love" as it is called. This led to the strange occurrences which I told you of in the terrible letter and which I certainly exaggerated there. But I thought then that you were engaged and I think now that it was that belief in good part which made me so fearfully sad then—for dear dear Fannie you scarcely know yet what it is for me to ...

Fannie to JLC (nd)
Although undated, this letter likely was written in 1852.

Sunday P.M.

O! my dear, dear friend, you do myself so utterly unable to remove from you one particle of your sorrow. I seem to be struggling and struggling with some terrible ill, while I am bound by a mighty spell so that I can neither move nor breathe. Would to heaven that I only had the power to bear your grief for you. Do not think anything of what I wrote in church this afternoon; I know not what it was; I only know that it must have seemed miserable mockery to you. Do not ask me to forgive you for revealing yourself to me, but you must tell me all do not keep anything from me; this anxiety and imagining wears me out. why should you not tell me all your feelings and why should that which was given us for our highest happiness be only a source of misery? it is not right Lawrence—indeed it is not. Do not reproach yourself for bringing any of your troubles to me. I want to know when and how you are suffering; but O! why is it that I can only cling to you and lean upon you and trust you when I would fain be strong to make you happy. I do not see that I have any of the influences over you that you told me I had; else why, why is it that when you are so full of woe, I can only come to you and press my poor, weak hand upon your brow and lean my head upon your bosom and rest upon your strength, and weep for you, without having the least power to remove your terrible grief. O! you do not know how wretched it makes me. But you must not look so gloomily upon everything; you think you do not, but you do. Tell me why you feel as you do, you cause me more unhappiness by such suspense as I seem to be in than you would if you told me everything. I entreat you if you are for me at all, not to make yourself so much misery through a mistaken idea of duty. Why should such a heart as yours be still? and why if it would be anything to you, would you forbid me from feeling any interest in you? What does it mean? tell me, O! tell me. I do not dare to go away and leave you in such a state of mind, and unless I can feel sure that you are calm and peaceful, I cannot understand why you should not tell me everything I am bewildered with a great deal that you say. I know what a heart yours is, and it is such a one as I cannot help loving—it is so generous and true. I have everything more to say but I am obliged to stop writing. With a heart-full of sympathy for you.

> Yours truly,
> Fannie

~~~)

Fannie to JLC (nd)
Also undated, this letter, too, appears to have been written in 1852.

Mon. P. M.

I have just received your precious, precious letter, but it almost killed me to see how troubled you were. O! do not be anxious again when you do not hear so soon from me, because I have more to hinder me from writing than you know of. I did not get your last letters until long after they were written. I must not say what I can hardly help saying to you now, for I must send this immediately to the office. God bless you, dear, noble heart. good bye Fannie

O! Lawrence it was you and your love alone of which I was thinking when I spoke to you of "man's love" I was thinking of you as a man, a strong and noble man and of myself as a frail, weak woman when I said what I did. I am sorry, sorry that you did not understand me better. Never speak of weakness in connection with yourself Lawrence. You are never, never weak, and you are manly just as I would have you be.

~~~)

Fannie to JLC, 1852

Do you not feel happier this afternoon than you did this morning? O! if I had only the power to comfort you as I would but I am afraid that I only make you unhappy. I shall not be happy when I am gone if I think of you as you were this. You are so generous and kind! You deserve to be full of joy and indeed you have a great deal to cheer you and fill you with hope. You must write to me often when I am away and I will write you only I shall be so afraid that my letters would not be much to you. I can never do anything right. I wish I could tell you what a strange, strange girl I am. I do not believe you know it. I meant to have written you before this but I could not. O! dear it was so terrible a letter that you wrote me this morning!

Fannie "Flees" to Milledgeville, Georgia

In February 1850, Sara Adams, Fannie's adoptive mother, passed away. About eighteen months later, Reverend Adams took a nine-week trip to Chicago that included a meeting on foreign missions. During the trip, he met and began courting Helen Root, a woman half his age and just six months older than Fannie. The day before New Year's Eve, the couple was wed in Reading, Massachusetts.

Within a year, the family dynamic was drastically changed by the arrival of Reverend Adams's new bride. Life in the household in Brunswick became unbearable for Fannie. She wrote of how Helen treated her as if she were a child and had even gone through her love letters from Chamberlain. Cousin Deb and another adopted daughter, Anna, had both left the home, Deb for New Jersey and Anna for Mississippi, leaving Fannie alone to bear all the unhappiness with her father and Helen.

Having spent several months studying music in New York under Helen's brother and noted musician George Frederick Root, Fannie had outstanding bills that Reverend Adams paid, but unlike previous expenses, he demanded that Fannie repay him. With Lawrence off to the seminary in Bangor for three years, Fannie felt she had little choice but to find employment that would allow her to leave the Adams home and earn enough money to repay the debt to her father.

In early December 1852, Fannie received word that Professor Root had arranged for her to teach vocal music at Miss Lucia Bass's female academy in the state capitol of Milledgeville, Georgia, and play the organ at the local

Presbyterian Church there. Altogether, the work would bring her $800 per year, an irresistible offer given her current situation.

A few days before Christmas, Fannie left Brunswick for Boston, where she would visit her birth family before continuing on to Georgia.

~~~~~~~

JLC to Fannie, 2/9/1853

Bangor Feb. 9th 1853

My dear little girl cannot see such a beautiful morning where she is. You must know that is has rained a week here and taken off every bit of snow and not many signs of winter were left, but now it has "cleared off" so brilliant and pure and mild that it seems as if the birds would be here next from the sunny south all but one, and the last rain froze upon the trees encasing them in ice so that this morning as I look our of my window it seems as if a thousand colors were actually alive in every tree and dancing and even singing about on the branches. Oh, it is so beautiful! and I have nobody to put my arm about and draw to the window or to go out with me and take a walk on the frozen smooth ground on the banks of this deep wild stream that flows near by.

Evening same day:
I have been at Mrs. Stetsons this evening, darling for this first time since that queer night how the sight of those familiar things so suddenly restored to my eyes all the scenes of which that house has been the witness. Although I was so very affable if the word is not somewhat assuming and tried to make my call agreeable to Mrs. S. as well as to myself still dear my thoughts were all gathered around the one image of my heart's earthly love and honor and worship. How I loved you then my Fannie darling when I thought of the room over that back drawing room where we sat this evening and then too I felt a still warmer flush and glow of affection when I remembered the other room. Do you remember all? Fannie darling, how your "husband" does love his gentle bird! Would that she could not be nestling in her own next. Think dear one how sweet it will be! Even tho' other things that we might desire be denied us, will it not be something at least if that one soon be granted! Good night love. He has promised to go to bed at half-past-ten every night and he must. One more kiss and a few more good nights! There dear! "Holy angels guard thy bed!"

Thursday eve. 10 o'clock

How he loves his darling! You would laugh to hear "somebody" when he makes his bed at night saying to himself, "I guess I know how to make a bed! I know who I learnt of! I guess she knows how! Darling bless her! Maybe someday she will put her now dear head on the pillow she has smoothed so sweetly for another head!" And then it is altogether pardonable if I do think that even now there might be soon enough in my bachelor bunk for somebody other than a dream. Fan, you do know how to make a bed and that is rather a rare thing really. And then if she is going to make "two little puddings" with her earnest honest heart all in the work just for my sake, I wont be so naughty as her as I was when she told me before. No Fannie, my wife, I will never be so stern to you as I was then. Since that time I have known you better and like you better too, my worthy friend, and I hope before long you will allow me the pleasure of buying the materials to be immortalized into Fannies first family pudding. Pardon me—I have no latent and lurking insinuation in my honest term family pudding. It shall be limited in its dimensions to the capacities of two eaters. Fan. I am going to learn "a lot" of stories to tell you by and by "when we sit side by side" Put your dear hand in mine now and sit down by my knee and lean on my bosom and we will have a mild dreamy story. And then she will sing a song for me and I will praise her wonderful deep voice that years ago thrilled the very depths of my soul. I don't know what we shall do then dear, but I suppose strange child, you will be climbing up to get your face a little closer to mine. Oh, I do love you very much Fannie, my lovely. But, tell me, in your very next letter, dearest, be sure that you forgive me for all my unkindness to you. Do forgive me, dear Fannie—not in words only but in deed and not in deed only but in words. Do, Fannie Good night to "my darling".

Thursday Feb 17th p.m.

How does my darling, darling do now; for it is a week who would think it since I wrote last in this letter. Why if my Fannie only did know how he does love her I think she would be pretty happy. At any rate if I was sure she was comfortable I should be happy now even with thinking about her. Bless the darling! I do love her. Fan, you don't know how much fun I keep up here. I made Prof Shepard[7] laugh fairly out at public declamation yesterday

---

7 George Shepard was professor of Sacred Rhetoric at the Bangor Theological Seminary, 1836–68.

with my drolleries, not in emending I mean but in other queer ways. You see I am critic of the declamations for this term and I find pretty good chances for fun. O if my precious darling were only here and was reciting to me (or maybe you would like me to say with me) in some of those things that we are going to study together, I should enjoy myself very much And then I am so happy how to see Father and Mother thinking so much of her. Fan, bird I want you to get your French all polished up while you are there, if you do not have to "rash" you "all over" as you used to do—or if your hair can submit to any less combing and frizzling truly formerly so that we can read some together. Darling! Wouldn't I love to take her in my heart forever my own wife?

That is enough I am sure to fill up one line as I am very sure it will be to fill up one life and one other thing that I can possibly think of a triditeral word beginning with G

Oh. I am a rogue, I know it, but then I must play with you because you know (we) I mean, am never going to have little playmates and you must let me play with you won't you? "my mother said I might come over and play with you this afternoon." Bless the darling, bless the darling, bless the darling

Friday eve.
Why does not my darling write to me? I hope its because she don't want to, and not because she cannot, for I had rather she would be a little careless of me than be sick herself. But then darling I have not really heard from you since you left Brunswick. You seemed to be in a great hurry when you did write and by the way if you did not get my first letter please tell me—I wrote it before I heard from you so that it probably awaited your arrival. Sometimes I have very sweet thoughts and hopes about you and then for a moment now and then I think you will not be very happy with me—there is not versatility enough about me—you would get tired of my dull dry barren sameness—though if you could look into any heart I think you would see some freshness and even some beauty and even beauty—changing in its seasons in the heart that loves you. I wonder sometimes if you will love me always and how you will love me. But after all, I don't know but I should dare to see the risk and maybe you could "make a shift" to love me some. I love you very much my precious precious one.

Your own Lawrence

JLC to Fannie 2/21/1853

[Antescript]No matter who wrote this letter

Monday Morning February 21st. I see, dear Fannie, on looking at the <u>dates</u>, that it is not three weeks yet since I had a letter from you and that circumstance makes me less concerned at not hearing from you; though I do not consider in general the fact of being <u>busy</u> as any reason or excuse for not writing a letter to a friend who sympathized in every phase of mind and every state of circumstances. I never make that apology for I never am and never can be so busy as that I can not find time to write to <u>some</u> of my particular friends. Taking the liberty to reckon you among that number, my dear lady I address you a few lines this morning, though not only severely pressed by my <u>business,</u> but also nearly abandoned by my natural and usual(?) good humor with myself and my mental capability thereby is suffering so serious a diminution that you will be called upon often to interpret according to the "analogy of faith" rather than by "the literal sense." You will permit me to say at the beginning that I have derived great pleasure from your acquaintance, and that it affords me more than ordinary satisfaction to believe our mutual interest has lost nothing by being occasionally rather extravagantly expressed—the reaction that might have been expected not having occurred.

This circumstance gives me the boldness and the assurance to measure upon a continuance of the blissful relation that has hitherto existed between us until some fortunate accident or providential arrangement enables you to look for sympathy and friendship and communion to one who will far better fulfill all these offices than a <u>friend</u> merely viz a <u>husband</u> I do not deny that I do somewhat in anticipation <u>envy</u> that by hypothetical and prospective individual. My feelings are a lot quieted much by the daily observation of what my fellow student Jotham Sewall experiences and enjoys. Be it known unto you that the aforesaid went over to Lewiston some time ago and returned in company with a miss Fanny Swett[8] whom he has deposited for security and for his private use and benefit at Dr. Pond's[9] the nearest house

---

8 Jotham Sewall (Bowdoin, Class of 1848; Bangor Theological Seminary 1854) married Fanny Swett in Lewiston, Maine, on March 14, 1855. He became professor of Rhetoric, Greek, and Ancient Languages at Bowdoin College and an overseer of the college while Chamberlain was president.

9 Rev. Enoch Pond held the chair of Ecclesiastical History at the Bangor Theological Seminary and became president in 1859.

to the fern (Mrs. P. is an aunt of hers I think) and I declare it does torment me to see him at the public meetings and lectures so _playing_ happy. Not that I envy him so much in _particular_ as I do in general. (You may apply the rules for "and of faith".) Now I tell you what it is Fan. Ch— if you don't write me a letter pretty soon, I'll torment you to death with epistolary racks and thumb-screws and whips and wheels and all imaginable things. You needn't think you are hid all so secret and smug just because you've got your head out of sight. Now mind you little rogue. I forget who sent particular love to you thro' me, but any how the medium assimilates it all into _homogeneity_.

JLC to Fannie, 4/26/1853

Quebec April 26th 1853

My dear Fannie

Here am I in this famous old city—waiting for a passage down the river. We left Montreal Saturday and had a glorious passage down the St. Lawrence, except that it was so slow. At last, however, the frowning citadel came in sight as if let down from the sky, and we "rounded to" under the friendly protection of the innumerable cannon which on every possible commanding position lie so sullen and watchful. As we came up to the wharf on a beautiful Sabbath morning with the English colors flaunting proudly above us, you would have smiled to see the immense motley crowd that lined the pier. All sorts and sixes and sexes (for there are more than two sexes here) and you would think all languages under the sun, greeted our coming as we were nearly the first steamer from the upper river. Well, after a while I got some what familiar with the city and dropped into the French cathedral where a pretty red-faced fair-haired priest was rattling off the catholic service in a mighty hurry. My attention however was soon called off from him and from the dense congregation to the beautiful little girls who eat around what I suppose is the altar all in which robes and all having a graceful white veil flowing down at each side—it really was exceedingly beautiful and the veils reminded me of some other sort of veil which I hope one day will fill be with a greater and better joy than even these white veils of the little imitation-angels of the French cathedral. In the afternoon I went to the English cathedral where I heard music that would have done you good. They manage the Amen well and with great affect. When the anthem ends be it forte or piano the final note is left square and at once then your ear is caught in the perfect stillness that succeeds by the slightest possible notes as if of very distant and very sweet music floating toward you—you feel it coming— on comes the rich stream from the organ nearer and louder and richer till all at once the choir catch up the notes in the same way and end with such a fervor that it inspires you. Well that will do for a journal—now to tell you of a few things in general, to rest you. This city is entirely surrounded by an impenetrable wall, through which the people of the suburbs (who by the way compose two thirds of Quebec) enter into the city proper. There are cannon mounted all along the wall on every side and two regiments of soldiers stationed here to keep things right. You will see also at almost every corner of the streets and especially at the gates old cannon set up in the grown for ports. The houses and all buildings are almost universally of stone. The streets very narrow and the people generally rather insignificant. The great deal of labor and skill and money is spent on the churches—in fact they are all magnificent even the old French chapel right opposite my window which is 300 years old is not bad. We have been on the plains of Abraham where the great battle was fought and I of course with my usual fondness for relics picked up a stone from the place where Wolfe "died victorious" as the inscription on the monument reads—I also went to the cliff where Montgomery was killed in endeavoring to climb almost perpendicular heights. I clambered up nearly to the place where he fell, but as I feared a fall too I did not attempt to go all the way so reaching up I "scaled off" of bit of the slate rock and "slid down". Yesterday we rode to the falls of Mont Morenci 7 miles below—and such a ride! and such magnificence! You must certainly see that sight. I cannot begin to tell you anything about it—I do not know how to describe the tremendous perpendicular sides of the gorge or the dizzy distance of the rushing white cataract. I crept along to the edge of the rock that overhangs the basin just below and looked down into the mist and the roaring. O, Fannie you must see this with me! I succeeded in breaking off a piece of the rock on the edge for a keepsake. About half way down to the falls is a beautiful cross erected—I should judge to the virgin Mary as the inscription is (in French) "O Marie who hast conceived without sin received us and pray for us." The whole country along our ride is very beautiful, much more so than the city. We took a turn on our return, around by the convent of St. Rock. Last evening we went into the Parliament. This morning we are to visit the citadel on the summit of the rock on which the city is built. I heard nothing but French at the house where we stop, and in fact that is the language of the place and is used even in the parliament. While I write, the girls are tripping about humming their French songs as gay as larks. I do not know when we shall get a passage down river—we are going more than 200 miles further and no ships as yet go down so far. We may however get a chance today. Father is delighted, and the falls set him in ecstasy. He said we must make another visit in the summer—I replied that it would do very well for my wedding tour—you would have felt it necessary, I suppose, to blush at that. I do not have a very good chance to write but I thought I would just let you know where I am. We shall have a hard tramp in the woods I suppose. Don't you think Father the other day said he should leave me in New York and I could come by way of Georgia if I liked! Did you ever? What a man. I wish you very much even here, dear Fannie, I do dream such dreams of you and more of them are very bewildering. You may know always that I am thinking of you that your name, breathed forth from my soul, blesses every place where my feet tread. I am very sure that I am day by day growing to you. You seem so refreshing and so fair to me that I rest thinking of you. You must not suppose this letter to be a fair species of my deceptive flowers, but only a little message to go, as I suppose you may be anxious about me. Do not be afraid of any ill to me although I am going into a wild country and among still wilder people. We are going down the river with a French (esquivacan), you never saw such a mass of blubber and miserable French. I manage a little French myself esquivacan and so we get along. I can't stop to explain the blots—with much love for the dear one who is my brightest and my beautiful earthly hope and joy

Your own Lawrence

JLC to Fannie, 5/4/1853

Remouski Lower Canada
May 4th 1853

Well here I am on the St. Lawrence yet, two hundred miles below Quebec now; and I don't know as I shall be anywhere else very soon. We have been detained by head winds since Saturday and there is every indication that the same monastery is in store for us some days to come. You need not laugh at this paper, for it is all I can get at Remouski—this place not being <u>exactly</u> at the head of civilization. Moreover you need not laugh at the writing; for I am obliged to use a steel pen, which as you know is not a favorite implement of mine. Finally you need not laugh at this letter; for my mind has been so withdrawn from everything having a tinge even of the intellectual, that mental effort is actually difficult. I have got quite black and coarse looking now—sixty miles riding lately from this place still farther down the St. Lawrence (which is a gulf here) in the very face of a cold wind and driving easterly rain would be enough to spoil my students' face with out the additional guaranty of forty or fifty miles footing it in the woods, now on snow shoes (the snow is three feet deep in the woods) now wading swamps and brooks, now trudging in some old road, now crossing rapid rivers on logs or fallen trees, and all that sort of thing. I wore every thin flimsy moccasins and my feet were wet all the time and then when I came to travel in the rough sharp icy roads with my tender feet took it seemed as if every step would be both a fish and a finisher. Positively I do not think I ever suffered such pain in my life. But I was determined not to complain and to keep up with the others. Father was very careful and kind to me, but there was no help and I resolved to "grin and bear it" I've found meaning in that phrase I tell you particularly the grin. It was actually a relief to me when in crossing a furious river on some logs that were floating down, I got on one that was too small and sunk in—it felt so refreshing. I concluded however that it was best to get out <u>from which place I now write to you</u>. I have got also quite Frenchy for it's all French here—you can't get along at all without it in speaking. I do not take the short course which was recommended by my friend the captain, "you sleep with French girl too might you speak French then very well" I content myself with rather more innocent flirtation and liaisons with the French country girls and some of them I assure you are very pretty. Only the trouble is, just as soon as they are grown up at all they are married and I <u>sometimes</u> make mistakes. Last night I had been sitting silent and sober some time, when a little French girl said to me in a French very archly and sympathizing "I am afraid your love is sad for you tonight" or may be more plainly "your sweetheart is only for you". I thought it might be so, but on the whole it struck me pleasantly it seemed so homelike to be reminded away here in this almost foreign land and too by a mere chance expression perhaps to rally me, of someone I need <u>never</u> to be <u>reminded of</u>. It made my dreams pleasant. Every new place I visit, every new thing I see—

every hardship I go through, every new experience I gain makes me love somebody more. What do you think of that?

JLC to Fannie, 7/16/1853

Bangor, July 16, 1853

Dearest Fanny

When you going to let me hear from you again, "idol of my affections." Here I've been longing and pining for the last fortnight or more—actually in a state of almost bowing or absolute desperation. However this may seem like anything but deep feeling—you'll know it's burlesque. Well, seriously—are you sick or well? Do you not know that the happiness of him you love as your own soul (aye far more than this, as you have always shown) depends upon the well being (the knowledge of it) of his own chosen loved one? But perhaps this is over anxiety—I ought not then to imitate my distrust of my darling or which is far worse—my distrust of Providence but I feel slightly blue today—and you know I am wont to do—and this must account for this miserable beginning—I wish Georgia new news—do not you? This p.m. hour be spent diff.y, I fancy, by both of us—What would we both give for even one hour together—for only one minute if we could have no more—for one <u>look</u> for me (?) etc— But let me not waste this paper and time in vain wishes for what cannot be—"Wait and hope" is an excellent motto— Let it be ours—

This morning I have been busy doing nothing—and now I am trying to rest myself. Sewall (I don't mean the Tutor—but a young cousin of his— whom I mentioned a while ago to you) is in here boring me and reading Smith's poems. He is a pretty good sort of a fellow and to tell the truth I like him. But then I want to be all alone when I'm talking with you. By the way have you read this new book of poems—it's received good reviews on par as I have read. I am perfectly carried away by it, as if we could read it together! We <u>will</u> some time—D.V. — It's full of the greatest imagery—great because so forcible—so plain—so simple. If I have time I would copy some passages—perhaps I will do before I close this letter.

For Fannie, this is me of that rascal Bill Sewell's work. He came in to have a <u>row</u> with me (as we sometimes allow ourselves to do) accompanied by that new modify of an English poet Alex. Smith. I took up the book and went on reading while he sat down at my desk and scribbled this to you in my voice. The scamp has missed some things however, that I fully feel about seeing you and reading together, etc. I confess that I have occasionally a sort of desire to know how you are doing, where you are etc; but I don't very often feel impatient about it, because I suppose you are well when you do not write. Only I get lonely and sad and strange when I have so little communication with you and I have read all your old letters over so many times that they are near "tongues end " there is no freshness now when I read them. Sometime I almost think there is no such person in this world as you—it seems to me all a dream—the past two years—and I feel again lonely and soul-sick as I used to before your beautiful love hung over me so like a gentle cherishing Mother over her darling baby. It would seem to me as if you were something more than the one whom I loved and who loved and who loved me—something like a healing, refreshing life-giving balm or breath of peace. It would seem so now if I could ever feel your influence as I used to. But you dear Fannie that I do not have much from you at all and so it seems so strange and unreal to me. But still after all and before all my heart clings to you with that same undying affection—that same confidence and fidelity which once we plighted to each other, and I shall be more than satisfied if your love for me is measured by my own to you. I miss too those intellectual conversations—those interesting stories which we were somewhat in the habit of carrying on and it is with nearly as much pride as pleasure that I look forward to the time when in the midst of worldly cares and toils I can have the sweet satisfaction of your companionship and communion. Forever very dearest one, your own loving Lawrence.

A good night kiss.

Fannie to JLC, 8/14/1853

Milledgeville August 14th 1853

My precious Lawrence did not dream that for a long fortnight past his darling Fannie had been sick, very sick part of the time. I did not imagine several days ago that I should be able to write you again as soon as this. And now I must not let myself write you a very long letter or I shall suffer for it, very severely I am afraid.

O! how I did long for you, my dearest earthly friend, while I was so ill and suffering so much. I thought that if you were only here to take me so tenderly in your strong arms, I shouldn't mind much if I did faint there. I had a fever such an unusual thing for me and a very severe attack of Erysipelas;[10] I believe that was what the doctor concluded at last to consider it, at first he imagined that I might have been poisoned by some venomous spider or other insect (is a spider an insect? how I hate even to write it's name!) My whole face and head were very much swollen, and for some days I could not open my eyes with the exception of a small crack in one of them. I was so suddenly reduced, that after a day or so, I could not be lifted up to have my bed made, without fainting; and then dear, my physician felt that my case required very prompt attention, so he resorted immediately to rather a violent and very painful remedy; and applied caustic to my whole face (nearly). If he had held my head in flames, it seems to me that I could have hardly suffered more. He wanted to kill the inflammation if possible, before it became seated upon my brain, but dear Lawrence I have been so troubled for a day or two, since a good, wise, old woman told me that the scars made by the caustic would always remain; others assure me that they will pass away in time, but I don't know what to think. You used to praise my cheek so, dear, and think it so pretty, that I cannot bear that you should see it altered. Don't be very much frightened though Lawrence, for it isn't very bad dear, and they all tell me that it looks much worse to me than it does to anyone else. A part of the time when I was sick, when my brain was somewhat affected, I was tormented with all the horrors of delirium tremors; hideous demons formed a circle around my bed, jeering so hatefully at me, frightful precipices yawned beneath me; and if I turned away, nests of sharp-pointed instruments were just ready to pierce me through; then an imp would dash almost a river-full of cold water into my face, and nearly strangle me. Satan himself was just about to appear to me when I leaned over a Bible that lay upon my bed keeping my eyes fixed upon it and he went away. Mrs. Orme tells me that they were quite anxious about me for a day or two, and that I have great reason to be

---

10 Erysipelas is a skin infection usually caused by group A *Streptococcus* bacteria. It often is accompanied by blisters, fever, shaking, and chills. Even if treated with modern antibiotics, the skin effects of the condition can last weeks.

thankful that the disease turned as it did. Dear Mrs. Orme, Georgia, and indeed all of the family, were very kind to me and everything was done for me that could have been done; only I could not help feeling that I was among strangers after all. I thought a great deal of dear mother, and the tenderness with which she used to watch over me when I was sick and of you too darling, and all your dear, loving devotion. Once dear Lawrence, I imagined that I grew worse and they sent for you to come to me, but when I looked up to see you standing by my bed-side, you appeared as a horrible monster and I shrunk away from you—then I seemed to become one myself. O! I did suffer very much dear, but it is all over now, and I have reason to be very, very thankful and I know how full of gratitude you will be to know that I am well again, or nearly so.

You wish me to write cousin D. I have written some weeks since, and I learn by a letter from her received several days ago, that my letter had been lying a fortnight or more in New York, when it came to her hands. I sent her the $10, which she so kindly lent me, and I was sorry to think it was lost. Did I tell you dear, that I had remitted to Father, $150, the first money I have received since I have been here? there is something more due with which I hope I can pay my board, piano-rent and so forth, but there is no knowing when it will come in. I didn't like that letter of "William Sewall's"[11] very well dear, what made you send it? isn't it funny that I didn't see that it was not your handwriting? but the manner of the thing was so unlike you, that I was really troubled at first; it seemed like what you would write if you "had been drinking" I was relieved when you really came at last. Miss Georgia was very much pleased with her note dear and Mrs. Orme thinks it is one of the prettiest things she ever heard; and I—I think it is darling! No matter dear about getting me "fern leaves"[12] and such books because you know they will be "gone by" in a great measure when I come to them and we will have enough other things to buy you know darling. Don't make fun of her so, when she is trying to learn to spell like a good child. Webster is my authority, I would have you to know, sir and he spells "respit" just as I do. Will you please dear be so kind as to send me by mail if you can easily

---

11 William Sewall graduated from Harvard University in 1849 and the Bangor Theological Seminary in 1854.

12 *Fern Leaves from Fanny's Port-folio*, was a collection of articles written by Fanny Fern (1811–1972). It was published in 1853. Fanny Fern was the pen name of Sarah Payson Wills of Portland, Maine, a humorist who wrote novels and children's stories. She was the first woman to have a regular newspaper column in an American newspaper. The book sold 70,000 copies in its first year.

a little of what Barret calls, "commercial note paper?" I cannot get anything like it here or in Savannah. You know what I want; it is large and thick and smooth. I cannot even procure any nice letter paper here in these outlandish regions. Please tell me dear what was the expense of the advertisement you put in the paper for me? I know you will laugh heartily at some things in this letter, you old comfort, but I don't care.

Adieu mio caro
Your Fannie

Was it you dear who sent me those musical paper? The note paper I speak of is nearly the size of small letter-paper.

⌇

JLC to Fannie, 8/19/1853

Aug 19th 1853

I wish my darling Fannie could be with me now through these beautiful days, and maybe through part of these glorious moonlight nights too. I miss you very much. I do not seem to be in a very good state of health after all this summer—though rather better I think than I was last. You know I don't have quite so much of a draught upon my strength as I did part of the summer! I have to go to bed now because I have nobody to sit up with. Sometimes somebody comes to see me there and I have pretty intoxicating dreams I am not sure how I shall spend the approaching vacation. I don't know whether to teach school somewhere, or to remain about my old premises here and keep my German classes going and preach (if you will let me) of the Sabbath in some of the surrounding towns. I should rather prefer the latter. But a new idea is in my head at present that is that grandfather wants me to go to Indiana with him. If I do I shall make an effort to slip into such a place there in some of the western colleges as we were talking of and not return till spring. I do not intend to set your imagination going by telling you any of my notions about it for it is all at present quite a contingency. You need not suppose that because I don't carry out and realize every thought and possibility I am therefore not doing anything. I feel pretty sure that the Providence which has hitherto led me by so pleasant a way will order all things so that I shall at last be in the right place. We should pray, I think that God will not suffer us to have our own way, but will lead us in his. We shall certainly be happier on the whole. Nobody can tell dear Fan. how I trust in you and how often my doubts and fore shadowed gloom are disputably the through of you. I hope you can be to me all that I make you in my meditations. Do not be troubled about any of the things <u>we have spoken of</u>. You may be sure that I will not be so sensual and so unkind as to expect of you so slavish a sacrifice—I want to give you an opportunity to be what you can be (so that if you don't it will be your <u>own fault</u>—isn't that selfish enough?) but dear Fannie, I hope you are well and happy. I was very glad to have you say "there were some pleasant thing about y'r present position." I trust it may be so now and still more hereafter. a great many send love to you through your Lawrence

Horace to JLC, 10/3/1853
Chamberlain's brother Horace wrote this letter about finances to him in autumn 1853.

Bowdoin College—Monday morn—Oct 3 1853

Lawrence the accompanying letters have come to hand this morn from Bangor in Peaslee's hand with a little note from Sae saying that I bought it over Thursday eve and she thought best to send it on then. She was well as it might relieve some anxiety.

Sam brought a tote for you from Sae that morn you left but it was of no consequence to you, only sending $7,00 to me says that Father had just answered I suppose. I would send you more money if necessary or Mother they probably got our letter Sat. and will forward you the amt. immediately. If anything comes here for you I'll send on for 1 week to Boston—A Adams[13]. The first lesson in Liby came off this morn. and the Greek is to come at 11. yrs. HBC

P.S. I shall not want any more money present HBC

---

13 Ashur Adams, Fannie's biological father, lived in Boston at this time.

Fannie to JLC, 9/11/1853

Milledgeville Sept. 11. 1853

My dear Lawrence,
What do you suppose could have caused such a delay in the arrival of your last letter? Why it was at least <u>nine days</u> after it was mailed, that I received it here. Are my letters ever so long in reaching you? I never count upon more than five days, unless something very unusual is the matter. I sat down a long hour and ½ day to write to you dear, but I fell into such an interesting day-dream, that I forgot that my pen was idle all the time. I wish I could tell you exactly what day dreams are, with me; for it seems to me that they are very peculiar. when I build "castles in the air," there are no tangible plans in the matter, but it is as if I were borne aloft and far away, into scenes, often times very thrilling and exciting, which are really at the moment transpiring and I experience all the emotions which would possess me in the reality. Do you think dear that I have an uncommon imagination, or what is the strange and great peculiarity of my mental constitution? Do tell me candidly what you think about when you write me again, won't you Lawrence dear?

You would quite laugh at your little "w—" if you only knew all about her "day-dream" this afternoon. It was all about our little home that is to be; O! I wish you could see the sweet picture that I did! The "<u>two</u> little rooms"[14] were all, but they were so tasteful and attractive, and all within the bounds of probability too! Then I was all absorbed in a pretty story about your coming home one rainy night, the first time you had ever been away without <u>me</u>; and I <u>actually</u> heard the noise of the wheels as you drove up to the house, and then you cannot imagine how dearly I had arranged everything, just as I knew you would love to have it. I dressed myself up just as prettily as I could, in a little new dress that was a present from <u>you</u>, and then wheeled up our little lounge near a bright, <u>home</u>-fire, brought your dressing-gown and slippers, and then I know what a little <u>scene</u> we had when we had closed the door of our dear home-room upon all the world! I was talking with Mrs. Orme about you a little the other day, and told her something about your temperament; how easily you were troubled—how

---

14 This phrase, often shortened to "two rooms," represented their idea of a home together once they were married.

sensitive you were, and so forth, and how fearful I was constantly lest I should wound you in some way, innocently. She told me that this thing would be a great source of distress to me, through life, with my temperament particularly, for that no wife could avoid doing something occasionally, that would not meet her husband's views, and would offend them perhaps. I do not think Mrs. Orme quite understood me at first, but whether or not, you do not agree with her, do you dear Lawrence? you do not think that we shall ever have that kind of trouble do you? O! tell me that you do not! for I cannot bear that thought. Now dear I want to answer some of your questions contained in the letter before your last; (by the way I'm delighted at your success with Prof. Stowe[15] thus far.) you ask if I would like to go into a new country like the west; well, the truth is, I am not certain that my preconceived notions concerning the west are at all correct; for I find the south so different from my anticipations, that I shall not in the future rely so much upon what other people occasionally say, but entirely (almost) upon my own judgment. Will the aspect of things in "a new country" necessarily be unrefined and common? (I mean that "common" in a peculiar sense, and no other word exactly expresses it) and do you think it quite certain, dear, that a western climate would be injurious to my health? As to the south, the thermometer never stands here so high as it does at the north, but of course there is less variety of temperature. The winters are less cold (full cold enough though) and it is warm later into the fall and earlier in the spring; that's all the difference, and I do not feel in the least confident that your health would suffer at the south. It seems to me that people here complain of the heat more from habit than anything else. I am surprised that there is such a want of refinement here, there is a lack of poetry, that I feel in everything, and I am most disappointed in that particularly. I think that the effect of slavery is incomparably worse upon the white than the blacks. Miserably worse upon the whites than the blacks. Miserably ignorant, vulgar-minded negros are the "bosom companions" (almost) of southerners from the cradle up; what could be expected then? It seems to me that Virginia or South Carolina would be far preferable for residence to Georgia; I don't know about Savannah though. I pine sometimes for companionship; for there is no one here who is really congenial. It is strange, but I have not met with a single person since I came here, who had any

---

15 Calvin Stowe, Bowdoin, Class of 1827, and husband of Harriet Beecher Stowe, was professor of Natural and Revealed Religion at Bowdoin. At this time he was helping Chamberlain find work as a teacher.

poetical thought or feeling; there is not the slightest hue of romance about any being or anything. I cannot entirely account for it, but it is even so. Georgia (to whom somebody keeps sending his love!) is a good, <u>clever</u> (in our Yankee sense) girl, with not one spark of original thought <u>beautiful</u> feeling; and I was surprised to find that she even had appreciation enough to admire your note to her; but she was pleased with the <u>attention</u>, and knew it must be beautiful, partly because her mother was so much pleased with it. Mrs. Orme says that your best way would be to come south and take a school or become known to the public in some such way; but I do not agree with her <u>much</u>. I wish I could go to Athens and see what sort of a place it is. The professorships there are filled by appointment as it is the "state university" Dr. Church, the president was a northern man; do you know anything about him. Mrs. Orme says that it takes <u>strong influence</u> to get in <u>them</u>, but the salaries are large and certain. What department do you consider most desirable for you, taking everything into account?

I admire your subject, "the melancholy of genius"! It is just what I would have chosen in all the world, for you and I. But I want to know what you said, dear. what is the matter with Helen[16]? to change the subject a little; Mary Dunlap writes, that the physicians now that they have decided upon her disease, have little hope of her recovery, although they think she may continue in the same state for some time. Poor thing! I am sorry for her! I am sure. Is she still in Bangor? Poor father! Poor father! It grieves me to think of his being so lonely and sad and changed. But he seems to have thrown me away, and I presume it matters little to him how I feel about it. do you think he really cared much when he learned how sick I had been? tell me dear, when you write again, for it may save me many bitter tears, if I can know exactly how he feels towards me now; but don't say the best you can, just to comfort me, <u>be sure</u>. O! those things he has said to me! they <u>almost kill me</u> even now. I never, never can get over them in this world. The mails have been entirely interrupted for a long time, in consequence of the heavy rains that have rendered the rail-roads and impassible so my letter has not gone before. I hope dear, you've not been anxious. From your own dear Fannie

16 Helen Root Adams, Rev. George Adams's second wife, lived into her nineties. She traveled alone to Boston at this time, when doctors told her she was "... run down from manifold cares and anxieties."

JLC to Fannie, 9/28/1853

In my blessed girl's own little room
Brunswick Sept. 28th 1853

From this sanctuary of my heart, my dearest Fannie, I shall write you a bit of a letter, sitting at your own table and surrounded by these precious relics and remembrances of you. Then when I have prayed for my beautiful girl so far away and entrusted her anew to the holy care of God, I shall lie down in her own bed to sleep and sweetly dream of her; oh my more than bride if I could only tell you how strong a tide of love flows towards you from the heart that once won you—may I say so? That once and long ago won you here! Would that I could only tell you about it and how I can see now that my love for you had grown larger and purer and deeper since I last pressed you to my heart in this sacred room. I slept in the dear bed last night—Mrs. Adams[17] was kind enough to let me and I talked myself to sleep with you, till a dream came and carried it all to heaven; for it brought you and you were my own dear Fannie just as you used to be. But my precious precious girl, I am troubled very much about you—especially as I do not hear from you quite so soon again as I expected. Moreover I do not think you had better stay there any longer after you can well get away. Father has taken the matter up now in great earnest. He and mother have come to the conclusion that you must not stay there any more and just as I came away mother was going to get father to write to you, making a proposal which they are sanguine enough to hope you will receive with favor. Perhaps our family modesty will prevent his writing. He was going to propose to you to come and teach Sarah and Thomas on the piano at such a salary as I think would satisfy most any young lady. It would be a pleasant home for you my darling, for a little while to be sure it is not a very refined or elegant society; but every advantage which father's large heartedness and mothers good sense and Christian character could procure should be yours. There are other advantages, which my own position and acquaintances together with your genius and beautiful character would ensure so come my own darling! I know it will be pleasant for you and of great benefit to me. I have been telling mother how I have missed you and felt the lack of your influence the past year. She wants you to come. We have plenty of room. I would not

---

17 Rev. Adams's second wife Helen Root Adams, essentially Fannie's stepmother.

plague you much. If you will come I will go for you at any time—if not this winter at least in my April vacation—The first I knew of father's plans was his outbreak to me the other day. "Lawrence don't you want to go to Georgia this vacation and bring home your girl?" Why no, father "yes" said he, "I'll fit you out well, for it" Where shall I bring her to "say I. "Why here to be sure" and then came the talk. He feels great interest in you and so does I. Do write and tell me about it. I am so anxious about you Fannie bird. I do not stay there, if it is not pleasant to you dear. Do tell me just as it is; which I fear you have not done yet and let me come and get you. My own darling will not rob me of herself by getting sick unnecessarily will she? What shall I do, if she loses her health? Think about it my dear and act as you think best. There are many advertisements this Autumn for teachers in New Jersey and some of middle western states. Maybe it would be better for you to go further north. But do tell me just how you are situated at Milledgeville. Perhaps by this time you are anxious to know why I am here. I came to get Horace[18] entered into college. You know I have fitted him in a year and that is rather a short time; but he entered with a clean ticket that is with no condition assignment of any study to be made up. I feel very well about it and darling I am received so beautifully in Brunswick that I cannot be very sad here except when I see some dear thing that reminds me of our early love. Then I go to you all anew and love you better and better. I did not think to be so well received here. All the college officers are astonishingly courteous and familiar and everybody seems delighted to see me. Did you know you have a great many strong friends at Brunswick? I begin to like the town again as I had ceased doing since you went away. I love this dear dear room. Might I just peep into the drawers and see the funny little things that look so much like "oo"? I expect every moment to see the dear child herself tripping in and punishing me with a kiss. Why, the door of the room is just the same as it was. That I suppose is from something in your drawers. I am going away Saturday morning and when I come again maybe somebody will come with me. My darling must be very careful not to work too hard as she recovers from her illness. It takes longer to get well than it does to get sick. She shall hear from me again pretty soon. If she writes immediately she may direct to care of Ashur Adams[19] (maybe you know him) Boston, as I shall be there in a while from today. But maybe you would not reach me

---

18 Horace, Chamberlain's next youngest brother, graduated from Bowdoin in the Class of 1857.
19 Fannie's biological father.

then better direct to Bangor as usual Mrs. Adams and father send love and sympathy. Good by to my blessed bride. Her own Lawrence.

JLC to Fannie, 10/10/1853

Boston October 10th 1853

My darling Fannie
Thank you for the dear letter. I was expecting it, having charged little Sa[20] to send your letters to Boston to your father's care. When I got in to town I was so tired I could not go out to Roxbury my fifteen hours ride in stage coach and cars from Fryeburg was a hard one, so Sunday evening after thinking and worrying about you, till I had got myself into a most superstitious apprehension, I walked to Roxbury and found not only the beautiful welcome but the <u>welcome</u>, <u>beautiful</u> letter. You may imagine what a frenzy I was in, when I tell you that because the bell was not answered immediately and I saw no light, I felt sure that you were dead and all the family were gone to the funeral and poor, sorrow-stricken I did not even know where it was. The great drops stood thick and cold on my face. Your mother came and taking my hand in both of hers asked "where have you been? Have you seen Fanny?"! I actually sink into a chair. but a few words set everything right; and I seized your letter and read it first hastily to see if you were well—but strange strange child, you did not mention one word about your health—how do we know but you are not well yet? I read some parts of the letter to your family (not the one you are going to have(!) for <u>he</u> had read it to himself twice) but to your "folks" You are very dear to me, darling, both subjectively and objectively—to speak philosophically—and I think my little genius of a "w___" will understand me. You show me to many proofs of your constant and sweet affection you need me so dearly, that I couldn't help loving you if I should try not to. And then you are the <u>prettiest</u> girl I've seen this many a day. Why I'm as proud of you as I can be. I like you so—you suit me so exactly! Then too I know that I couldn't feel quite so strong a <u>passion</u>—such a kind of dreamy, voluptuous delirium for any other girl; no matter how seductive she was; and my darling Fanny only

---

20 Chamberlain's sister Sarah, whom the family called "Sae."

can make such a passion other and better and sweeter than a mere physical sensuousness. Why, what strange talk! But you see I love you with all sorts of love and with something more than anything which most people call love. You need not be afraid—I shall not plague you quite as I used to. I am getting quite steady! Your "day dream" was very dear—and it is all and altogether within the reach of probability, and can scarcely be failed of except by our own fault. We will never let such a cause cheat us out of so great happiness, will we my own love? You ask me about your "mental peculiarity." I do not feel quite bright enough to analyze your character, but I should say it is a strong rich imagination in repose; or rather, perhaps, too strong for so slender and delicate a constitution—not having such a balance of actuality or activity in temperament as would work up some of the dreams into living, in perishable expressions. I am going to take you in hand with a course of studies that will make a goddess of you. Ah! I'm proud of my beautiful little "w___". Maybe you'll think I don't allow you enough in my hasty "critique"; but I don't want to praise too much that already over strong quality in your mental character. I recognize the richness and beauty of it; but it will be richer, even more than ever, when it is brought out bye and bye. So be a good girl and dream as many things as you will. bye and bye the dreams will burst forth into life and loneliness—yes, rogue, I suppose you will plague me some—not so much as Mrs. O. thinks though and maybe you won't feel very much pleased with me too, sometimes—we shall probably have to forgive things in each other once in a while—such maybe the case. I don't say it must be. I am going to make a solemn resolve not to have the first unpleasant thing between us so far as I am concerned. O, it's just as we make it that's the amount of it all. I am forbearing and so are you. We'll get along well, I am sure—as for Athens, I have no desire to go there. I don't know yet what will come about, but I don't want to stagnate in the South. Yes, my love, your father did care about your sickness. He feels grieved too that you do not make more of him. I am going to try to have a better understanding between you. Do write to him just as you feel—then he will show you how much he cares for you. Your father at Roxbury too is very anxious about you and sympathizes with you fully. I have a thousand more things to say, but no time. Please tell me about the paper. Tell me too about coming home. I must have a little bit of a letter from you in a fortnight—sure. One "honeysuckle" kiss, more for my darling love from her own Lawrence.

JLC to Fannie, 10/23/1853

At home Oct 23 1853

My dearest Fannie,
It seems so strange to me to have you away that I hardly know what to do with myself. When I think of what you are to me, of what sort the interest is that I have in you, I can not reconcile myself to the thought of your being away. I miss you very much—I feel the loss. I am losing my acquaintance with you. You are to me now what I make you in my own heart. I hear so seldom from you, that there is not continuity enough for any great growth or progress in acquaintance or mutual influence. In writing to you I write more to a blessed memory or still more blessed hope, than to what you are at the instant. I do not think it is well for you to be away. I am sure it is not dear Fannie; so do manage to come home pretty soon, or else, darling, write to me a little oftener. You must, Fannie. I cannot pretend any longer to get along so easy without you. To be sure, dear, I am in the midst of friends and there are some that love me dearly—but I long for you, my darling, my generous-hearted and noble-minded girl. I want your counsel and your sympathy. I want to talk with you about a thousand things which I cannot so freely discuss with any other person. I cannot study without you. I want you to talk with. And I need too your moral influence. Do not laugh at me Fannie, I want you to keep me from temptations, which I am liable to have—when if only I could come to you and love you, they would cease their drivings. How could such temptations come to a heart that is full of you? Cousin Annie[21], whom I am beginning to know a little, keeps or rescues me from many a dark and dismal hour of sadness or temptation; for I have enough of both. Ah! too much—too much. But I see her often and she is such a treasure to me! But I want you too, dearest, and you should see if I did not love you more than your heart imagined. Come to me, my own Fannie; write to me as you used to as you do darling—only more, for I need it.
Wednesday 26th yes, darling she did write to me! And I was so glad to get the letter. Are the poor dear eyes so bad that she cannot write just such dear letters even if they might be a little shorter some what oftener? I think her "L___" as she roguishly calls him sometimes would be much better every

---

21 Annie was Hannah B. Chamberlain, the daughter of Jefferson Chamberlain, his father's younger brother. Her family lived in Bangor, a short walk from the Seminary. See letter of December 26, 1852.

way if he could have such a letter as this pretty often. Are you not a little surprised at cousin D's proposal to your father? Is it or not a tacit or implied confession of having been in the wrong? It was however (i.e. the "however" in the sense of the word in Butters analogy at all events—in any case) it was, I say, very generous in her. As to the other things you speak of—the "woeful words" I have not one word to say except that I hope and shall do all in my power to effect, that there will be a complete restoration of confidence and sympathy between you and your father. I talked of the matter with y'r own parents in Roxbury. I think I do not now know exactly how this will come about, but I trust it will. I did not congratulate you about the $150.00, I know dear but I was so anxious about you that I could not pay much attention to the miserable price at w'h you are selling all your present comfort and I fear me something more. How is your health my Fannie, you do not say—I can only advise you to do as you think best about staying at Milledgeville. I had rather you would come farther north—perhaps y'r balance y'r next profit would be as great. However I think that unless you find yourself able at the end of this year to pay the full amt. of the fine, you might well consider that it was not very profitable to teach at that place. I will tell you my whole and only feeling about you and your labors. Spare yourself. I have something better for you to do than that wearing wasting profitless anxiety. (I don't mean any roguishness now, about something better for you to do—you need not scold me) don't get worried and discouraged my darling, about not being able to accomplish all that you would. Do what you are well able to—there is not hardship in that. Leave the rest to me and all to God. Keep bright and rosy and smiling there are ten thousand unavoidable delights for us yet. I trust you and love you fully. I have a stout heart for you to lean on if there is any manliness in me, it is yours. You seem miss rogue to be rather curious about my financial concerns. Don't be concerned lest I can't support you and the (!) I shall not be immediately dependent on my salary. But it is true that I don't have much money of my own now. I don't want much now. By and by an extravagant little wife (!) will—make it very delightful for me to show her that her darling love and care for me is not unappreciated nor unreturned. Why Fan. I own 400 acres of land and a fine black horse at any rate!! What do you think of that for a student? Now don't laugh at me. When so many rich and splendid men would like to put you beyond the reach of a thought about money—only to have you for a wife. But you preferred poor me. Thank you, darling, once more for that generous love and sacrifice. Let us hope that sometime your poor Lawrence will be able by the smiles of his dear darling Fannie to do something worthy of her. On my next letter I will try to answer more questions in your last letter. Did not say very much any way! Why dear? To these troubles let me say for John Crosby[22] that he did tell Cummings to carry "them" home. I wanted them but they are in y'r father's bed chamber. May be we shan't want any. Forgive me I couldn't help that one! Lawrence

⁓

JLC to Fannie, 1/18/1854

Bangor Jan. 18th 1854

My dearest Fannie,

I am just as busy as I can be but it never seems to take up much time to write to you; or if it does I can't make it seem like lost time exactly. I think I have not acknowledged your last <u>good long</u> dear letter (or Dec. <u>number</u>). I must thank you for such a dear letter—I had waited for just such a one a long while. You seem to be considerably astonished that I don't forget you and fall in love with somebody else.

Now you know, Fan, that <u>that</u> was in now part of our stipulation. I never promised to forget you as soon as you were out of my sight. Besides if I <u>hadn't</u> promised to love you I <u>know</u> you and there, I declare Fan I <u>love</u> you and I can't write a word to you without almost stopping ot tell you so for the thousandth time. I do see other girls and (to confess) for an instant I do sometimes feel a very peculiar sort of a thrill or drawing or stirring or something and—but I'm not going to get you mad with me by telling the whole mischief. Yes I do "see" a great many girls but I don't see any that do not make me love you more. You want to know what I am reading now-a-days. I think you would laugh to see my course of reading. Old musty tome in outlandish languages and some in harder English that have been quarreled over for ages—a few Hebrew books some Greek—more Latin— half a dozen medical books, a manuscript lecture or two—these constitute my reading at present. All the beautiful books that I know of I am keeping to read with you. I have a very diverse little library, for us bye and bye. I think I am doing something in the way of solid acquirements this year

---

22 John Crosby was a graduate of Bowdoin, Class of 1863. There were two Cummings in the same class: Ralph W. and Ephraim C.

though I cannot for my life make any sort of regular system of study but when I take a fancy to one particular book and any particular time why I just sit down and go at it. That (you may not know) is not my usual practice. Fannie, would you object to my taking a place as assistant instructor in Hebrew in a Theo[logical]. Sem[inary]? Not this one—I suppose you would not at all consent to that—but for example in the new seminary in Illinois (or somewhere out west I declare I don't know where now) I should like such a place—the advantages of it would be great in giving me time to perfect myself in other things and then I should be in the way of preaching now and then. I should like very much to stay at Bangor in such an office, but somehow I am afraid that we should not find it altogether so convenient though I should find less difficulty probably in getting the place here than elsewhere. I want to mention the matter to your father; but I am afraid he will not approve of it or that it will not be best I don't know what else to do than to keep where I am and so all I can every way. I feel as if I could do something with the support and sympathy of my blessed Fannie—I do not think she will hinder me from doing what I can do and being all that I might be. I look forward indeed with some painful apprehensions with some shrinkings; but I can not think of damping all my fathers hopes of me and defeating all my mothers prayers. I must and will do something and be something. And you too darling oh my darling I do not get along very well without you. I get sad and lonely—so lonely, dear one, and nothing seems to satisfy me or soothe me. I am sorry I cannot see you darling, once in a while now-a-days. I miss you. I cannot bare you away from me much longer. I am wondering how you will look when I see you again, and whether I shall be afraid of you. But if my precious one could come to me tonight and rest in her own place I would try not to be much afraid of her. Poor little girl, it is a great while since she came to her "own house" and it is a great distance for her to come tonight, but maybe she will come in a sweet dream and maybe too the dream will be only a foretaste of a verity! Pretty soon she will come and will not go away again. Only love me now, love me, darling, and speak lovingly to me for I need your sweet words to keep me. Write to me, Fannie love, as you used to in the days of our earlier love. Do not leave me to guess and to hope only but tell me—come to me—blend with me and let the perished fragrance of the dear honeysuckles once more live and float around us. Lawrence to his own.

JLC to Fannie, 6/17/1854

Bangor June 17th 1854

My dear Fannie,

I have got home again—that is—to my room at the seminary, and I am not very well; being in such an unsettled state too, in every respect <u>almost</u> makes me quite at a loss for any comfortable feeling. I am wishing very much to see you my Fannie you are very dear to me all this long, long while that I do not see you and I am anxious to take you as soon as possible to your own home forever. I have considered the matter you propose to me and have come to the conclusion that if I could get the place you spoke of I would be willing to undertake it. I have asked the opinion of some weighty persons and am advised on the whole to try it. It is however very difficult for me at this distance to make any thing like a favorable impression on the authorities; though I can command any amount of <u>testimonial</u> so far as that goes. I went to Brunswick to lay the case before your father, who with parental kindness not only approved and seconded my wishes and flaws, but offered to take the lead in the affair so that the preliminary steps are in his hands. I think they are as sure of success there as anywhere. You can have no idea of the <u>intensity</u> of my determination which I manifested to your father in such a remarkable degree that he seemed scarce of knew me—to leave no honorable means unattempted to carry this point if possible. Fanny I <u>know</u> I could sustain myself. All, <u>all</u> I want is to get the place. My father and mother are anxious I should not be longer here (in the <u>sem</u> I mean) than is necessary and they are desirous of seeing me settled as soon as possible. (Don't think them selfishly looking for <u>grand</u>.........!) And Fan, if I don't succeed as your father seems to think probable after all our efforts why I'm going to try the next opportunity and so on. I have a good many compliments now-a-days in the matter of my general style and promise, but I know the other side. I am glad your mother at Roxbury thinks her baby is going to do well. O, Fan. if you only could be with me in these days and help me and cheer me I should be better. I do love my darling child just as dearly as always, if I <u>don't</u> write such sweet letters to her. I'm sorry I have been writing naughty letters to you, dear, when you are already so troubled. Don't, darling, be anxious about anything if you can help it, for I will do everything that you want me to, and I do not want you to be wearing out with unavailing care. Now cheer up, my own love, and be happy for it will be only a little while now, before she will come to him—to her own place. Tell me, dear, would it kill me, do you supposed, to go to Georgia from here in the summer? For example, now? I am much disposed to be bilious since my poisoning affair and any such change of climate, I fear would give me a bad turn.

I think your father may have written to Mr. Orme in relation to the place at Athens. If so, I hope (and need not doubt, need I) that he will take the best measures to open the matter to Dr. Church. Your father thought he might send the letter he wrote directly to Dr. Church and then if there was any chance at all we should know it at once. I think we have taken the best and most strenuous means consistent with any degree of modesty. I am expecting to know by the first of July or a little later whether there is any hope at all. You see there may be many applicants nearer and known and of some standing. But if I only had a trial in an objective sense I mean—I am sure I could hold my place not very disgracefully. I am doing something every day darling to make me stronger and greater and I have improved so much you would think better of me than ever. Maybe though after all I am not worthy of such a darling girl as—somebody.

JLC to Fannie, 7/6/1854

Joshua wrote to Fannie shortly after the death of her biological mother Amelia. Fannie's sister Charlotte also was ill, and the death of her mother worsened her condition. Charlotte lived until the following year.

Bangor July 6th 1854

My darling Fannie,

I suppose you may have had a letter from me a few days ago, but I want to write you often now, dear, when everything must be so sad to you. Perhaps you have heard from Charlotte more direct than through me; but in case you have not, I must now tell you all that can be told as I gathered from Dr. Adams' account. She was getting better when I saw her, but the shock of her mother's death affected her as we may suppose. She is prostrate again. George[23] sits by her night and day. She wishes no other hand but his to care for her and he is as delicate and gentle as if he were born for no other object.

---

23 George Wyllys Adams, the oldest brother of the family.

It is feared, my dear, that Charlotte may not recover. Some think she may not continue more than a month. I fear this last opinion is most probable. She seemed bright when I saw her, but it was a frail brightness. Your father bears it as those who know him would expect. In all he does or says he bears that dignity of sorrow—that large nobility which could only mark such a soul as his. Mrs. Crosby told me he wrote a most beautiful and elegant letter when he announced to Deacon Adams the death of your mother.

I feel, my darling, as if I had lost something—something I needed and which I can not easily or ever make up. I feel the solemnity—the weighty— teaching of these days of mourning. I trust, my blessed child, you may take it to heart too, and in such a way as she that has departed so earnestly wished. Fannie, the last time I saw her I sat with her alone until eleven at night. It was a time of tears. She was talking of you, my dearest, and how she was longing for her dear daughter to live in the light that was cheering her heart through dark and troublous times. We both were hoping and praying that you might not fail of that without which everything else is nothing.

If you care to have me answer the questions in your last letter which I had waited for nearly two months, I will tell you that I went to Providence with mother and stopped in Boston on my return. I left your little picture for them to see. They were glad to have it. I am especially glad now. Mother had a very pleasant visit in Boston—in Providence I meant to have said, but it is true of either place. From Boston I went to Brunswick to see y'r father about the place at Athens. He very generously offered to take hold of the case immediately and to write to Mr. Orme or Mr. Alexander (a classmate of his) such a letter as he thought would be best with the expectation that it would be forwarded to Dr. Church. You may be sure the matter is taken hold of as energetically as it can be, at this distance. For my part I am extremely anxious to go, now. The objections you refute are not the serious objections I had in view. Those I am willing to waive or to meet. You remember, Fannie, I asked you if I should go to see you this summer vacation. You said no, I understood from your letter. It is too late now. However I do wish I might be there now; for perhaps I might do more in person than by any amount of letters from any sort of persons. I don't know how it may be if I only had one friend there who would spare me those thing which in me would be immodest and egotistical. I might perhaps make more impressions.

I hope you will write to me soon—if you hear of any way by which I could make more successful movements. I am anxious to succeed in this. I feel more than ever competent. I am giving my studies a little turn towards history and think if I pleased I could weary you with details of all my "interest in the enterprise" you speak of and of my "scholarship" which is fair or if you want to know I have made more advancement in scholarship than nine tenths of our liberally educated men. I profess to be something of a scholar, dear. I shall be very anxious to hear from you often.

As to that question you ask me "looking into your eyes" to answer, I won't answer it little rogue—you know well enough yourself. Do let me hear how you are every week which the cholera lasts. Do. I shall be very anxious all the time. Tell me all about things that concern you and us.

JLC to Fannie, 7/23/1854

Bangor July 23rd 1854

My own darling Fannie,
You will not find any fault with me I am sure for taking this big sheet to write you a letter—I suspect I shall fill it if I say all I am wanting to say to you now. Tell me first of all, darling, how you are—if you are well and loving me just as always, in your loneliness and sorrow. I wish I could see you. I sit down as just now in the twilight on a Sabbath evening and think about you and love you with all the warmth and beauty of our old love (old in time, not in spirit) but when I begin to write I think of so many troublesome and harassing things that it spoils the freshness of all I had in my heart to say to you. Be sure of one thing, my own dearest darling, that I do love you as I always have, and must ever love you. I long for you. You? Why, my Fanny, do you remember who you are? Do you, sweet darling? Come now dear and sit on my knee and talk with me, this Sabbath evening. I am alone in my chamber. The windows overlook the most of the city—or would if the foliage of the great clouds did not make a sort of ambuscade of our peaceful dwelling. Now it is growing dark and there comes a rush and war bearing clouds through the sky—the hot air is cooling down and the branches of the trees are fanning me gracefully and mournfully—as if to say, we love you, we

pity you; for you are all alone and your poor heart needs its mate. We will soothe you, will rock your spirit to rest. I am weary dear; for my "Sabbath" is a burdensome day. You know I have to "play" which is work then I have a large Bible class in Romans in which I literally toil—then after afternoon service I go three miles to a Sabbath release I have got up "out in the woods" almost. Of this I have the whole general care and a class of women besides. It is hard, but my heart is in it. For years it has been a notorious place—the resort of certain young men from the city—who keep mistresses out there, etc. In visiting officially a day school there, I was pained to see those beautiful little girls growing up to certain sin. So I gathered a few faithful teachers and started this school. I have a class of many whom are known to be girls of the lowest character and who have hitherto spent the Sabbath in entertaining their visitors. I feel for them deeply, painfully. I try to be faithful. I feel as if God had given these girls souls into my charge. I blush, it is true to recognize them in the street; but I think of one who shrank not from the touch of the lowest of the lost and did not cease though "the disciples marveled that he tabled with these woman". I will not tire you dear, but those are my extra duties every Sabbath besides the regular services of the day. Now, dearest it is evening and you have come and sat upon my knee and leaned your head against my bosom and listened to me all this while and I have been telling you many things that are not written here and I am rested even now. Only I am not sure how you are feeling yet for you have not said anything yet, and I am looking down to see if her dear breathing is a half sobbing, and her eyes are full of sorrowful tears. Look up now and tell me. Tell me all the grief's that make her heart beat so against my bosom. Oh, yes, I know she is sad—I know her lovely heart is struggling with its swelling tears. Dear darling! Come closer to me and rest; lean on me—you used to say it was a strong breast that pillowed your head—it is stronger now, dear, and better and larger, and yours.

Did it grieve her that I did not come to see her? She knew why I could not didn't she? Is she sick now darling? Do write and tell me. I wrote your Father yesterday asking him about our going to Galena or to some Western college. I feel very sure he will catch something of my earnestness and that I shall know at any rate what can not be done. I am studying faithfully. My health is good. I feel some hope sometimes that there is good for us yet. Only be patient, darling, trust me, rely on me, come more and more to me as one and another of those dear to you are failing from your touch. I am with you. You are <u>mine</u>. I am on the point of writing a letter to your father at Roxbury expressing my sympathy and share in this great affliction. Yes dear I saw your Uncle Harold.[24] He manifested quite an interest in you and maybe will go to see you. Tell me dear if you would not come home this summer if it were convenient and pleasant. Mother and Sarah want very much to know you before you go away with their boy. They want to see you. I do not know but mother may have written you before this—she said she was going to. O. I wish you <u>could come</u> darling, darling; then we could understand each other and I know something would come for us and then you would be near me almost as much, except—the two rooms—as you could be.

Love me, dear, and write to me very soon; <u>do, do write to me</u>—anything—anything only write.

Your Lawrence

⟋

JLC to Fannie, 2/28/1855

Bangor. Feb 28th 1855

My own Fannie
I am going to write something now in answer to your beautiful letter, though I feel so miserably this morning that it will not much resemble yours. I think you will be a pretty nice little wife, after all. Yes, <u>"after all" your</u> doubts, expressed at sundry times and in regard to <u>sundry things</u>! You remember, Miss Mischief? I think you will be a dear sweet comfort to me pretty soon; for I get sad and oppressed with thought and bewildered with strange dreams and I want to go and sit by you at such times and let your gentleness and freshness draw me back to life. My little wife doesn't know much about the <u>mind</u> she is coming into such close contact with, does she? <u>Perhaps</u> she may reciprocate the "pride" <u>he</u> will feel in her. I do not think I am a very great genius, but I sometimes think such thoughts as are drifting thru my head may sometimes be turned to good account. You will appreciate me Fannie, perhaps I am sure there are not many who <u>can</u> know me.

---

24 Harold Wyllys, brother of Fannie's birth mother.

Last Monday evening, dearest, (is is a sweet word?) I delivered an address before one of our societies, in public, on the "Genesis of Mythology," in which I brought out a new theory, or at least one that is not generally entertained in regard to the origin and growth of early religions. I think you would be interested to know about it. I can't tell you of course what I said in all the forty pages of my piece, but I rejected the common theory that Mythologies are mere corrupt tradition and took the ground that they had their fountain in the human soul and are the attempt of man to fill the great void in his heart where God had vanished. This accounts for the similarities in all Mythologies—the diversities are accounted for by the various circumstances, genius, or necessities of each people. I cannot tell you how I carried it out and illustrated it. Only it seems to have set everybody into perfect astonishment, to think that I could have written such a piece. A gentleman who told me my philosophy was all wrong—that I had not touched the posit, said nevertheless that it was a "perfectly elegant and classical production—full of beauty and sometimes absolutely sublime." As for the theory, I am going to think more and write it over again—not to modify it, but to prove it still cleaner. I am not very much elated—not at all—but I take some courage from the issue of this and hope a little more.

You ask if you may be independent? Why yes you little rogue—I will warrant you will be independent enough in spite of us all, but I am afraid sometimes we may not happen to agree on that topic. I mean you will get to be independent of me as for my "bearing it" I spoke in bitterness—in despair. I could bear anything not "so easily" as you say. I would bear it if every heartstring of mine shivered to atoms. That is only my spirit. Nobody ever should know I was disappointed. But what is the use to talk about impossibilities. Get on all your youths and bloom and girlishness, now for you are coming home pretty soon. I am trying to get fat—for I never was so thin. We all are pretty well. Many people send love to you. I've forgotten who. I am going to Mrs. Stetsons tonight or tomorrow night. Be a good wise sweet little wife and by and by you may put just as much "insertion" into your _____ as you want to.

JLC to Fannie, 4/25/1855

Bangor Apr. 25 1855

My dear Fannie

I have fallen in love with you all over again—I don't mean that I haven't loved you always; but the sensation of <u>falling</u> in love is quite peculiar—for I have just dreamed about seeing you at church looking so beautiful and rosy and tempting that I was completely charmed. I thought you were not having much to do with me, but after meeting just go into a carriage of Mr. somebody's and rode off—though I did manage to speak to you and ask you how long you were going to stay at that hateful <u>school</u> where I thought you were teaching. Oh said you, I have it go half through yet—you wouldn't go home with me, but went right off in a manner which I think you won't be very likely to do after next July—3 <u>months</u>, by the way. Now although you don't write to me, still I suppose you entertain some notion of coming to see me this summer, and doublers have some idea which would be of advantage to me, and I wish you would write to tell me what you "sink o' sings" and when you mean to come and what you want to do. You know in July I shall be so busy with my <u>preparations</u> of all sorts that I can scarcely speak to you them. So I want to know what you intend or wish to do. At present my mind is divided between going to the west, remaining here as I have intimated to you, or going, if they will let me, to a pleasant little village nestling in among the hills, about fifteen miles down this river, to preach temporarily. Don't be frightened. You know I can tell them I have a very <u>peculiar</u> wife and they must not plague her by expecting her to do all the works of mercy and self-denial for all the women of the place. They shouldn't plague my little Fannie; no, no. There papy will take care of his little baby, yes he will. How will that do? oh, mercy; I forgot. You will think I don't mean <u>you</u> but_____; let me take it back quick—it <u>does</u> mean you—it <u>does</u>.

Fan, are you handsome now? I dreamed you were. How do you do your hair now—the same old way? Well that is pretty good. Only maybe we shall have to have some curls somewhere—can't we manage it. O I wish you could read German with me. Do you suppose you could ever learn? And <u>would</u> you? I read it a great deal. I am reading that strange old romance

---

25 A character created by Friedrich von Hardenberg, a Romanticist who wrote poetry and a novel under the name Novalis.

"Heinrich von Ofterdinger"[25] I want you to read some of these things with me—I wish you could sit and read the German to me when I am tired some evenings, sitting close to me. Can't you? Fannie I have changed so since you went away that you do not know me at all, as I am now. Not that I have changed in looks so much as in mind, and habits of thought. To be sure the grey is visible on my temples, but people that speak of my looks, say—I tell you with a sadness and strange foreboding—that I am "growing more and more beautiful every day." My expression they mean. It has been said by several. But this change is in my mind. Maybe you would not love me now. Do you think you would. Write and tell me darling; and do be good to me and love me; for you must.— There is meaning in the must. Good bye, dearest and write to me soon. I send you the little poem from my cousin Annie see if you like it and please send it back.

JLC to Fannie, 6/19/1855
Amid the challenges of his schoolwork, the feelings of her family toward him, and now the impending return of Fannie after a separation of nearly three years, Chamberlain wrote to his fiancée with decidedly mixed emotions.

Bangor June 19 1855

My dear Fannie,
I cannot make such a complete and particular answer to your letter as I wish to. Mr. Dole (our pastor formerly) has died—I have been with him for a week more or less and now have his funeral to attend and so it takes all my time. I would be glad to answer your letter. It admits an answer. But my present letter must be chiefly confession. I will however premise by thanking you for the unusually long letter you wrote me last. You have not written so long a one for a great while. I believe the old Latin poets were of opinion that love conquers all things; but I think that this time— something else had done what love could not do and you have written me a long letter. Still I know that after all such a terrible scolding you do love me, and as I love you too, I don't see any need of quarreling. I confess I have written and seemed strange to you of late—just as I have to everybody. I am strangely changing—I know it. Not that I love you, or anybody, less than ever, but I don't know what it is about me that makes

me so different. Maybe you wouldn't love me any if you were to see me now; or I mean when you do see me in a few weeks you won't love me— I am so thin and pale (I believe I wrote "thin" "thine" but you may believe both.) I confess I have been indefinite and contradictory in my statements about my flaws but I can only say now you must not blame me for that— I cannot bear it at all. Don't if you have any regard for my welfare, say anything about my place of residence or labor at present. I am sorry I ever said anything to you about it, till I was sure of something definite. Fannie dear you must bear with me—you must. I tell you I cannot endure one particle more of trial and burden. If I don't seem to you to be well do not reproach me with it. I can't help it. I am—have been—killing myself I know, but I could not help it. You must bear with me till you see me, and then you will forgive me all. I have not perhaps even a subject for either of my orations and they come in a month or more. I am very sorry I can't go for you darling. Can you come home alone? I am afraid to have you. But darling you must come now. I did not expect I was to have the masters oration; but now I am and you must come. Of course I cannot see you much and it will be hard for me not to see you, but I want you and you must come. We will be married just as soon after commencement as you please. I will see that I am ready. You will come Fannie, darling. Write letters. Forgive me all my naughty things for I am too troubled to feel very well, but shall not be when you come

as ever yours Lawrence

JLC to Fannie, 6/28/1855

Bangor June 28 1855

My dear Fannie,
I believe I have told you about the masters oration and the graduating exercises since your last letter was written. There is a weeks interval. I suppose the exercises at Brunswick will begin as usual on Monday. They are—I scarcely remember what—but at all events you had better come on in season—I think, for a little rest before commencement. It will be a severe journey. I would like very much to have you at Bangor, and if you come

here it will be from <u>Boston</u>. You would wish to be here by Saturday July 21 or at any rate on the next Tuesday. If you come best take an <u>outside boat</u> Friday P.M. at 5 from Boston—the outside is best as no change in the dark will perplex a young lady like you, not on that dismal wharf (<u>but maybe I would go for you after all.</u>) If you only wish to get here in season to hear my part take the inside next Monday P.M. from the Maine depot to Portland and thence "change" to the boat at 9 ½ P.M. Get a ticket through to Bangor. If you only go to Brunswick you would need to be there Saturday—July 28 in order to be rested by commencement time. You see at all events you must leave Milledgeville immediately. My dearest Fannie I shall be glad to see you and all the time now I am just as fond of you as ever; but I am in such a state of mind that existence is a burden to me and the very pain of living almost insupportable that must excuse my strange actions. Do not be grieved at me. God has some great end in these severe afflictions but human nature is so weak that if I dared to die I gladly would rather than bear any longer. Your last dear cheerful letter brought a smile to me and has been very precious. Do not imagine I am in <u>professional despair</u>—I have the offer of this place of Hebrew instructor if I wish it, and of every assistance in getting another if I prefer. But the faculty want me to preach; if I stay here I can supply somewhere the salary would be small but no matter—it would support us. I am longing to see you. I have not touched my "parts" yet. But don't fear. I have been and am too ill, but I shall have all done at the time. <u>Write</u> and come <u>immediately</u>.

Sae to JLC 9/7/1855

Brewer Sept 7th

Dear Lawrence,
We were very glad to hear from you so promptly. Mother is getting the package ready and I think we shall send it tomorrow, (Saturday). I am not sure that this will reach you before the package, but think it will. I wished to write in season for you to receive the letter before the arrival of the things that you might know when to go for them could not tell until now when we should send them. There is no blanket. Mother says that if you need one you will have to buy it for really we have none. I believe John and Horace

both have one. And as to your things at the seminary, I did not quite understand you. You did not mean to say that we <u>should</u> move all things, did you! But before we had heard from you in relation to it the news came that Evarts Pond[26] had moved out all your things, and taken possession of the room. I was exceedingly surprised as you said they could remain there with perfect safety until the commencement at the most time. Mr. Wallace called him and said that Mr. Pond wished to secure the room. Everything was put into the old bedroom very <u>carefully</u> I should think. But I would far rather have removed them myself. Wasn't it a little curious for him to do it? It struck me so. The books were all piled on the bed. If he must have removed them I should think he could not have done it better. I went over to see about bringing the books home, for I didn't exactly like to have them there though I suppose they would have come to no harm. Mr. Wallace met me at the gate and went up with me. The door was locked on the inside. Wallace got in at the window and opened the door. Mr. Ponds room looks very nice indeed. Everything looked as though he might have been there years. Mr. Wallace offered to pack the books so that we could bring them home and I hardly saw how I could refuse the offer. So he did, and Thomas went over and brought them and the secretary home. I think you told Sam not to touch anything until he had orders from you and having heard nothing directly has done nothing. I told him, twice about the picture, which still hangs there. He has not carried it yet. I think, however he will soon. He has been away a good part of the time at Bucksport. Miss Foster and her brother are at the Gardner's now. I guess you had better write Sam what to do with the things which you wish to sell. I am afraid they will be injured. The sofa especially which is in the entry. It is well to have everything taken care of. Don't be in the least anxious about your books. I will take the best possible care of them. We thought we would put the secretary in the <u>piano room</u> that was. It was so much work to carry these up stairs, besides we have no carpet for the garret. Taking everything into consideration I thought it was best to let them be downstairs. I shall write Fannie by the same mail with this. If she comes we may change them upstairs, if you think best. I suppose I ought to have written her before, but we have been very busy. Mother is worried to death about Horace.

---

26 Jeremiah Evarts Pond was three years younger than Chamberlain. He graduated from Bowdoin in 1853 and from the Bangor Theological Seminary in 1856.

Would it be a good thing for you to write to Mr. Reed to know whether he has heard anything, and whether he feels anxious? Mother wishes very much to hear from him. Of course you will do as you think best about it. Aside from mother's worriment isn't it about time we <u>did</u> hear? Thomas is getting better—his <u>health</u> I mean. I wish I needn't limit the expression to that.[27] I am glad he is contented. He must write home soon as well as yourself.

In haste
Sarah

S. L. Hook to Horace, 9/22/1855

September 22 1855

Mr. Chamberlain
Sir being called upon to pay my bills by those who have furnished me with groceries I am obliged to ask you if you will take the enclosed bill and hand it to your father I need the money very much by the first of the week

Truly yours
S L Hook

Mr. H. B. Chamberlain
To Mrs. S. L. Hook
Jan 25 to boarding 12 weeks at $2.50 per week.........................$30.00
May 5 " " " " " 2.12 ½ per week...$12.75
Rec'd Payment 42.75

S. L. Hook

---

27 A humorous reference to Tom Chamberlain's reputation as a sort of black sheep of the family.

J. S. Sewall to JLC, 9/27/1855

Winthrop Maine
Sept. 27. 1855

My dear Jack,

I am just on the point of discharging at you a business letter—will it frighten you? It's a precious little thing to make a matter of business—but yet I imagine you will be willing to dignify it into either 'business' or 'pleasure' for the sake of an old friend (not so very old within if anybody says I am old—just send him to me). So jump in the medias (I "scratch out both one's eyes" ride Mother Goose's melodies) I have a box in Prof. Cleave's[28] hands containing a few specimens of chalcedony which I wish to get. Prof. Cleave promised to send them home by Everett Webb[29] when he came up after commencement but did not see him—and now I want to ask you—will you be kind enough to get them for me and send the box to me by Express directed to "Winthrop, Maine," so that I can receive them before leaving for Bangor a fortnight or three weeks hence. If you will I will be ever so much obliged to you—I will do you a good turn whenever I can. Would you like a piece of news Jack? Your most humble obdt. sevt is engaged! Just think of it! It only happened a day or 2 ago—so you see my warm temperament ran the gauntlet of beauties for more than a year after returning from the E. I. before it yielded. I am engaged to Louise C. Benson—a daughter of S. P. Benson (member of the House of Reps. for Maine—and residing here) a most noble womanly Christian of fine taste, education, and manners—of very superior mental endowments—not very pretty but most perfectly guiltless and good. You can imagine I am very happy in the present and in anticipation of the future. But I can't stop to scribble more for it is nearly midnight and I am tired. I close my duties here tomorrow and leave Saturday for Kennebunk, Lynn, and Oxfordville, N. H. where my father lives—I shall return in a fortnight and go on to Bangor to enter. Please do my little errand if you have time and I give my kind regards to all my Brunswick friends

Yours—J. S. Sewall[30]

---

28 Professor Parker Cleaveland taught Chemistry, Ministry, and Natural Philosophy at Bowdoin from 1805 until his death in 1858.

29 Francis Everett Webb, Bowdoin, Class of 1853, tutored in Greek during the 1854–55 school year.

~~~

Wellington Newell to JLC, 12/8/1855
Rev. Wellington Newell, a Methodist Episcopal minister, was a classmate of Chamberlain at the Bangor Theological Seminary (Class of 1855) though twelve years his senior. He was a minister in Brewer, Maine, from 1862–69 and in Greenfield, Massachusetts, from 1877–86.

Frankfort Mills Dec. 8/55

Dear Lawrence; I take my pen to write in haste respecting a school here needing a teacher. It is the village school here at F. Mills—a large school needing a <u>man</u> to manage it. The teacher they employed is sick.
Mr. Pierce, the agt. will be in Bangor on Tuesday (11th inst) and would like to visit Mr. Arthurs at the Hatch House at 2 o'clock P. M.

Truly Yours,
W. Newell
JL Chamberlain
Bangor
ME

PS
Please let me hear from you respecting "matters and things"
W

~~~

---

30 John Smith Sewall graduated from Bowdoin in 1850, sailed with the 1853–54 U.S. Expedition to Japan, and then returned to Maine, where he graduated from the Bangor Theological Seminary in 1858. He became professor of Rhetoric, Oratory, and English Literature at Bowdoin from 1868–75, then professor of Sacred Rhetoric at the Bangor Theological Seminary from 1873 to 1903. He was a trustee and overseer of Bowdoin from 1875 until his death in 1911.

Fannie to Joshua (partial), nd (roughly 1854)

He does not consider exactly how it is with me perhaps; and then Helen influences him in the matter a great deal; however she means right I suppose, and I mustn't blame her. I was obliged to borrow Cousin D's money that she sent me for purchases, and pay her back with the $10 that Father sent me afterwards, and then of course he couldn't realize that I needed anymore unless I was being very extravagant. Forgive me dear for filling up my paper with these particulars; but then you remember that you asked me about all these things when you wrote me a little while since. I wish that I could help being so anxious and troubled in these matters; for it actually makes me sick—wears me out sometimes. I have not been well lately, I have had no appetite literally, and I became so weak that I was unfit for everything and the least little anxiety or annoyance made me cry until I was weaker still; but I am much better now dear, and you must not be troubled about me, for I shall come home very bright and rosy? I know we shall be so happy this summer together! Almost too happy I'm afraid dear. I have a pretty little new bonnet to show you; a cheap one, but then it is very pretty we think. It is chaste and beautiful enough for a "bridal hat" they say, and I don't know but that I shall have to be married for it's sake but then I cannot find anyone who is willing to take me, and so—I'm very sorry—but I'll have to give it up. I've got something pretty for you, only don't tell that I told you, but Oh! if you don't like them, I shall be so sorry! and I shall come and lean my head on your bosom and cry; perhaps he will think it is a very little thing to cry about, but then it isn't little to me, when he does not like what I do. O! I have been thinking lately Lawrence, that there never were two dispositions so exactly fitted for happiness together as yours and mine; and it is such a comfort to me to think of it, for I am learning more and more, how few there are in the world with whom I am brought in contact who do not make me unhappy in one way or another. But then we never could have a hard word together I know. O! we shall be too happy together darling! never fear lest the cares of life harden us! they cannot touch us, for we shall be everything to each other, more than everything. Will he please tell Cousin D. with my love, that I cannot tell exactly when I shall be at home, and I will write Sarah as soon as I find out certainly. Anna does not appear! Where can she be? I am so troubled because my darling isn't well! O! take care of your health my noble dear one, if you love your Fannie.

The Cousin Annie Letters

During his time as a student at the Bangor Theological Seminary, Chamberlain struggled with the absence of Fannie, who was away in Georgia. At the same time, he had accelerated his studies in order to graduate early in order to start his new life with her. All the while, he was working wherever he could, teaching languages, bible study, and even choir in order to avoid becoming indebted. In the summer of 1854, he wrote to Fannie saying, "I get very lonely and I do not know how to bear it sometimes. I can not study even unless somebody cares and loves me all the time, and knows just what I am doing."[31]

To alleviate this loneliness, young Lawrence paid frequent visits to the nearby home of his father's youngest brother, Jefferson Chamberlain. Jefferson had five children, and Chamberlain became smitten with the oldest, a daughter named Hannah whom the family called Annie. Only two and a half years younger than he, Annie had attended the German classes he taught, and the two cousins shared a number of similar interests.

After only a few months at the seminary, he began to describe to Fannie his new friendship. "I went with my cousin Annie, dear (the dear is for you) and I suppose you won't be jealous—she won't even let me kiss her now as she used to though I want to kiss her sometimes just to keep me steady, but you with your experience wouldn't think that a very remarkable quietus to my warm blood."[32]

Nearly three years into his studies in Bangor, he wrote to Fannie that "Cousin Annie, whom I am beginning to know a little, keeps or rescues me from many a dark and dismal hour of sadness or temptation; for I have enough of both. Ah! too much—too much. But I see her often and she is such a treasure to me!"[33]

By describing Annie as someone "I am beginning to know a little," Lawrence was drastically understating the extent of their relationship. The contents of more than a dozen known letters between them reveal an intimacy that went far beyond friendship or familial affection. In October 1854, Annie's father found a note that Lawrence had written to her and was deeply concerned by the nature of it. Within a few weeks, Annie was sent away to teach at a female academy in Newton, Massachusetts. Alarmed and embarrassed by the revelation of their correspondence, Lawrence sought an interview with his Uncle Jefferson and then reported the results to Annie in a letter dated November 10, 1854.

---

31 Chamberlain to Fannie, 7/30/1854 (Radcliffe Institute, Harvard University).

32 See letter of 12/26/1852.

33 See letter of 10/23/1853.

In it, he told Annie that he had kept the truth from her father so as not to add to his pain. "I could not grieve the heart of your father, my own uncle whom I know and love, by speaking of things which he could not control and which would only distress him in vain." *Instead, he allowed her father to assume the relationship was purely innocent.* "So I was willing, though my spirit chafed under it—to allow him to regard me as a simpleton—our affection as a silly blindness and indiscretion, rather than to pain him by alluding to the causes of all the troubles"[34]

Letters written by Annie after she was sent to Massachusetts indicate that Lawrence secretly visited her at her school and that the two arranged to be together on other occasions. The exact nature of their relationship is difficult to determine from the surviving letters, especially with only the small number written by Chamberlain, but a letter he wrote to Annie's sister in August 1855 sheds light on how Annie's family treated him as "an object of pious detestation" in a home where his name had "scarcely been mentioned with ordinary courtesy or kindness for some time." A week later, Chamberlain escorted Annie, probably secretly, at least part of the way to her new home at Bradford Academy in Massachusetts.[35]

Sentiments expressed in their letters seem to indicate that the two were very close. In that November 1854 letter, Chamberlain wrote, "I will sooner be blotted out of being than ever let you go." In her letters to him, Annie calls him "Darling" and describes herself as deeply heartbroken by their separation. Nearly a year later, their feelings had not abated.

In October 1855, Lawrence apologized to Annie in a letter, saying he was sorry if he had made her "sin or sorrow" for knowing him. Replying soon after, Annie wrote, "My Darling—You have made me love you—If that is sinning—you have made me sin deeply. Oh! How deeply! But you have never taught me to call that sin—"[36]

Chamberlain kept his letters from Annie, and they have survived through his family's care so that many are now held at Radcliffe College's Schlesinger Library; eleven of them are part of the collection published here.

The last of the most intimate letters came from Annie, who wrote to Lawrence in December 1855 begging him to come to visit her before he married Fannie. Unbeknownst to Annie, however, it was too late: She was writing the letter the day after the wedding had occurred.

---

34 JLC to Annie, 11/10/1854 (Radcliffe Institute, Harvard University).

35 JLC to Martha Chamberlain, 9/5/1855 (Radcliffe Institute, Harvard University). See Annie to JLC 9/12/1855.

36 Annie to JLC, 10/24/1855 (Radcliffe Institute, Harvard University).

Though with less intimacy, the correspondence between the two cousins continued throughout their lives. In time, Annie married Luther Keene, was widowed in the 1870s, and married again. With her second husband, Gilman Smiley, she had one child, whom they named Elizabeth.

Cousin Annie to JLC, 3/4/1855

Lasell Seminary[37]
March.4.1855

Mr. Chamberlain:
Your cousin Annie has been quite ill for several days, not able to sit up. — And fearing she could not write you this week at her request I write a few words for her—her chief object in wishing me to do so is to send a letter which she thinks you may need.

The physician thinks it is a severe cold settled on her lungs and says by care and quiet may be well in a few days.

She wants me to <u>charge</u> you not to mention it to her mother; and she only speaks of it to you because you might think it <u>strange</u> should she send you the letter without a word. <u>She</u> says she is <u>very</u> lonely and you <u>must</u> write her every day if you can. And her "<u>must</u>" was one of her most emphatic ones!

She will write to you <u>herself</u> the <u>first</u> <u>moment</u> she is able to.

Very respectfully
Her other "Clara"

My darling—
They have all gone down to tea and will not know it and so I must just tell you how lonely and very sick I have been and am now.— My head is almost bursting—so I can only just speak to you— I put my "<u>letter</u>" safely in with my own hands—They say it has been a beautiful Sabbath but the window has been darkened that I could not see it—but just now I made them open

---

37 Lasell College was founded as the Auburndale Female Seminary in 1851 in the Auburndale section of Newton, Massachusetts.

the blinds for I <u>would</u> see the sunset—Oh my darling I am so <u>sick and lonely</u> but don't tell <u>them</u>—I shall be better—I am afraid they will come and find me writing and the Dr. said I must keep <u>very</u> quiet and not ever sit up.

My closing—good bye
Your poor Annie

~~~

Annie to JLC, 3/6/1855

Auburndale March 6, 1855

My blessed darling—
Do you know that those words are a whole letter in themselves, if not another line were written?

Three times I have got up from my bed to try to say some little thing to you and in all those times have written only these few lines—I have not been down stairs for five long days and I am so mad now that my spirits and courage are almost gone. I am so <u>very very</u> lonely and sad away from "done" and "due" just as soon as I am able I shall go in town and see Dr. Clark. Maybe he will do something to cure me soon and he <u>must</u> for I never can stay here so— I have tried to be happy and cheerful because you told me to and for the <u>reasons</u> you told me but I have not been so always. Darling I could not when I was sick could I? Whenever I have dreams or <u>thought</u> of you lately it has been in so strange a way that I can't help telling you can I? I seemed to be in a <u>strange</u> place alone—a very much changed from what I am now yet the same—and dressed in mourning—sitting alone and <u>you</u> come—<u>so</u> changed! from far <u>far away</u>—all warm and <u>pale</u> and kneel down before me and lay your head in the old stillchen while I wipe from your forehead and face the drops of sweat and the tears—never speaking all the while—only sitting in the same strange way and always looking at you. —The dream or whatever you may call has come to me again and again until it seems to be so true so like a <u>very</u> <u>prophecy</u> that I <u>must</u> tell you since I may "tell you everything" this is my birth night do you remember my darling?[38] It is not a very glad one for many reasons—for you ask me if you must go to the Lanes— It will hardly do much

---

38 She turned twenty-two years old.

good to tell you now for you are already there— and sister Clara wrote me some days—a week or more since— that you had "promised to go" —so I must have answered the question "yes" or have greatly disappointed both you and her—So I suppose you are there— I see you as if I was close by your side, everything is bright and beaming and joyous. The music is beautiful and you are all very happy. I know you must be—I hope happier than last year, for after all it was a sad time for me and for you too, was it not. Love will think of me every time you look up at the green on the knolls, or at the clean old arm chairs, when you listen to the reading and the music and when you go away and leave it all you will miss me, but you are alone in the "zimmer"[39] again. I will "kommen[40]" yes tonight, of all the nights of my life, I must "kommen," my birth night, and so sick and so far away and so comely. "How does Auburndale seem to me"? Not very "schon"[41] not much like my "home" yet. It is very beautiful here now for all that. When I look out of my window at night, as I have been doing tonight, the sunset was so soft and like those of June, I wondered if you were looking at it too from our "zimmer." I thought you must be tonight, for it was my birth night!

My darling fellow, I wrote to Peasly[42] because I had promised to do so very soon, and I had not time to write to you both then, afterward I was too sick, besides you would not care much for such a letter as his. I am always writing to you though you may not always see the words I write.

Now I will tell you what you may do, for my birth day present, and you will not refuse—You may—The next time you write "tell me the Traum"[43], the very one and all of it— "do, do just me". I will tell you everything may be at "home... ... . is"! Another thing, do explain that mysterious work at the close of your last letter, it makes me feverish, particularly please not to forget this.

Now the other—

What a "böse"[44] letter you sent me, it makes me shudder every time I think of it. Is he a friend of yours? and if you call him an honorable man? Lawrence what effect did you think it would have upon me? What did you think I should say? It only makes me more afraid to trust—— anybody. But

---

39 German for "room."

40 German for "come."

41 German for "beautiful."

42 Peaslee Badger Chamberlain was a classmate of Chamberlain's at the seminary. If they were related, it was distantly.

43 German for "the dream."

44 German for "evil" or "wicked."

for all that I thank you for sending it to me for it tells me <u>how</u> you trust me and maybe do "lieben" me. —

About the piece— "Did I like it" Yes I loved it because it was "desire" and because it was beautiful. You have made it more so, I thought you would. I wonder if you attend the places such a silly child as I would? I cannot visualize it by just hearing it. "When I hear it again I will. Though my poor praises will be nothing when you are so * with those from other and "<u>high</u> <u>places</u>". You will hardly need or have some for mine, will you liebling? I am afraid not, afraid <u>not</u>.

"When may you come" when you <u>will</u>—<u>only</u>, ——Mr. and Mrs. Whittier are going to Bangor the first of April, <u>maybe</u>, and Hattie says "Annie you shall go home with me on Friday and spend Sabbath and then if any body comes you shall see them." But don't wait if you can come before, I want to see you always and it seems long, very long this time, when will you come? Tell me <u>when</u>, Lauren go to our house pretty often, I will tell you only when I see you. It is enough now that mother mentioned you not calling for two or three weeks as the reason you had not received the picture. So you love the picture, I am so glad I gave you that one. What did you and "Gordon" say about "it and me" I want to know that because he doesn't know me, doesn't even know that he has ever saw me. I hope it will be a good sweet letter child to "Du" and make you happy sometimes and tell you of me when I am gone. My poor L— you were sad when you wrote me the letter, like the morning you talked to me at Nesa's, you were sad and had nobody to talk with. I am so sorry and have so much that I might say to you, but I am to sick thought, besides I cannot write what would comfort you most, you know what some of the things would be, if I could see you and you will see me soon. Then I will be something to you, some comfort, which maybe you will remember till the spring is gone. Then you will not be so sad perhaps.

Good night, I must go now, but I remember when you have gone "home", and are all alone I shall "kommen" over, you will, you must know, and feel what I am after, for Lawrence I am very very sad and lonely always and your letters are sometimes "good sends" to my heart. Tell me all the tings, please do not forget it.

Annchen

Hattie sends much love and would to know if you go to well often?

~

Annie to JLC, 3/21/1855

Auburndale March 21/55
Sunset

My dear cousin Lawrence,

I hope I shall not say anything to grieve you in this note—don't let me I beg of you but I feel dreadfully and so may say something which may seem unkind. I do not feel unkindly though.

I received a letter from Clara today and she told me in it everything that has happened to or about me since I came away. If you didn't tell her please forgive me and grant me one request—don't mention my name to her again while I am here. I know how many many and hateful things I am doing every moment of my life and it is all I can bear to feel that you and those I love know them and are troubled and mortified by them, but I cannot and will not be reminded of them by her and everybody.

It is a shame for her to ask me why I direct "Lawrence's"!! letter to Peasly. And then that she was willing "you should stay away from the Lane's for my sake!" I know you said so to me in your letter—and I tried to half believe it—because I know I was so "sick" to believe. So though of course even you did not mean me to think that was all the reason. Of course it was not—for you didn't know I was sick till afterwards—but to know that she is explaining to my friends and all the world the reason of your absence and to hear her tell me that "She was willing" as if she had anything to do with it. But about the letter I feel the worst—if you didn't tell her —forgive me but if you did—tell her or anybody—anybody. I do think you might have punished me in some other way— I could have borne most anything else. I will say no more about it—only trust her with your own things but remember do not mention my name—The other "news" I will omit—I am not angry— no not that but I think it is all too bad; forgive me everything. It is a great deal I know but not much to ask "Du" —Remember I am not angry— but everything is so hard for me and not one thing comes to help me. — I am not offended with Clara—she has been kind to me and is and I thank her for it. She didn't mean any harm—but she has done it.

Martha even asks if I didn't make some mistake in Peasley's letter. ? Every body knows it! But they shall know no more! — Mrs. and Mrs. Whitham go to Bangor tomorrow "Konest Du kommen"? I know it cannot be— it would be too much good for me— write quick and tell me it will not be though— I know it will never be.

Many things in your last letter I cant speak of now— but shall soon— I should have told you myself who "the other Clara" was if you had waited without so much wonderment and enquiring— There is no use if it now— If I am wrong in— anything tell me and forgive me—forgive me—I am not displeased only discouraged and sorry that everything must be so to me. In great haste but "wurmen."[45]

"Annchen"

Annie to JLC, 6/5/1855

Auburndale June 5/55

I was so overjoyed at the light of your letter this morning dear darling. I was in the midst of my examination so that I could only look once at the direction—to be sure—and then put it away till I came up here to see you in it. You were good to write me such a little letter. Last night darling I was sick all night long and didn't sleep any—Miss L. came up in the dead of night to do something for me. She was good—I think it partly the disappointment that made me sick for I was so sure you would come and then to see the whole day go without bringing you!

I am sick today and oh! darling so lonesome. It is terrible for me here since I have seen you but I will try to be something even here and without anybody to help me.— I will be "your own noble Annie" if Oh! if I can— but it is so hard without you or somebody— but I will remember you every moment and that will help me—.

Are you coming to Boston? You told me so and you would not tell me just to comfort me if you were not sure of coming. Write and tell if you are really

---

45 German for "rankled."

coming. Do—do come will you darling—You must—To think you are in Boston <u>now</u> and so near and I cannot see you or speak to you.

Yes! Dear Darling why do you not talk to me <u>more</u> when you do see me— I thought you would tell me so many things this time—but darling it has all gone—<u>not in vain</u>. I am sure in my love— for I am more and better than when you came but I did want you to tell me all about yourself—<u>Sometime</u> you <u>will</u>.

Lawrence I never will come back to Bangor to live again—I could not after this fall—think how terrible it will seem without you—for I only remember it with you there.

Would you stay here next year and <u>will</u> you let Sarah[46] come to stay with me? <u>Don't</u> let her go alone to one place and I to another when <u>she</u> is the only cousin I have—I mean the <u>only</u>—you know! Please do darling let her come to be with me if I stay—If I leave Auburndale where shall I go or what shall I do dear? Stay <u>home</u>? I can't do that so I must come back here and Sarah with me <u>please</u>.

Mattie Ripley came to Auburndale last Friday to spend the night with me— it was very unfortunate that I should have been absent—she had written me a note which I never received. <u>So darling</u> I saw you instead of her. —

I am afraid you will get home before this poor miserable note—but I did as you wished me—I have written as soon as I had your note. You will write <u>very</u> often these five weeks will you not. I <u>will</u> be good if you will only write and tell me how. —

You are going home and in two hours! Shall you. Remember last year—as you are darling, all alone working? <u>I</u> shall remember it <u>all</u> when I think of you. —

Fannie Stowe brought me some beautiful Lilies of the Valley yesterday—I will lend you the little cluster as I did once last summer. May I? They are <u>very</u> sweet now—I wish you could see them here in my vase. <u>Do</u> write whenever you can.— Write <u>kommen</u> and "leiber mien" kommen.—

I would write more only darling I am really troubled to do so—only darling—you are going away from me—in two or three hours. Do for it seems I almost came in town this p.m. if I had known where you were.

<u>Write</u> to me—

---

46 Sarah Chamberlain, Joshua's sister, known as "Sae" to the family.

Annie to JLC, 9/6/1855

At Home
Sept 6th 1855

"Changed!" New rubbing that is it, You are changed and I feel it more than you even. Every thing you will do or say is unlike "due", that unless I am beside you and looking in your face I do not know you—your face is the Love dear face it used to be and not is all. I do not complain, perhaps you have yours more and better in the change—only I have not learned, I know you in it yet.

As I was looking over a package of letters today, I found a little Briefchen[47] from you written more than a year ago. Such a strange süss[48] one it was too—And it looked so fresh as if it came but just now from the "Stillchen." The very touch of it upon my hand—took my strength away and such a terrible fondness come over me Liebling that for a long while I could do nothing. You will call me a foolish child and I am—I am—but you were so much to me. And <u>now</u> I am so alone! You <u>know</u> it all—

The picture has not come. Why is it? I could not go away without it, if I should be called to Bradford again—did you <u>forget</u> to send it? Thank you for writing to me. I hear Athens is a beautiful place and that a situation there would be desirable—I should prefer to go to Virginia though. Mr. Manley—Pres. of the Richmond Female Institute (to whom I wrote) is a friend of Mr. Caldwell and I would like to go there, but he has been visiting at the north and I am fearful has never rec'd my letter—I <u>must</u> go <u>somewhere</u>.

<u>10 o'clock—</u>
Father has just brought me another letter from Bradford—they offer one $200 in addition to board—"<u>they</u>" think I had better go—so I shall—but shall engage for no length of time merely <u>one</u> quarter— for I <u>must</u> go South— I want to go <u>far</u> away darling—How shall I see you? I shall go the first of the week Tuesday or Wednesday— Can I get a word from you before that time? I must for I must see you—Father I know will say I must go boat.

Can I see you one more visit darling? Do you think I can—write and tell me but write to <u>Nesa's</u> or somebody. I mean send it to somebody darling. Remember I must see you in some way. How could I go to that lonely place and never see you to say good bye. Write to me soon and tell me what I must do—for I am so sick. I cannot think alone—

---

47 German for "note."
48 German for "sweet."

Write my darling,
your "Annie's kind"

Tell me how I direct your letters—Friday Morn—
I am so afraid I shall have to go by boat— I have written that I will leave
Bangor Tuesday or Wednesday—probably Wednesday— how can I see you?

~~~

Annie to JLC, 9/12/1855

Bradford[49] Sept 12 1855
Oh! Mine Liebling

Come and see how beautiful I am tonight. I mean how beautiful it is here,
in and <u>around</u> my new zimmer—perhaps my arguable disappointment
makes it seem so to me and it will move away in a little while but I hope not.

I arrived safely darling—spent the night at Rev. Munroe's who has a
house full of pictures, books, and quaint things that I like. And then he and
his wife were so good to me that I guess you will like them some when you
come zu sehen du kind[50] in her new home. When I was introduced this
evening my family consists of 25 young ladies whose sole guardian I am.
Presiding in the parlor at the table at all times and places. <u>So</u> my darling
you <u>must</u> come soon. Don't wait for Rachel, I can "play" <u>gooden</u>[51] then she
and don't say you are too busy. You will come pretty soon.

I am very tired tonight, but I have hung up your picture and found Mrs.
Browning[52] and read "sweetest eyes" and wanted to copy it for you. Do
you want me too?

Were you lonesome going back all alone—and remembering that I was
going all alone too—and <u>so</u>—<u>so</u>, heavy hearted though I didn't seem so—
Would I could see you. What did you do and think about all the way? My
darling, I don't want you to be "wild" any then with that "Hayes boy!"
You are too old! and too "<u>wise</u>" for <u>him</u> or to be "wild" with anybody. You

---

49 After a brief visit to Bangor, Annie moved to Bradford Academy, a school for young women in what
   was once Bradford, Massachusetts, and is now part of the city of Haverhill.

50 In German, "to see your child."

51 "better"

52 Elizabeth Barrett Browning (1806–61), a well-known Victorian poet. Her poem "Catarina to
   Camoens" repeats the phrase "Sweetest eyes were ever seen!"

know I used to scold you—on Teresa's and Clara's account, but in these days my dear darling, I thought you couldn't be so—I couldn't love you so. Maybe though it only told me, and show me he had been honored with an invitation to your room—

Don't let anybody make you vain either. Prouder you could not be—! but I am afraid they will spoil you too much. You mustn't let them spoil you darling. Keep good darling!

I dread the coming of the time when I shall be all settled and rested—For then will come that terrible loneliness and utter desolation that I have felt at home and at Auburndale sometimes. Now I am too tired and too excited to feel anything only that I do "leiben mein"[53] and want you "zu kommens"[54]— and every night I put my arms around jemima's neck and go to sleep "in du stillchen." Did you tell me ever I might?

Good night now. You will not be busy I mean too busy to write to me very often will you? One letter this week darling. Direct to my own "self" Bradford Academy. Burn the foolish letter right up. I am so tired and such a silly child tonight.

Good night Mein Leibling.
"Annchen"

⁓⁾

Annie to JLC, 9/19/1855

Bradford Sept 19

Is my mother sicker then when I left her, dear Lawrence? Tom startled me so terribly this morning that I could not oblige and dismiss my class early and come home to ask you—and I "must be good to her"—those words killed me almost—I have not been good to her—? Do you think I have not? I know you did not mean to tell me that— I do not suppose you thought it of me— But now that I have asked you what do you think?

I was glad to get the letter—I had been hoping all morning that it might come—for I had not yet got one yesterday and that lonesome rain—When

---

53 German for "my darling."
54 In German, "to come."

I sat all day long and all the evening—with nobody to speak to and yes Leibling—my new position is a fine one I suppose—my duties in school are pleasant—the young ladies at _____ house! Treat me with every mark of respect and affection. The people of the town receive me with much cordiality and kindness.—but the small place there is not <u>one</u> soul I can speak to— Lawrence—I sometimes wonder if <u>all</u> the year s of my life are to be like these? If they be—it shall be a terrible—terrible thing to live—I almost wish I <u>need</u> not— Why did you make that strong explanation? I did not want you to do so—I wish you had not—It seems so much like not trusting me—I only said what I did wholly in sport—I was very tired that night and did not know what I wrote—I only <u>remember</u> what I <u>wanted</u> to say and what I wanted you to be always—It was foolish in me to speak of it at all—I was not <u>thinking</u> of reproving you for anything—How would I—when I had just <u>seen</u> you—seen you in such as _____, precious way— Excuse it all—

Lawrence dear—I wish you could send me your sermons—or written some little sermons I'd read to my children on Sabbath morning—Last time I was obliged to deliver one of my own—and without even thinking for one moment on the subject before I entered the room—there are a great many strange and new things for me to do here—I wonder sometimes—I ask myself if it be <u>really I</u> here. Please tell me what Italien reader is best for a beginner—only think I am teaching Italien. I am ashamed of myself to say it—Don't forget to tell me about the reader—only also What German dictionary is best—and now for myself—<u>What</u> shall I read here—What shall I do to keep myself able to stay here—tell me Liebling—unless Mother is sicker I shall not go home in vacation—if I can <u>make</u> myself stay—Is Louise well? I did not see her to speak to her before I came—She called to say good bye <u>or</u> to bring your note—That was all. Clara gave her the idea that I was perfectly happy in Mother Ripley's visit and I had no time for anything also—At least I judged that from a note she sent me—congratulating me on Mothers my happiness in living here—as I cared anything hardly for <u>her</u>— does Louise—I have written a miserable letter—but it is all I can do today—I am not myself and I wonder if the day is long—if I was always so <u>tired</u> and <u>worn</u> out and lonely—I do whatever I am supposed to do and I try to <u>care</u> for it all—but—write to me only if you are <u>too</u> busy—as ever feel carelessly to me—don't write <u>then</u>.

Annchen

~~~

Annie to JLC, 10/4/1855

Bradford Oct 4th

My dear Lawrence;

I can conceive of but two reasons why you could have written the strange short note I received this morning. One—that you are very angry with me—the other—that you supposed me too ill to read a letter myself. The first reason I know cannot be true after all for I have done nothing deserving your displeasure—So I will comfort myself in believing the letter until I hear from you. It was rather a shock to me at first I confess but I will not let it worry me. I will remember the last dear briefchen instead of this. Did you want me to answer your last note soon or are you fearful I had never received it. That you were so anxious about it? I have wanted to answer it any day but Lawrence I have had nothing to write I have been too lonely and too nom to write. I have been waiting till it gets a little brighter and lighter about me. It wasn't of much use to wait but I was hoping that by doing so I could write something which would be worth your reading and more than that might perhaps be of some comfort and pleasure to you—instead of the poor miserable notes I send you lately. I hope you are well and pretty happy darling! Now I have the letter or the few questions you Sarah—I am afraid to write a word and was just wondering if I ever really should call you so did I Lawrence sometimes I don't know the time turns so long so many years since I saw you or spoke to you—you can't be angry with me, no I am sure so I will not think about it and yet how the waiting in that permits me you must be yet though I know for I am must the some "kind" to your when will you come? In this the Indian summer surely will you come. Let it be on Friday. Tell me if you will not come soon. A year ago pretty soon I made that little visit at your house and you remember I have been wondering today when I should go again! I am pretty well only I have a love tremor all the time and yet all tend out every day so that I am good for nothing in the evening. I can only sit down and sit up my eyes and think that it is time for me to go and say good night and my children you won't delay answering this note will you? I will try and then write something for you when I have time.

~~~

JOSHUA AND FANNIE

Annie to JLC, 10/24/1855[55]
Fannie returned to Maine from Georgia, October 8, 1855.

Bradford Oct 24, 1855

Oh! This weary—dreary night! With the rain washes down and the wind soars so among the trees! The clouds are dark and heavy in the sky—and it is so desolate here—I do not even know where you are this terrible night or whether you remember me in it. I can do nothing—I can only remember and keep repeating the poem I read the other day—

"Rattle the windows winds!
Rain drip on the 'pane!
There are tears and sighs, in our hearts and eyes,
For the life we live in vain.
The gray Sea heaves and heaves,
on the dreary flats of sand;
And the blasted limb of the churchyard tree
Shakes like a ghastly hand.
The dead are engulfed beneath it,
Sunk in the grassy waves;
But we have more dead in our hearts today
Than the Earth in all her graves—"

Where are you this wild night? Why do you not come to me by one word at least—to tell me where? —How can you leave me alone so long? You are not angry with me—you cannot be—when only a year ago just this day— we walked through the fields together—that beautiful—still autumn afternoon—I had been sick before that you know—Sometimes now I wish that I had died then—

You are not forgetting me—you could not after these years of loving me—You will need me sometime again—So you would not forget me so soon. Nothing can have happened! My letter sent two weeks ago has come to you? Then why are you so silent and so strange—Yesterday and today when the letters were given I sat with both hands pressed over my eyes—I could not see them all given—and not one to me—So I only sat and hoped

---

55 Courtesy of Schlesinger Library, Radcliffe Institute, Harvard University.

till the last one was gone—the teacher needn't have said in her careless way—"None for <u>you</u>" I knew it—Today I [word illegible] again and sat in the old place—I was <u>sure</u> it would come today It was well that my eyes were shut tight—nobody saw the hot tears that would come—Shall I go again tomorrow—and wait—and <u>trouble</u>—and hear every name but mine and then go away to struggle through another day? Cheerful I must be of course—and with a bright word for every body I "who ought to be so happy—who have everything to make me so" and I <u>have</u> been cheerful—I have borne the whole day with my pupils—have received them kindly in my room tonight—so much so—that I have wondered at myself—have bidden them all good night—while they wondered if I "ever have anything to trouble me—now that I am <u>not</u> a school-girl but a teacher with everything I want—and everybody to love me"! and I say "Oh! yes sometimes" and let them go—and come back to my chair and to myself—no word from <u>home</u> or no word from <u>you</u> for two long weeks! <u>Has</u> anything happened? <u>Do</u> tell me if anything more is coming to me—

Sat morn.—

Your letter is here—And all my anxiety will seem foolish to you—but the <u>suffering</u> has been just as <u>real</u> and <u>terrible</u> to me for all that—

    Why do ask me to forgive if you have ever "made me sin or Sorrow for knowing you"? Why will you <u>distress</u> me so—by asking me so often? You know <u>how</u> that question comes to me! My Darling—you have made me love you—if that is sinning—then you <u>have</u> made me sin deeply—Oh! <u>how deeply</u>! But you have <u>never</u> taught me to call <u>that</u> sin—Do you think it a sin—<u>Tell me</u>—"Your griefs you cannot tell <u>me</u>!" Can you tell <u>anybody</u>? If I cannot know your sorrows and try at least to help you—then—I can be <u>nothing</u> to you of course—It is what I <u>must</u> not know? What I must not? Oh, Lawrence!—

    You ought not to be very unhappy now—with Fanny to help you—I would of course have excused you for not writing—and would not have worried so—had I known she were with you—You must not be grieved <u>now</u> dear—

    You <u>will</u> not come to see me this long time—Well! I will try to stay—but it is terrible here alone—I will <u>try</u> to—to believe all you have ever been or said to me—You tell me I may do you not? And I "am good to you" I <u>pray</u> for you <u>more</u> than for myself—You <u>know</u> that I am good to you—or would be. —only if you are happy tell me so—I like to know when you are—Another time I will tell you about in letters—Read [three words illegible]—if you have not darling—Oh! what <u>could</u> let you neglect me so long—don't I beg you, do so again—What and how I suffered—I cannot tell you. Almost three weeks to wait for a word from you! Be sure to send that note back to me—Why should I "verbrennen"[56] it? Oh! Lawrence what makes such a gloom over the sky and over everything today?

~~~)

Annie to JLC, 12/8/1855[57]

Bradford Dec 8 1855

Yes you did not write to me last dear Lawrence—a whole <u>month</u> ago! In the letter you said "I will write again soon even if you do <u>not</u> answer this I not foolish enough to think that perhaps for <u>some</u> reason—you did not wish me to write answers—and therefore I have not and should not—Had I <u>not</u> received the promised letter. I have waited to hear from you—and wanted to write— <u>more</u> than <u>you</u> can ever know—but I <u>kept</u> myself from writing because I thought <u>perhaps</u> I might. But vacation closed last Tuesday. I cannot tell you about it this morning—for I am not well—and have not been lately—besides I don't care anything about it and you would not—I <u>cannot</u> write much now— only to beg you to come and see me before you are married—Do come—

Mr. Haskell of Dover Mass. husband of Lucy Dickey wishes me to invite you to come and preach for him—he wanted me to <u>urge</u> you to do so—also invites me go too and spend the Sabbath with you— I tell you because they wish it so much.

Oh! Lawrence—your letter was so <u>hurried</u>—are <u>you all</u> having a business too? It makes me sick and feverish to cook at the house visiting—yet I am glad—glad to see it once more. I "<u>am</u> not <u>well</u> or <u>happy</u>" when I "do not write to you"—I could not be when I know nothing of you—Will you not come <u>once</u> more? You <u>surely</u> can spend the <u>time</u> for me—Do come.

I cannot write—
Annie

~~~)

---

56 "Burn" in German.
57 Courtesy of Schlesinger Library, Radcliffe Institute, Harvard University

Annie to JLC, 1/5/1856

Bradford Jan.5.1856

My dear Lawrence;

Let me assure you in the out set that it was from no freak or foolish whim that I so long delayed replying to your note of two months ago. I need however enter into no explanation of the true reasons. The spirit, or as you called it, the mood in which I did at last write was the same in which you have known me for the last three years. If I have been a source of trouble and distress to you during that length of time I regret it very much yet cannot but think that you should have made some effort to help me see my fault, and to change me. As it is I have been indulged in it so long that all you can do now is to bear patiently with it and with me until I can change myself. It seems strange to me that you should have asked me to write to you in Brunswick much now so that you should give me any encouragement about coming here when although my letter was written in the same hour yours was received and reached Brunswick in three days after yours left you were gone before it came I am sorry you did not tell me you expected to leave so soon—then you would have been spared the distress and mortification of receiving and I of having written so unnecessary and foolish a letter. As it was I looked for you day after day until your letter came last Saturday. It brought me rather a surprise as you may judge and of course I can look for you no more so I will do all that is left me to do and as you wished me I will write to wish you a "Happy New Year" and to tell you how sorry I am not to have seen you here once. Should this letter leave to have been written in one of the moods you so much cannot I beg to believe that it is only because I do not quite know how to write now and whatever my letter may be I am only what I have always been to you. About going south you know how strongly I have always desired to go—so when you hear of a situation please let me know of it I shall go as soon as I can the distress makes but little difference if I must be separated at all from my friends. I shall like to go the early part of next autumn. Don't you think dear Lawrence, my vacation which was of two weeks only was spent in visiting mostly among strangers. I did not enjoy it much but in some instances the invitations were extended by persons out of town whom I had never so much as seen but I felt obliged to accept from courtesy—I passed a Sabbath with Mr. and Mrs. Packard who are living in Groveland five miles from here—my visit there was a quiet but very happy one and I felt the good of it for weeks after—the Sabbath before Mr. Jordan preached. If I had only known him in Bangor perhaps I should have seen him for I would have gone to hear him. I might see him once in a while here too for he is in Auburn only a five miles from here. How very sorry I am that you never brought him to see me. Isn't it too bad Lawrence I know I should like him—everybody in Groveland loved him for the good sermons he preached.

I am sending Horace yet and doubt I am learning to speak the German from Marie Knower our teacher of music who sits by my side at table and says I shall go sometime to full a week I said to the young ladies and talk with them a little when I am not too tired and on Sunday evening had to them those sheet sermons of Mr. Chegins. Besides this I practice one hour a day usually in the morning. These glorious winter mornings when I ought to be so glad and bright I have aroused some beautiful new things though I left your letter to go down and play Sherbests serenade for this howling mind and stars would not let me here alone. Is it not beautiful? It leaves so to me tonight when I heard above its music the wind swelling and then dying away.

So much like some of its passages for ask me how I am and how it is with me. I am pretty well only not strong and my throat troubles me very much—it is almost constantly intoed and painful. sometimes I am pretty happy—never very—I am almost always cheerful because I must be then again I feel and know that I am doing some good and may be getting a letter. There again I am happy once in a while in merely living and caring somebody in seeing the blue sky and the stars and the thought that some beautiful day may come to me soon I shall be happier that you want me to write to you often and you will not right me again for a whole month will you my dear Lawrence? And next Autumn remember I am coming to see you at commencement. I shall bid on the anticipation of it so do be there and do not forget to let me come with you. Give my love to Fannie sometime I hope to see her. Sarah need not excuse herself again I did not feel so much hurt at her disregard for my letter as if I had not written it at her earnest request.

Be sure to give my love to your mother when I go home in the spring I shall go over to see her. Yes, I would go to your house but let them know of course that you remember they have not call on you. And now my dear Lawrence good night. I look very soon for a letter—very soon.

Annie

CHAPTER THREE

Marriage and Family

As 1856 began, the newly wedded Chamberlains settled into married life while Lawrence continued his search for regular employment with which he could support his new family. Boarding at a Brunswick home in an apartment that Lawrence referred to as "Mrs. Stanwood's closet," he began a second term as instructor of Logic and Natural Theology at Bowdoin College, a position far lower in prestige and salary than that of professor. Meanwhile, he bided his time hoping for a better opportunity and at least pondered other opportunities.

Among the most assertive suitors for Chamberlain's skills was the Congregational Church in Belfast, a working port on the Maine coast that was a couple hours' steamboat ride from Brewer. The outgoing pastor, one of several who had passed through the new and unstable congregation in recent years, was retiring due to ill health, but the absence of a guaranteed salary and risk of failure amid the unrest there led Lawrence to decide against accepting the offer.[1]

Chamberlain's decision to remain in Brunswick was rewarded when Bowdoin appointed him professor of Rhetoric and Oratory for the fall term. The appointment came none too soon, as Fannie gave birth to their first child, a daughter they named Grace Dupee, in October.

---

1   Edward Cutter to JLC, 2/18/1856, Adams Collection, Schlesinger Library, Radcliffe College.

W. Newell to JLC, 1/8/1856

Rev. Wellington Newell, a Methodist Episcopal minister, was a classmate of Chamberlain at the Bangor Theological Seminary (Class of 1855) though twelve years his senior. He was a minister in Brewer, Maine, from 1862–69. In 1856, he wrote to Chamberlain about recommending someone for the minister's job in Belfast should Chamberlain decline it.

Frankfort Mills. Jan. 8/56

Dear Lawrence,
You know the thoughts of some people are always coming along a day after the fair—

It occurred to me this morning to suggest the idea to you of naming brother Jordan to the people of Belfast, or to Mrs. Field,[2] for an introduction there, in case you should decide not to accept a call there. Would there be anything objectionable in your mind to doing that?

I name it for your consideration

Fraternally yours,
Wellington Newell
Rev. J. L. Chamberlain
Brewer
ME

C. Chesley to JLC, 3/27/1856

Charles Chesley, an attorney in New Hampshire and a Bowdoin classmate of Chamberlain's, wrote to say that he could do worse than accept a position as a minister in Wolfboro, New Hampshire. He addressed Lawrence as "Jack," a nickname given to him by his classmates at Bowdoin.

Dover New Hampshire
March 27, 1856

---

2 Rev. Dr. George W. Field of Bangor was a graduate of both Bowdoin and the Bangor Theological Seminary. "Mrs. Field" likely refers to his wife.

My dear Jack,

When I was at home at "election time" I had occasion to speak of your Rev. self in connection with an anticipated vacancy in the Cong. Church in the town of Wolfborough. The accompanying letter will explain the rest.

You must not judge of Wolfborough from our illustrious classmate Allen.[3] He's not a fair representative. It has been my fortune to be in seventeen of the states and the two Canadas[4] since we quitted Brunswick and with one exception I have never been in so pleasant a village as Wolfborough. It is situated upon the shores of Winnepasge—(can't spell it) lake.[5] There are two steamboats upon the lake and in the travel season W. is filled with strangers in search of health and pleasure. The society is said to be choice. Churches and academies are the pride of the town. Don't, pray don't judge from Allen: he don't live in the village. I am not aware that you are desirous of preaching: perhaps you have a professorship in view. But if you would like a church I can think of one in the country preferable to the one in question. If you sh'd happen to go there I shall consider myself entitled to some of the credit you are sure to gain. Qui facit per aliums facit per se[6] is the foundation of all laws of agency.

I am reading in an office in this city. In the course of time I shall "go forth conquering and to conquer" ready to rob men and women too according to the most approved plans of Blackstone and Chitty.[7] I have been informed you are a married man. If you are, accept my congratulations; if you are not, get married immediately.

I am stealing this time and can't even glance back to rectify

Reply immediately and please return your cousin's letter TO ME NOT HER. Please write a note to "the Convent" if you have any ideas of accepting "a call."

---

3 George Franklin Allen, Bowdoin, Class of 1852, was from Wolfboro, New Hampshire, and went on to Harvard Divinity School before becoming the superintendent of the Children's Mission Home in Boston, where he stayed until his death in 1860.

4 Prior to its independence in 1867, Canada was described in two parts: "Upper Canada" and "Lower Canada."

5 Lake Winnipesaukee in New Hampshire.

6 "He who acts through another does the act himself," a Latin legal term.

7 Sir William Blackstone's *Commentaries on the Laws of England* was reprinted in 1832 with an analysis of the work, a life of the author, and notes by Christian, Chitty. It is sometimes called "Chitty's Blackstone."

Yours till death
C. Chesley
where's Bill Owen?[8]

∼)

E. Beaman to JLC, 5/13/1856
*The church in Belfast, Maine, strongly reasserted their interest in having
Chamberlain become their pastor. Edwin Beaman was deacon of the church.*

Belfast May 13th 1856
Mr. J. La Chamberlain

Dear Sir,
It has been my intention ever since the rec't of your letter, giving your
reasons more fully for the course which you saw fit to take respecting our
call, to write you on my own account—not officially, but giving my own
private views and feeling in respect to your becoming our Pastor, so long
time perhaps since you wrote us, that possibly the interest which you
manifested for us may in a measure have pass'd away, but I hope and trust
it may not be so far past but that it may be received for I assure you that
many if not nearly all who became interested in you and desired to secure
your service are still so—I think I express the true sentiment and desire of
our people when I say that they are disposed to wait your own time if you
will consent to give an affirmative answer to a call—We understand your
term expires next August, and that you will then need a long vacation—we
will say take as long a vacation as you please as you feel to be necessary—
only allow us to depend upon your services whenever you feel ready to
assume the pastoral care of this people. Mr. Haply is now supplying us but
was engaged with the express understanding that we were indulging
expectations of securing you that as were intending farther negotiations
with you any impression is that Jun. H. is not quite suited to our place tho,

---

8 William Henry Owen graduated from Bowdoin with the Class of 1851. He taught in Mississippi and
Tennessee for a few years before becoming a civil engineer in Tennessee from 1853–58. He returned
home and served in the 3rd Maine Volunteer Infantry, rising from lieutenant to colonel during the war.
After working as a lawyer for a few years after the war, he joined the U.S. Quartermaster Department
in Washington, where he worked for the next twenty-six years.

he is a good little man and seems very anxious to do good—should be happy to hear from you however at best your convenience.[9]

Y'rs Truly
E. Beaman

~~~

Horace to JLC, 8/2/1856

Horace returned to Brewer at the end of his junior year at Bowdoin and wrote, with his usual touch of humor, about the news in town.

Brewer Aug 2nd 1856

Dear Lawrence;

I arrived at home on Thursday by the cars as I at length concluded to go. I am glad I did; it would have been tedious to loaf about Portland and then not get in to Bangor till the next day noon. My arrival at home and surprise to the folks was a little ludicrous—I marched up to the front door—it was about eight o'clock and I rung the bell and waited soon I heard as I thought, Sarah's foot in the entry I arranged my hair and hat to the best advantage—prepared a good speech, which I had got on my tongues end and had my hands ready for an embrace of welcome when the door opened slowly and a little suspiciously and out popped a candle into my face and a pair of Irish jaws squawking out "Lord, Hooray is it ye?" "Yes Mary it is I, but where on earth are the folks." "Shure ain't they all gone to the city. Every mother's son of 'em." But I hadn't waited two minutes before over came Tom with the carriage and Susan Brastow.[10] They had all gone to hear a lecture from Rev. Dr. Hamlin.[11]

Every thing is well here and looking very decently. The hay is about all in and the fields look finely. I called over to Annie the other day. She doesn't look so well as she used to, I think. Sam G[ardiner]. is here of course making

---

9 Rev. Wooster Parker became minister instead and served for fourteen years.

10 Susan S. Brastow was their cousin (their mother's niece).

11 Cyrus Hamlin, Bowdoin, Class of 1834, and Bangor Theological Seminary, Class of 1837, was a missionary in Turkey, where he founded Robert College in Constantinople. He returned to Maine in 1876 and became professor of Dogmatic Theology at the Bangor Theological Seminary. He became president of Middlebury College in Vermont in 1880. His younger brother Hannibal Hamlin was vice president of the United States under Abraham Lincoln.

"Spacious Yawns" and writing Fremont Songs for the Brewer Club. Mary Wheeler is considerably better than she has been for some time. She was down here the other day. Addie is here also. She is in her turn ill, or at least she has been and is now getting better. Pratt was here day before yesterday. Sae and I had no little fun with him. I told Sae afterwards that she told him lies enough to sink the whole family, but she insists that I told two to her one— Rev. H[orace]. P[ratt]. thinks that if he can get matters adjusted he may be at Brunswick this com[mencement]. I say that for your special consolation.[12]

The folks are anxious to see you and Fannie here this vacation. I don't know whether it was your intention to have Fannie go on to N.Y. this vac. or not, but at any rate you must come home part of it or all. Mother will not survive if you do not. She in particular is very anxious to see you. Sae is here twice as good natured and funny as ever. Only one thing, I advise you not to attempt to disagree with her for you will surely get the worst of it. She is as sharp as Dr. Johnson. Sam Gardner thinks of going on to commencement Tuesday I believe. So I suppose you mean to come immediately. I left the good city of Brunswick in some haste and doubtless there are many things of ours there which John will have to see to.—

Among these are such things as taking up the carpet and putting it into the basement, throwing the most valuable books into the drawers and such little things as occur to him. I don't think of anything more. I told him I would send him on some money, but it is a little tight just at this particular juncture. I have been trying to collect a little note ever since I returned and finally the cousin concludes he will pay it without fail next Tuesday or Wedns. But as this is a little late for him I should like for you to let him have five dollars or so, if you have it to spare, and when you return I will hand the same to you. If Fairfield is there and calls for my exhibition bill will you please pay it if he can and Tom Coe says he wants his paid and will refund with thanks. I don't think Fairfield is there tho'. I came away and forgot to pay him. Please let John bring home my examination theme. I don't think of any thing more— Hope Sarah B[rastow]. will have a good time. With regards to all yrs. Horace B. C.[13]

---

12 Cousin Annie Chamberlain. Samuel Spring Gardiner, Bowdoin, Class of 1858, and a lifelong friend of Chamberlain's. John C. Fremont was the Republican nominee for U.S. President in 1856, and singing at events was a popular form of campaigning in the 1800s. Mary Wheeler was a family friend (see Mary Wheeler to JLC, 12/15/1858). Addie was cousin Hannah B. Chamberlain, Jefferson Chamberlain's oldest daughter. Rev. Horace Pratt graduated from Bangor Theological Seminary in 1848.

13 Hampden Fairfield and Thomas Upham Coe were classmates of Horace at Bowdoin. Sarah Brastow was another cousin and Susan Brastow's sister.

～〉

Ashur Adams to JLC, 10/21/1856
Ashur Adams, Fannie's biological father, was a regionally known artist and map maker. This letter followed the birth of Grace Dupee Chamberlain on October 18, whom the family called "Daisy." At the time, Ashur was seventy-nine years old.

Boston Oct. 21st 1856

My dear sir,
On my return home yesterday, my heart was gladdened by a line from you announcing the safe arrival of your daughter and my dear little grandchild, and that both mother and child were doing well. We have been very anxious about Fannie, as some of our officious friends have troubled us with gloomy predictions; but as the time of pain and difficulty has past away we will thank God and take courage.

I wrote Fannie some time ago and having received no answer was fearful that you had no good news to communicate but the good news has come, all in good time and is a matter of joy to the whole household.

We are all as calm as usual, excepting "the old gentleman" who feels the infirmity of age coming on somewhat rapidly—please say to Fannie that many will write her soon.

With love to all concerned

Yours very truly
A. Adams

～〉

John and Horace to JLC, 11/24/1856
Chamberlain's two younger brothers, then enrolled at Bowdoin, wrote from Brewer about the news at home and college business while on break.

Enclosed $40.00
Brewer Monday Nov 24th

Dear Brother

I write you this morning to get you to settle up one or two of our term bills and enclose for that purpose $40.00 an astonishing amount for us to collect nowadays but times are a good deal better. Papa is in Canada. Heard from him yesterday says he shall remain there at $5.00 per day till January to see to a lumber operation.[14] Did not expect to remain where he went but is needed. We are getting along <u>very pleasantly</u> this winter I am going out to the Wiswell settlement[15] to get a school after breakfast—a fine school. The folks want to see you and <u>family</u> very much. Expect the pleasure of it, at the last of the week.

Aff.

John C. C.

Shall hear from you soon.

Mother thinks you had better come as soon as pos. Can take better care of Fannie here.

Dear Lawrence

Sir the folks have concluded to send you some money to pay term bills—I don't know as it is best to pay any of mine probably. I am already some one hundred dollars <u>under</u> to them and I don't know as its best to meddle with it till I pay it all up. You are at liberty I presume to bring it back if you think best. There is some $18 in the house now. I can't tell whether there is anymore coming at present or not. My plan is, in pleasant weather to prepare for a stormy day. But Mother cannot rest content so long as there is a cent in the house of course. Father seems to be doing pretty well in Canada and if debts do not come in there is a chance of our doing pretty well within the money line this winter. He writes that he wants us to come home and keep quiet this winter. As for myself I shall do the best I can for it. I think my health and spirits are a little better than when at Brunswick. Is rather strange that I haven't seen the first about the Prizes nor the exhibition either. Seems to me there never was one came off before without having some sort of a notice in some papers. Perhaps you are unaware that

---

14 Father Chamberlain often worked as a surveyor timber cruiser, locating, planning, and supervising timber harvests.

15 Part of what is now the town of Holden, Maine.

Luther Brastow lies at the point of death.[16] Folks are feeling very sorrowfully about it— We shall all be happy to see and yours. Affectionately to all,

> Your aff. brother
> Horace B. Chamberlain

~~~

Annie to JLC (nd/1856)[17]

Dear Lawrence—
Please tell Fanny that her letter would have been sent long ago had I not been so unfortunate as to lose the key of my post files where it was carefully locked up. I have been looking for another these two weeks and here had so much trouble in finding one that I began to look upon the account as a sort of omen that I should not write her at all— I haven't found a key yet— but am going down for one by and bye. If I find one shall—probably consult my own inclinations in place of the omen—about sending the letter—in case I don't succeed—I will send her the portfolio with its contents as a sort of legacy some day—

I saw Mr. Douglass yesterday. He enquired patiently for you— and I couldn't help telling him that you were looking <u>tired</u> and pale when I saw you last. He says you always needed somebody to take care of and cautioned you for working too hard. I am thankful Fanny is with you again. She will <u>make</u> you rest.

> Yours
> Annie B. C.

~~~

Mother to JLC, 6/1857
Chamberlain's daughter Daisy, had gone to visit her grandparents, aunt, and uncles in Brewer, and his mother wrote soon afterward.

---

16 An extensive published genealogy of the Brastow family includes no one named Luther.
17 Harrisburg 1995.459.7.19

My Dear Lawrence

I am very sorry that I am not able to put more into this valise, also that I could not send it before. The corned beef, we must save for another time. I hope the cake will be good and get there unharmed. Poor children I wish I could afford you more assistance—t'is a great undertaking to entertain so large a company, try and make it as cosey for yourselves as possible. I sent the recipe for the cake and frosting. I have written about Willie and Daisy in John's letter. Fannie you must not be troubled about Daisy at all, if all was not well with her we should of course let you know.

Lawrence you must be careful of your health are you careful about your food? And what about the Wilde house have you bought it?

When you see Prof Everett thank him for his attentions to me and Daisy in the cars.

~

Sae to JLC, 6/15/1857
Sister Sarah wrote that Daisy would be returning to Brunswick soon.

Brewer June 15th

Dear Lawrence,

I write hastily to tell you that you may expect Daisy and me next Saturday in the cars unless it should be very stormy in which case we will come Monday. I send a little picture.

In haste—
S. B. Chamberlain

Daisy went to meeting Sunday behaved perfectly well.

~

James S. Blake to JLC, 6/25/1857
Having purchased their own house on Potter Street near the Bowdoin campus, the Chamberlains set about decorating their new home. The marble slab mentioned in this letter was likely a fireplace surround.

Boston June 25, 1857
12 Cornhill
Mr. J. L. Chamberlain

Dr. Sir,
We shall forward your marble tomorrow by the Steamer Eastern Queen. It will be the same slab, which has been put together very neatly, and which we will warrant to be as durable as any other. It is a beautiful piece of marble.

We enclose 67 cents in stamps for the mailing.
Yours respectfully

James S. Blake
Lut. Davenport

P.S. We shall pay the freight.

~~~

Receipt for Hod's Bills, 8/3/1857

This document was receipt for Horace's Bowdoin bill. Commencement usually occurred the first few days of September and was followed by a break until February.

Received of H. B. Chamberlain one hundred and twenty five dollars 20/100 in full for his Term Bills to Aug. 5 1857 inclusive

Jos. M. Keeny Treasurer.
Bowdoin College, Aug 3 1857

~~~

Thurston and Parker Circular, 8/27/1857

Two alumni of the Bangor Theological Seminary sent out a circular in an effort to raise funds for repairs to the main seminary building. Thurston was Class of 1825, and Parker was Class of 1832.

Dear Brother:

In the Circular we recently sent you please read PROPORTION instead of "proposition," as printed ... a mistake strangely enough overlooked. What we ask is, that you sent us $10.00 IMMEDIATELY. The repairs on the Seminary building need to be made THIS VACATION.

Stephen Thurston, Searsport
Wooster Parker, Belfast,
Aug. 27, 1857

~~~

Mother to JLC (nd/1857)
A worried mother asked her eldest son to look after her second youngest down in Brunswick.

Dear Lawrence—

I [am] sorry to trouble you but I feel terribly worried about John—to leave the poor boy in Brunswick alone is too bad. Is he not sick—I thought he seemed dispirited. Will you see to him get him what he needs. O the times for money![18] We shall have some soon but have to wait wait wait for it. Father says whatever you do for John he will refund when you come home. You had better take what books you will need this winter stay here till the commencement of the next tern. I would not buy any provision they will be much much cheaper bye and bye—we will be at the [railroad] cars next Monday.

Mother

~~~

Sae to JLC (nd/1857)
Sarah wrote of the family's efforts to help the new homeowners set up house.

Sunday night

I have just got home from meeting and although it is quite late I feel as though I must write a word or two. I tried to do just as well as I could about the

---

18 The financial Panic of 1857 began in September of that year.

carpets. I think the stairs carpet is a beauty and it was reasonable as to the price $1.11 per yard. You will see that it is a good one too. It was by far the handsomest one in the city. I should have selected it for myself. If you don't like it they will take it back and refund the money. I could not find anything at all like your parlor carpet. I remember the pattern. I should like very much to see you. There are a great many things I should like to tell and ask you. Dr. Field and Mrs. Page are looking for Mr. Field tomorrow night in the cars.[19] He spends one Sabbath in Portland, perhaps he will make you a call.

I shall write you soon. Love to Fannie and Daisy. Don't she talk any?

Sarah B. C.

Chas. Kimball to JLC, 2/12/1858
Apparently, curtains for the new home were more expensive than the Chamberlains expected.

Boston Feb 12th 1858
Mr. Chamberlain

Dear Sir
Yours of the 3rd has come to hand. As regards the curtains you write me that you think I have made a mistake in reckoning the price. Below I give a statement

Damark	18.00
Farrels	5.28
Hooks	.90
Corners	4.12
27 yds. Linens 12 ½	3.37 ½
Making 3 set curtains	6.00
	37.67 ½

---

19 Rev. Dr. George W. Field of Bangor was a graduate of both Bowdoin and the Bangor Theological Seminary.

$2.00 is a very low price for making of the curtains. Our price for making in the way they were made being $3.00 per window— It is so long since that I can not remember whether they were intertwined or not but if they were they were sold at to low a price allowing they were not interested they were very low. I am sure that there could be no mistake. We are always willing to rectify mistakes and careful to do business in an upright manner. I feel very sorry that there should be any misunderstanding about this bill and hope if you should favor us with any other orders to do them in a satisfactory manner

Respectfully yours,
Chas. Kimball
681 Washington St.

Sae to JLC, 7/4/1858

Sunday noon, July 4th

My dear Lawrence,
I decided to write you by the next mail and as I couldn't do so yesterday I think it not wrong to write today. I have scarcely had one moment of time to myself since I returned. If I could have found out when I could go to Brunswick I should have written before. I cannot go until week after next perhaps somewhere near the fifteenth or sixteenth of the month. I wanted to go before but it seems impossible.

Mary Brastow[20] is to be married tomorrow evening and when that is over I shall feel a great relief. I have been over there a good deal and haven't had time to get myself ready to leave home. I have just read John's letter and your note. I think I can get the carpet, but perhaps I shall have to give four shillings for one good enough. I wouldn't have a poor one. They don't pay, I will do the best I can for you. The shirts we haven't been able to touch yet but they shall be forth coming.

We are expecting Aunt Susan's family the middle of the month just the time that I go. I want to suit your convenience entirely in relation to my

---

20 A relative on her mother's side.

visit. If you prefer that I should be there through commencement to my returning with you in September I will come at the time I specified. It is barely possible that I might make it a little easier for Fannie if I was to go now. I have no choice for myself but it seems to me that Aunt Susan and the children might have a more pleasant visit here if I were here. Perhaps they won't come quite so soon as they expected and in that case they will be here when we return. Mother seems to think that you rather I would be with you now than in the fall. Do not give one thought to us or our circumstances, but if you want me to come the middle of the month you may expect me at that time. Fannie knows whether I could help her any thro commencement I want to come just when you want to have me. If I had time I think I could be lonesome. It seems desolate here. Mr. Gardner is very feeble.[21] He was taken with the dysentery last week which reduced him very much but he is better of it now. He doesn't sit up an instant. Mary told me he selected the hymns to be used at his funeral a day or two ago. She was "what is the thing of greatest price, etc." Mrs. Gardner tried to persuade him that it was not quite so suitable for the death of a Christian as many others and we replied that he wanted to make an <u>impression</u>.

He has a foolish idea that he likes to see me and they all have been very anxious that I should not go away but if he does fancy he wants me to come in every day to see him I think he will not live two weeks longer. Dr. Field says he is liable to die at any moment. I want to see you very much indeed. I have almost forgotten how it would seem. Fannie and Daisy too. I wish you would write me soon about my going. I feel as though you would conclude that I better go now. I shall be getting ready

Love to Fannie and noisy.[22] S. B. C.

Sae to JLC, 10/24/1858

Sae wrote to her brother two weeks after the birth of Fannie's and Lawrence's son, whom they named Harold Wyllys Chamberlain.

---

21 The Gardiners were close friends of the Chamberlains. Sam Gardiner, a son, was a close friend of Joshua Chamberlain.

22 By "noisy" she sarcastically meant Daisy, who was very chatty as a child.

Sunday night
Oct 24th 1858

My dear brother Lawrence, I cannot let another mail go without writing you.

In the first place I am glad that I have a little nephew and especially that Fannie is so comfortable. I should like very much to be there and help take care of you all.

What do you think about my coming? Mother wants you all home to Thanksgiving and in that case it would be hardly worth while for me to go to Brunswick before that time. You see that I mean to make a long infliction upon you. And then what about the things, mattress, etc.

Do you want them before that time? The pillows will go in a trunk.

I got four yards of flannel for Fannie all-wool at .45 per yard. I judged it would be more nearly what she would want than anything else he had in the store.

They had little blankets but they were very nice and $3.50 per pair. I am making little Grace a quilt that will be so warm and will do about as well. It is not partly only warm. I have made the little new comer a lot of diapers. Tell Fannie they are just like the ones Daisy left here only not ragged and torn. They are just as soft all made out of old shirts.

I am afraid she needs those now. In the girl you have a good one, and what kind of a nurse is she after the old stamp that you and Fannie used to laugh so much about.

Mr. Newell exchanged with Mr. Cummings today his sermons were just ordinary.[23] He said his little child has the whooping cough. It is a wonder Daisy has escaped all those things.

Horace and I rode down to Bucksport one of those heavenly days last week. We took dinner with Ada. Mary is just getting about house having been sick abed there some months. little Alice is growing a little less fat but you would laugh to see how much it looks like Eben Gardner. Don't you remember one of his eyelids droops a little over one side of his eye. It is exactly so with the baby. It is getting too dark for me to see. Love to Fannie and write this week about yourselves, myself, and the things. I shall write John this week. aff. Sarah

---

23 Rev. Wellington Newell was the Episcopal minister in Brewer, while Rev.Ephraim C.Cummings was the pastor of Brewer's Congregational Church.

Sae to JLC, 11/16/1858

Sister Sarah updated her oldest brother on the news in Brewer.

Brewer Nov 16th/58

Dear Lawrence,

My finger is most well though I cannot write with much ease as you will perceive. John wrote that it was possible that you and Daisy might come home to Thanksgiving. We all are anxious that you should. I can assure you that you will have a more pleasant visit at home than at your last visit. All is as pleasant as possible.

Your things can be sent any time but if you are coming perhaps you better take them with you. That is as you like of course; they are ready for you whenever you want them. I finished the pillows today. My finger becomes sore at a very inopportune time. I was in the midst of all kinds of work and it was a long time before I could do anything—not even to dress myself. To say nothing of the agony I suffered with it. We are all glad that John is coming home. Father says he rather he would be here than anywhere.

Father has gone into the lumbering business pretty extensively and is in hopes to do well. He bought two yoke of oxen and sent them up river last week. He thinks he has secured himself against a failure—says he shall save himself at all events.

Horace is all unsettled yet. Do you approve of his going to Oregon? We are very unwilling he should go. I wish you were here to advise him.

Mary Brastow is here making preparations for going to housekeeping. They are feeling a good deal alarmed about her eyes. She hasn't been able to sew one stitch since she was married. Dr. McRuis thinks there is danger of her becoming blind. I do not know whether any of us have written since our choice of deacons. I think you will be a little surprised. They elected Joe Harriston and Mr. Jeremiah Skinner. Mr. Brastow had <u>one</u> vote. It is doubtful whether Mr. Cummings will be allowed to stay another year. He has improved a good deal in his preaching to my mind though mother fails to perceive it.

He enquires after you frequently. Dr. Page is here now and is in high spirits about Rebecca's talent for poetry. Have you seen any of it? She writes for the *Journal of Missions* every month and occasionally for the *Independent* she signs herself "Alice Auburndale Mass." I think I will send you her last piece. It will be no matter if you have read it. Is the nurse with you yet? How do you get along with two babies. I dreamed of Fannie and the little boy the other night. Nothing will happen to my blue mantle will it. I left it in a trunk in the unfurnished chamber. And my blue cord and tassel is there somewhere.

I wish you would write soon about the things and whether you are coming home and whether it will be worth while for me to go to Brunswick etc. etc.

Much love to Fannie and to John.

Yours affectionately
Sarah B. Chamberlain

Mary Wheeler to JLC, 12/15/1858

A letter from Mary Wheeler, a friend of the Chamberlain family in Brewer. She married Horace Chamberlain in May 1859 and mourned his death in December 1861. This letter indicates that she too was romantically attracted to, and perhaps involved with, Chamberlain when he was at the Bangor Theological Seminary.

Bangor Dec. 15th

When I tell you Lawrence that your letter was to me <u>all</u> I wished and knew it would be—perhaps that, more nearly than anything else, will tell you how gently and soothingly your heart spoke to mine and yet after it all—may be <u>because</u> of it all—I sat a long while, dreamily thinking, conscious all the time that an aching had crept into my heart or rather up from its own depths to the surface life of every day. Then I tried to detain and analyze the feeling to see why the being so sweetly comfortable had left such a vague indefinite reaching—out of the soul after something—<u>something</u>. ——And I fancied it might be partly the yearnings that come somewhat to all which are never answered till the spirit is "<u>free</u>" and more because your words of sympathy though few, were so much more to me than the many, which others had spoken—though they were meant in all kindness and I accept them as such— me they never touched—I listened and replied—without a ruffle in the deep under current of my soul—and then I thought how few can call out what is best and noblest within me—so the aching may be—was—that the very depths of soul to which your words reached, only showed how great the difference between what I am and what I should be, under other circumstances showed how much of me fails to be of its full use to any one— I do not feel blame for this—I am only conscious of the power when its waters gush out so joyous, full and free in answer to the charmed words that bid them flow—Don't think I am complaining in any way about my life—or that such thoughts trouble me very often—I know I shall be all in this life that God made me to be—and that others will be to me all He sees I really need to have them. For the rest—for what I might be—oh how sometimes it comes to me what it will be to have the whole being called out—and satisfied.

One of these days came to me while I was sick at B. this summer—I couldn't help writing "him" about it and waited till I should be better to finish the note—but I was well all at once and Addie needed every moment and I thought I would wait till I came home—but I put the letter away so safely that I forgot it but you shall have it when I can get it again. —

I was glad for what you said about the <u>understanding</u>—it has troubled me a great deal—troubled me that I could not treat you with a common respect—hardly with decency—without having it more than intimated to me that it was from feelings I ought not to have or that Fannie would feel badly about it or that at any rate she ought to—or that all the affection you had or ever had for me was nothing more than you had for every girl you happened for the time to be with—I did not of course believe these insinuations but at the same time you can well imagine that I did not feel quite at ease about them especially as those from whom they came knew much more of Fannie than I did—I felt sure that you would do me the simple justice to believe that never even in thought, have I wronged her who is dearest to you—your wife—when I have stooped so low as that, I shall at least have no claim on your friendship—I tell you these things only that you may see why I have not known sometimes what it was best to do—for I felt willing to do anything as far as you were concerned rather than to cast one shadow over Fannie's life, or that others should think I had any wish to have things different as to you and Fannie's relations to each other—for the wish never came into or went out of my heart—I did not think you would misjudge me so, for I was certain of that, which we both equally know—that whatever we were and are to each other was <u>never</u> in expectation of any nearer relation a something to remain when marriage vows and marriage rites have passed away forever—a something which no one and no time can change which even our own wills may not control. I have spoken very freely

In August 1862, Joshua L. Chamberlain was appointed lieutenant colonel of the 20th Maine Infantry Regiment after declining the colonelcy. (Pejepscot Historical Society)

Joshua Lawrence Chamberlain, Jr., his father and namesake. He died in 1880. (Pejepscot Historical Society)

Sarah Dupee Brastow, Chamberlain's mother, died in 1888. (Brewer Historical Society)

Horace Beriah Chamberlain was born in 1834. Called "Hod," he became a lawyer and died of tuberculosis in 1860. (Bowdoin College)

Chamberlain's only sister, Sarah Brastow Chamberlain was born in 1836. The anchor of the family, she died in 1921 at the age of 84. (Pejepscot Historical Society)

During the 1850s, when this image was taken, Chamberlain graduated from Bowdoin College and married Fannie Adams. (Pejepscot Historical Society)

Educated and artistic, Frances "Fannie" Caroline Adams, shown here in 1858, married Chamberlain in 1855. (Pejepscot Historical Society)

Rev. George Adams and his second wife, Helen Root. Adams adopted Fannie in 1829. (Pejepscot Historical Society)

Chamberlain, shown here in 1859, first was named professor of rhetoric and oratory at Bowdoin in 1856. (Bowdoin College)

Professor Chamberlain, shown here in 1860, was later elected to the chair of modern languages at Bowdoin, but soon felt an "irresistible impulse" to serve the nation during wartime. (Pejepscot Historical Society)

In early 1865, President Abraham Lincoln brevetted Chamberlain to the rank of major general.
(Pejepscot Historical Society)

Daisy and Wyllys Chamberlain in the daguerreotypes and cases Chamberlain carried during the Civil War. (Pejepscot Historical Society)

This political cartoon by Thomas Nast appeared in the February 7, 1880, issue of *Harper's Weekly* just after Maine's "Count Out" crisis. The cartoon's caption reads "The Smiths Gave a Great Deal of Trouble. POWHATTAN BLAINE. 'Just let me give him one whack to show how strong I am.' POCAHONTAS CHAMBERLAIN: 'No, Don't, Jim; you'll make a mess of it.'"

In September 1866, Chamberlain, shown here around 1871, was elected governor of Maine by the largest margin ever. (Pejepscot Historical Society)

In 1914, Chamberlain died at age 85. He is buried in Pine Grove Cemetery in Brunswick, Maine. (Pejepscot Historical Society)

and frankly to you Lawrence—I do it that for the future there may be no possibility of any doubt—treat me as frankly will you not and if it troubles any one at all—or if in any way it is not best that there be any manifestation of the feelings I have and ever shall have for you, you will tell me and I will see to it that there shall be none—but if not, it certainly would be a very great comfort to me—to seem friendly and affectionate and to have it known that it is not based at all on your being married or unmarried but because you are what you are and I am what I am—

Thank you and Fannie for your kind wish for me to come and see you and be cheered by you—I want to—so very very much but cannot just now—Uncle is very anxious for me to stay here awhile and help the boys in their studies—I hardly think it would be best for me to disappoint him for the sake of my own feelings—Sometime I will come—the future—my future is very undecided—I am and have been troubled and anxious about it as long as mother was here—though the home was gone I expected to be with her—but now—I do not know what is best. Auntie would like to have me stay with her—but without entering at all into details, you know me well enough to see why it could never be a "home" for me—I wish I knew what I ought to do about something else too—but I cant write it so I'll wait before I ask you—much love to Fannie—I wish she had written as she thought of doing—but she must be very full of care—direct to Bangor

I thought somehow you would send to Brewer before and so did not get your letter for nearly two weeks after it was written.

bye bye
Mary

~~~~~~

Horace to JLC, 12/24/1858

Bangor Dec. 24th/58

Dear Bro:
No doubt you have been very anxious to hear from us in relation to Mother's going to Brunswick but we have hardly known what to write. At first she thought to go immediately and we were only waiting to let you know the day, but since then everything has seemed to throw distractions in the way. It

seems almost impossible to get ready and then mother's health hasn't been very good so that with one thing or another, the time has got so short that she hardly thinks it will be of an object to you for her to come so late. Still if you continue to want her as much as ever she will go just as soon as possible—say the last of next week. So we shall wait to hear from you again. We hope the baby is better now—mother says it is no uncommon thing for infants to be in just the same state you say yours is in for some three to six months and the main object is to keep them as quiet as possible so that their system may have a fine opportunity to strengthen. They should not be exercised much by washing, rocking or tossing. Of course I cannot tell how valuable this advice may be not being supposed to be posted on such matters but certainly it looks reasonable. We all want to see the grandson and nephew very much but I suppose we must wait or certainly all but mother. Aunt H[annah]. seems a good deal exercised about him—I really wish she could see him—think it would do her more good than any of us tho' undoubtedly it wouldn't do the baby so much. We are passing the winter quietly and pleasantly. All at home but John who is teaching at W[est]. Corinth and doing finely so far as we can see. He has been down once and made a very satisfactory effort. He is a good deal amused at the manner of living in the family where he boards.[24] They seem to be somewhat behind the times. The old man tells John if any of the children get in his way just kick them out of it. He didn't mention whether he had found occasion yet to put his advice into execution. The wages are rather low—five shillings a day— they prefer to hire by the day. The school will be considerably too long for him and I think he had better get back to Coll[ege] as soon as possible after the com[mencement]. of the term don't you? The prize theme comes on then for him. I am anxious for him to do one thing at least. What a pity he was not on last term when he had so much leisure, instead of loafing why didn't he write it then at any rate? But no matter now. The idea is for him to get one of the prizes. Then perhaps he had better not lose the chemical lectures. Father is at home this winter. Got pretty large operations in the woods but I think pretty safe ones. As to my ongoing proclivities I have almost made up my mind not to go till after I have practiced here a year or so. So that I shall feel quite at home in a new country alone. Besides, there is every sign that business will be better here next season than for a few years back. I suppose you heard of Sam Lamb's death. He died on a voyage from the West Indies

---

24 It was very common for students at the college or seminary to spend their break teaching at local schools where they would board with a local family.

and was buried at sea in the latitude of Charleston, S.C. It was his first voyage as master. His mother feels it very deeply—please let us hear—mother will be happy to go if you can arrange it—tho if it will not make much difference to you perhaps she better not. Affy. H.B.C.

~~~~

Horace to JLC, 1/18/1859
While their mother was visiting Chamberlain and his family, brother Horace wrote of news in Brewer and of packages he was sending to Brunswick.

Bangor Jan'y. 18th 1/59

Dear Bro:
Fred Stevens is going to Brunswick in the morning and by him I was thinking to send the things to Mother, but Sarah has not got them quite ready so I have concluded to send by John Appleton the latter part of the week. I took a parcel to Mrs. Crosby's for Dr. Adams to carry to you but I have learned that no such gentleman has been in town or is likely to be, so I think of demanding the buck and Sarah is to put something more in the parcel and then send immediately.

We are all very well at home all that is Sarah and I and Tom who constitute the Chamberlain family just at present. Father is gone up river for a week or so and the great family of Chamberlain is somewhat restricted— leaving Sarah and Aunt Hannah sole occupants of the Castle—Tom and I do not get home to dinner he taking his at Uncle H's[25] and I carry mine just now in court time.

The Jany. turn of events is a very busy one because short.— I think I shall be admitted this term however and let up and shall farm for a while at least.[26] What do you think of it?

John is doing a good thing in his school as far as I can learn from all country men. I want him to get back to teach again though just as soon as possible. Don't you think it indispensable for him to be back soon? He has not been down now for two or three weeks, so has not seen the New Year's presents.[27] Sarah thinks he will never need it for whenever he has any money

---

25 Uncle Horace Brastow.

26 By "admitted," he meant to the bar to practice law.

27 At that time, it was customary to exchange gifts on New Year's Day.

he finds a shorter road for it!— We are all very much pleased at them— Father's was just the thing—Mother's imminently <u>ditto</u>. Mine was just the thing I have been teasing everybody to get for me and finally concluded to get for myself, but you were ahead of me. <u>Tom</u> however thinks his rather an anachronism—and speaks of it with considerable <u>disdain</u>—

We hope you are all very comfortable this inclement winter—Mother I hope will try to make it easy for herself as possible and reserve her health— She must not give herself any trouble about us—We get along nicely—and tho' we miss her much, yet everything goes well. Aunt H. does marvels— never did so well before in her life. All the things are doing well—Fred is waiting so I will not write more—will write by Appleton [Hall]—please write us after commencement and believe me yrs.

Affly Horace B.C.

Sae to JLC, 4/4/1859
Sister Sarah wrote to her brother while her niece Daisy, who was about three years old at the time, was paying another visit.

Brewer. April 4th 1859

Dear Lawrence,
I ought to have written you long before, but "don't say a word" as Aunt Hannah says. I am writing now; let that suffice. Do take the most important subject first. Little Daisy is as <u>interesting</u> as one could desire but she thinks she is rather plain as she says. When she is interested her face lights up, particularly her <u>eyes</u>. I think by and by she will look very well. She has learned to talk very fast since she has been with us. I believe she says everything now at my word she <u>knows</u> everything. We are trying to break her of a great aversion to men. Lewis and Sam Gardner called here one evening to see her and she insisted that she didn't want to see a man. At last she consented to go into the parlor but the instant she saw them she reiterated "Daisy don't want to see a man at all" "not at all". She is very much preoccupied with Mr. Cummings.[28] Indeed there seems to be a mutual

---

28 Rev. Ephraim Cummings was the Congregational minister in Brewer.

attraction for he is extremely interested in her. They spend most of the time exchanging vows and kisses. The saying "Daisy owns Cummings" he is to blame for. The seeming want of respect and giving him peppermints. We keep them for her distribution. She admires to see ladies, and always behaves well before strangers except that she is afraid to talk. She usually displays Papa's photograph kissing it once or twice herself. Lately she can't tell yours from Horace's but never mistakes it for any other one. We try to keep you all familiar to her. She always loves to look at Fannie's picture she noticed that one before any of the others. She loves to hear singing but cares nothing at all about playing. I must now assure you, we have taken the best possible care of her and have tried not to indulge her too much. She makes it very manifest that she has a will of her own sometimes. I think she needs a very firm hand with her. Let her understand that she will always find you the same under the same circumstances and there is no further trouble. We have had a hurricane of wind for two or three days and she seems to have taken a little cold, but she has been perfectly well all the time. There is one thing more so funny I must tell you. Sam Gardner was showing her the photographs in Horace's album without noticing particularly who he took out and asking her if she knew that "no dont know the man at all" every time at last he pulled one out and the moment she saw it her face lighted up and she reached out her hand and took it from him and turned it all round and looked at it and finally burst out "That's Cummings, that's Cummings" It proved to be Prof. Everett! and it was all the more funny because Cummings himself says he looks like Everett and it was all the more funny, because Cummings himself says he looks like Everett.

We feel sorry for you that your party was so thinly attended. I think it is more pleasant to have all come that you invite. But then you have the satisfaction of knowing that you have invited them to your house. I had a letter from Mr. Roberts[29] who went to the Ascension Islands the other day. I had no particular acquisition with him what do you suppose made him write? It was directed to Mary Gardner and me. He commenced it on board the Morning Star and wrote a little from the Sandwich Is. and some from Strongs Is. and closed it at the Ascension Is. His description of the Islanders was exceedingly brief contenting himself with saying "that the females and children of both sexes were entirely in the nude state!" No comment is needed. If you are like me your mouth will have widened sensibly by the time

---

29 Charles W. Roberts, Bowdoin, Class of 1851, was the son of a Bangor lumber baron.

you read the exclamation point. He sent his regards to Prof. Chamberlain and mentioned that he had a thermometer which belonged to you. He said it got into his room he didn't know exactly by what means. He didn't mention the reason of his carrying it to Micronesia. I saw Miss Anquata Mann the other night she enquired minutely after you. Mother was much pleased with the notice of your venture. Write us soon.

Sarah

~~~

Horace to John, 6/16/1859
Horace married Mary Wheeler on May 11, 1859. A month later he wrote to his younger brother John.

Bangor June 16th 1859

Dear bro John;

I send you by Sarah my Upham on the will. Might have sent it by [Professor] Appleton if I had known of it. I only saw him one moment in the street and did not know how soon he was to leave. He said nothing about it and I supposed if you wanted anything by him you would let me know. The fact is, I have been extremely busy lately as Sarah will tell you, in fixing up my house and moving into it. It so happened that in the default of promises by painters etc. I had most of the work to do myself—painted seven rooms myself and had to race after masons etc. look after them so that I didn't see my office for about ten days, even. Thank fortune, I hope I am about established now tho, and Tom, who dined with me Sunday thinks I live in pretty good style as to tables at least. The house is furnished not elegantly, hardly neatly, but comfortably and commodiously for the present. "When I get rich" it will be better!

You are about finishing up your own Coll[ege] course now—I hope you have done a good term's work. I would by all means put in so as to pass a good examination. There will be a good deal of watching and prophesying [sic] on that occasion by outsiders who form there whole estimate of a man (rather unfairly) by that one appearance. As you have got so far no what you can see through, you can look back on just what you need to improve. I have no doubt you will make a good appearance, you can if you will. I see by the papers that little Bradbury has been appt. as the orator. Rather unexpected to me but I hope he will work. I wish you would save most of my old books and bring home to me. They are <u>pleasant after</u> a few years of absence—my astronomy, chemistry, Poly and Butler, etc. There is one very valuable book of mine that is missing. It is a blank pass book or acc[oun]t. book that I used in Europe as a sort of journal. Red cover about half an inch thick and about eight inches by four. I would give a small reward to see it again. Contains all my notes etc. I am not quite sure as it is in Coll[ege], but can't find it anywhere else. Will you interest yourself a little about it and see what can be done?

Jan 17—I have just recd Franks letter. Don't know whether Emery will present it. A good many of the bits would not be appreciated here, especially since there … [letter ends]

Horace to JLC, 6/17/1859
After updating his brother John, Horace invited his oldest brother to pay him a visit in his new home.

Bangor Jun 17th 1859

Dear Bro Lawrence
I am rather tardy in composing your so very courteous invitation I admit, but in gratitude to your kindness I can only express my regret at the utter irresponsibility of my accepting at that time, and extra to you at the same time a similar invitation that you with your family will pay me a visit in my own house! We do not insinuate that we are "elegant commodious," but comfortable and free. Whoever comes into my house has it at his disposal with its contents. In fact I flatter myself that I am a tolerable host aiming as I do not at the tinsel and trifles of fashion, but the value substantial such as our grandfather and the men of his time even brought up to. My endeavor is to take no less of a man than led Josh, senior[30] as a jury in the countries of the mansion and for me, I think no style so courtly or so much. Our furniture is rather common but "when we get rich," you know, why then we shall see wonders of course! Probably you will not be able to visit us before commencement but if you want a short visit you shall be warranted the same at my establishment. Tom dined with me last Sunday and thinks <u>at</u>

---

30 Joshua Lawrence Chamberlain, Sr., their grandfather.

the table we can't be beat. That's one item certainly of no small importance in housekeeping. When one wants to recruit. If you are not able to come before, come after com[mencement] and the honor is yours.—I have had to work mighty hard as Sarah can tell you but in just four weeks from the hour I was married I was altogether established in a house of which I alone hold the fee and have not taken a meal out of it since. I said that often during Mothers, considering that I did not get possession till something like a fortnight after marriage. The question is generally asked How do you like the married life? I have only one answer to that—I think it the natural way for a man to live. A man better be asked how he likes an unmarried life. In my case it doesn't seem like anything strange—hardly any thing new—I have known Mary so long and been so intimate with her always that there is no romance at all about it, and I, who am naturally quite the opposite find myself quite a matter of fact sort of a man. How long this blissful state of things will continue tho I can't tell. If you remember why you didn't write pleasure or literary letters last vacation you will remember as I do the reason I didn't answer your so friendly letter of a few weeks since. Visions of truant painters, masons, etc. haunt that shrine with me. Still I am not at liberty now and shall be happy to let you hear from me very often. Write me if you can get a chance. Aff'ly tho in haste. H.B.C.

~~~

George J. Blake to JLC, 9/2/1859
The Chamberlains continued to fill their house with more furniture.

12 Cornhill
Boston Sept 2nd 1859
Prof. JL. Chamberlain

Dr Sir,
We have this day sent to you by Rail Road one arm chair. We thought the chair has been sent to you a long time ago.

    Yours respectfully
    Blake and Davenport
    Geo J. Blake

~~~

Susie Hildi to JLC, 9/13/1859
A school in Deposit, New York, asked Chamberlain to help convince his sister Sae to teach there. Sae took the job.

Laurel Bank Seminary
Sept 13th 1859

Mr. Chamberlain
    Dear Sir
    I enclose a note to Sarah as I believe she is with you—
    We want to secure her services as music teacher for the coming fall and winter, at least Miss Sturd must leave us at the close of this term—I hope Sarah will come as I should be very sorry to have a stranger—so far we have had a learning community of old acquaintances so that it has hardly seemed like living in a strange place but if Sarah can not or will not come perhaps you can recommend someone who would be suitable and available. It is hardly necessary to say that we do not want a person whose only recommendation shall be proficiency in music. It is of no little consequence to have a person who shall be an agreeable companion and shall exercise a good influence in all respects. But if I do not need to go thro' with that cant as you understand it as well as I. Please do use your influence to induce Sarah to come—we will take good care of her—and I will solemnly promise to abuse her in no manner whatever. of the latter clause is not included in the former. I am half blind with weariness and shall go to sleep if I write another word.

    Your respectful friend
    Susie Hildi

P.S.
That, dear sir was an after thought which accounts for its being put on to the jag end of the line—not at all spontaneous you see—if Sarah is not in B—will you do me the favor to forward my note to her immediately with all the arguments you can add to induce her to come

~

Horace to JLC and John (nd; ca. spring 1859)

The brothers informed Chamberlain of news in Bangor and Brewer, including some published in the Jeffersonian newspaper.

[... page(s) missing ...] Jeffersonian in which "civil" letter was published does not circulate much in the city nor is it read much here. Still I will see what I can do with it—a good many of the bits are good, especially the one on insects and the tri-daily meeting of the association to dissect this quest.[ion] and the "Anti-Peanut Soc." tho not many here could apprehend the full force of them ever. Most of the readers of a daily paper are unlettered businessmen who know little outside of their own sphere. Still I think a good many could appreciate most of it and I will try Emery on it. Frank says you won't want the Upham— I hope you have not bought one, I was thinking of sending it by Sarah— and perhaps I had better. If it isn't written you can send it back or bring it yourself when you come— I presume you will come home to 4th of July. You know they are going to lay out 15 hundred $ here on that occasion in Public sermons Fire works etc.. I believe the term classes clear that time so you could do so if you want to. Young Hersey with a friend of his called in to the office the other day. They say they want you to go up and make them a visit. You could have a good time no doubt. The programme for the 4th in Bangor has not fully come out yet. Tho they will have a percussion military parade etc.— at any rate.

Law business is rather full here now tho the lumber business is v[er]y good river full of vessels etc. I don't know just how Father is off for money now but I guess not very flush— If you are coming home at all before com[mencement] You had better put in and get your part done so as to come immediately on close of term. I don't know whether I shall be able to go on to leave or not but shall if I can possibly. You will hear from me now further after as I have leisure now.

Affly Horace B. C.

[side marking] John + Lawrence

~~~

JLC to Fannie, 6/17/1860[31]

In May 1860, Fannie gave birth to a third child, a daughter, whom they named Emily Stelle. Both mother and daughter were ill a month later, when word came by telegraph that Fannie's eighty-two-year-old birth father, Ashur Adams, was dangerously ill. With Fannie unable to travel, Joshua made the trip to Boston to be with her family.

Jamaica Plain June 17 1860

My dear Fanny;

I had to depend on my sagacity in getting out here, for nobody gave me any direction. I found my way though and got here at 10 last evening. I did not see your Father there, as he was asleep. He had been rapidly sinking since the letter, we had, and for the most part did not know any of his friends. Early this morning the nurse told him I was here, and he called out for me I went in and he seemed not only to know me, but to be very glad to see me. He brightened up a great deal. Said a great deal of you. "If you were here," he said, he "should have all the chickens here." Katie says he has not seemed so bright since he has been sick. I felt a great encouraged that he would live until you could see him; but I fear there is not much ground for such a hope. As the day advances he seems to sink: indeed since I began to write he has had another ill turn, and the family do not expect him to live through the day. What a noble head and face as he lied there so patiently! and all the elegance and courtly grace which marked him in his best days seems to be such a deep element of his nature that this outward weakness does not in the least affect it. I was going to mention with what particularity he inquired after you and Daisy and even the little one "if she were as beautiful as Daisy" etc. he talks a great deal with me, about various things. His mind was perfectly clear. I tried to pray with him. I felt there was great need for prayer for me, but of praise for him. One inarticulate feeble breath of his how much more availing than any prayer of mine! I have been up to see him again since I sat down to write. He seems to be sinking, but as he is so quiet I will keep on writing. No one could have better care and attention or more expression of reverence and affection than he has here. You will be glad to hear me tell you when I get home, how delightful it is here. Mr. LeCain seems to be and do everything that could be desired in a man. I am greatly pleased with him and shall not forget this cardinal greeting and continued courtesies. Katie has been reading some poems she found of Charlottes and your mother's.[32] They are very beautiful. I have a great many things to write and might keep on so all day but I will stop awhile now, till I see how your father is.

---

31 Harrisburg 1995.459.11.21
32 John A. LeCain was the husband of Fannie's niece, Mary Cate (Katie). Charlotte was Fannie's sister.

Evening 7 o'clock
I have been with your father and talking with him a great deal this afternoon. He has a great deal to say of you. He suggest names for the baby and "sends a heart full of love to you." I think he is sinking tho' and shall write to you by every mail until I come. I am going to sit up with your father tonight. He seems very glad to have me near him.

Lawrence

Much love to the dear children from Papa—Let the darlings stay with dear mama all they can.
If you are sick send me a dispatch
57 Hanover St.

~

JLC to Fannie, 6/18/1860[33]

Monday Eve 6.50

Dear Fanny,
I write in haste because I said I would write by eve. mail. I watched with your dear father last night but he has not received to know any of us much. They all say it has been a great comfort to him to have me here.

He does not sink rapidly but it is thought surely. We must prepare for the worst.

I have been over to Forrest Hills today and shall have something to say of that when I get home. I have also been looking over George's things and shall bring you some of them.

I intend to come home by boat Wednesday morning. Be very careful of yourself my darling wife—when I come I will be careful for you. Love to the dear ones and to Rebecca

Lawrence[34]

---

33 Harrisburg 1995.459.1.3
34 Ashur Adams died a few days later.

CHAPTER FOUR

The Civil War

D espite his new place on the Bowdoin faculty and his growing comfort establishing a home and family, Chamberlain began to grow uneasy as the country descended into civil war. With so many Bowdoin men leaving for the war—he wrote that "Nearly a hundred of those who have been my pupils, are now officers in our army"—and the public mood taking on an ever-increasing martial air, the young professor's earlier thoughts of a military career were stirred.

"The flag of the nation had been insulted," he wrote, "The honor and authority of the Union had been assaulted in open and bitter war. The north was at last awake to the intent and the magnitude of the Rebellion. The country was roused to the peril and the duty of the hour."

By the spring of 1862, the country had been at war for nearly a year, and Chamberlain felt an "irresistible impulse" to serve the nation. At just that time, however, Bowdoin gave him a lifetime appointment as professor of Modern Languages, a promotion that included a $500 bonus and a two-year leave of absence to travel to Europe. While he accepted the offer, he quietly put other plans in motion. In a letter to Israel Washburn, the governor of Maine, he expressed his desire to serve and offered himself to his state.

"In pursuance of the offer of reinforcements for the war," he wrote. "I ask if your Excellency desires and will accept my service." Explaining that he had just received the college promotion, he wrote that he was "entirely unwilling, however, to accept this offer, if my Country needs my service or example here."[1]

---

1 JLC to Gov. Washburn, 7/14/1863, Maine State Archives.

Describing his motivations, he told the governor, "I fear, this war, so costly of blood and treasure, will not cease until men of the North are willing to leave good positions, and sacrifice the dearest personal interests, to rescue our country from desolation, and defend the national existence against treachery."[2]

But college professors were not plentiful in the 1860s, and their value shaping the young minds who would lead the state for generations to come far exceeded anything they might accomplish as a single officer on a battlefield. To this, Chamberlain wrote that "I am sensible that I am proposing personal sacrifices, which would not probably be demanded of me; but I believe this to be my duty, and I know I can be of service to my Country in this hour of peril."[3]

Three weeks later, the governor sent him a brief note that read, "I hereby tender you the office of Lt. Col., 20th Regt. ME Vol. Adelbert Ames, Commander of a battery and native of Maine as Col. and a superb one he will make."[4]

That the appointment was to the second in command came as no surprise to the young professor. In fact, he had preferred it. Weeks before, the governor had offered him command of a new regiment, but Chamberlain had declined, saying it would be wiser to "Give the colonelcy of the regiment to some regular officer now in the field. I will take a subordinate position," he said, "and learn and earn my way to the command."[5]

By mid-August 1863, the newly sworn members of the 20th Maine Regiment began to assemble in camp across the Fore River from Portland. By the end of September's first week, they would move by train, steamer, and foot to a battlefield on the banks of a Maryland creek known as Antietam.

JLC to Fannie 8/20/1862
Soon after formally joining the army, Chamberlain wrote from Camp Mason, just outside Portland, where the new 20th Maine Regiment was being formed.

Head Quarters 20th Reg't
Camp Mason
Aug. 20th 1862

---

2 JLC to Gov. Washburn, 7/14/1863, Maine State Archives
3 *Ibid.*
4 Gov. Washburn to JLC, 8/8/1863
5 JLC, undated autobiography, Bowdoin College

Dear Fanny,

I do not have a very natural place for writing but I sit down on a box and take a piece of paper on a board and in the midst of a furious drumming on one side and ever so many men talking loudly on the other I say a word keep so as to myself in mind of you comfortable people at home.

I find I need a good many little things—towels, pins, etc. I forgot. By the way make me a needle and thread case will you, shirt buttons etc. included. My flannel for shirts I have not got yet, but will send or take myself when I come. The Col. [Adelbert Ames] is not yet here. Soon after he comes, I shall go. I had a call from Dr. and Mrs. Bacon yesterday[6]—they were very pleasant. She got your letter but had not time to answer [… letter torn …] is better, Mrs. B. is going to invite you to come here as soon as her house is repaired. I shall <u>probably</u> be detained there three weeks by lack of transportation, as the roads are so crowded by soldiers all the way to Washington. So you can make me a visit, and I will return it before we go. My two nights on the tent floor were not at all uncomfortable, but not quite so soft as my double spring bed. I like the major much, we are together now.[7] We have had over a thousand men, but have let so many go to the old Regts that we are short now. I wish Brunswick would send us more and make up her quota. Aren't you ladies going to make us a color, or something?

I shall be home Friday or Saturday I suppose—<u>not</u> with company unless with some notice. Stockings and drawers, you know would come into play for <u>me</u>, and those you can get.

I have to keep up a conversation all the time and can't write very well, when I get into my own tent it will be better. <u>No chance to wash much now!</u> With much love to auntie[8] and the darlings and hoping to see you all soon.

"Yours truly"
J. L. Chamberlain

Write me at
"20th Regt Maine Vols"
"Camp Mason"
"Portland"

---

6 Elbridge Bacon (Bowdoin Medical School, Class of 1839) was a dentist in Portland from 1840–95. He and his wife were friends of the Chamberlains.

7 Charles D. Gilmore transferred from the 7th Maine Regiment to receive a promotion to major in the 20th Maine. He proved to be a dishonorable officer who disrupted the command structure of the regiment through the end of the war.

8 After the children were born, Cousin Deb became known as Auntie.

JLC to Fannie, 9/3/1862

From Portland, the 20th Maine took a train to Boston, where they boarded a steamship for their trip to Washington, D.C. (then known as "Washington City" though often referred to simply as "Washington").

Steamship Merrimac
at Sea Sept 3 1862

My dear Fanny,

Here we are heaving and rolling about in this great ship with two full Regiments on board numbering more than two thousand men. Fairly off and stretching our way for the scene of strife. It is a splendid day and we are all in good spirits, and eager to do our duty in turning the battle against the foe. The news when we left Boston was bad for us; but it makes us all more eager to move on. We go to Alexandria our ship is too large to go up to Washington. You could have gone with us if you wished. The accommodations for officers are fine. I cannot say but that you might have been a little sick. You may judge from this handwriting what a shaking we are getting.

How dismal it was on that field where you and I passed our last night! I am sorry you had so unpleasant a taste of soldier life, and I am more so because the associations will be disagreeable whenever you think of our parting. I was quite proud of your behavior during all the dreary business.[9] I knew very well how you felt, and how I felt, but I knew too what must be, and we managed to brace up very well I think. How kind your father was. I feel very grateful to him. You will please thank him for me.

I had a very hard day yesterday. When we reached the ship the Col. soon went up in town and I had to superintend the embarkation. You would not believe it was so much work. It required fifty men for police duty on the wharf and with all our good order and expedition we were two hours in embarking. I saw Mr. LeCain and Uncle Swett.[10]

I offered my horse to the Col. [Ames] to ride through Boston and he accepted. But we could not get at the horses. In fact they could not be taken

---

9 The night before the 20th Maine departed the Portland area, rain and wind swept the regimental campsite. Chamberlain shared a tent with his wife and father-in-law until reveille awoke the camp at 3:30 a.m.

10 John A. LeCain was the husband of Fannie's niece, Mary Cate (Katie). They lived in the Jamaica Plain section of Boston, which was then part of West Roxbury. Nathaniel Swett married Sarah Brastow, the youngest sister of Chamberlain's mother. They lived in Arlington Heights, just northwest of Boston.

in this ship and are to come on in another tomorrow. My horse attracted a great deal of notice as he was brought along by a boy who has him in charge.[11]

I am surrounded by ever so many officers on the floor sick, and a boy is cleaning an oil lamp right under my nose. I with both elbows stretched out to the utmost to make a good base am dashing off these lines better perhaps than what I would like to have something [... letter torn ...] in case we break any [... letter torn ...] to let you know how well I am, and how content and satisfied that I am in the way of duty.

Whatever may befall me, I feel that I and all you who are so more than dear to me are committed to the care of a merciful God and all will be well. Pray for us and be full of peace and hope as I am.

Your ever loving husband
L.

~~~

JLC to Fannie, 9/nd/1862
A letter to Fannie, probably written in late September. Chamberlain's birthday was September 8.

Now, darling, I wrote you almost scolding in my last, because I thought you were worrying about money affairs. The only thing is, Birdie, I didn't want that pretty face to get care worn, and those two little lines perpendicular just between the eyebrows, I didn't want those to come out at all. I think I will write Rich Melcher to take care of you. Where is my photograph? Saturday Eve.

I knew you would write me a birthday letter and what a one! You are a blessed prize of a girl. You have been reading my boy-letters, have you? Well I just loved you then—I did not know you much, and I didn't care— respect, friendship, growing into affection and ending in a respectful, friendly, request to marry me—why that was not precisely the way the thing went. Oh. I can't tell you about it tonight. I am too tired to analyze that eager boyish love. How I love you now I am not too tired to tell you, and never can be. As I know you, blessed friend, whether you were man

---

11 Prominent citizens of Portland gave Chamberlain a handsome dapple grey horse as a going away present. He named the horse "Prince."

or woman earthly or angelic, I would cling to you forever. And, truly, after all, I love you better and more, in the same way, than years ago. I know how to love now.

I just had orders to be ready to march early tomorrow morning in case anything should happen (we make a reconnaissance towards Culpepper courthouse) so dearest I bless you once more. Do give my warmest love to that blessed Daisy and to noble Wyllys. How I love you all. May God keep you.

L

JLC to Fannie, 10/12/1862

The surviving portion of a letter that Chamberlain wrote to Fannie describes events in the field, including a review of the troops by President Lincoln near Antietam.

… your letters, that you are not having a very good time. Perhaps it is because money is not very plenty with you. <u>Very soon now</u> my pay will come in and you will find something at the bank for you. My note (the only one I think) comes due at the bank soon, but I write today to arrange about it without troubling you. Be sure and have a pleasant time and give the children a few extra indulgences—only <u>obedience, always, instant, and entire.</u> Those are my orders! That is the way to save children. But give them every comfort in the way of <u>clothing</u> and of <u>toys</u>. Toys are necessary. You need not make anything for me. You can't think how few my wants are. I could "get along" with only the clothes I stand in. I can buy what I want in the way of clothing from quarter masters and sutlers.[12] None of my books are in the old college room. The carpet is mine—not worth much—the table and cloth—the glass—and all the things in the bedroom. Mr. Tacker would not take any books, I think that were not charged to me in the library register. I forget whether we ever settled for the books I got for the library and the one he "<u>took</u>". I will write him.

---

12 Sutlers were merchants who followed the army selling goods to soldiers.

Oct. 12

A gloomy morning made more so by the sad intelligence which came post haste in the driving dismal rain last night that Capt Andrew of our Regt. had just died in the hospital there. He was an only son—young, brave, enthusiastic. His career was short. We all feel sad at losing him; but you could scarcely believe how the value of life is lessened in estimation, by familiarity with these cases. I should scarcely feel a death here that would break me down at home. If Tom now were to get hit (he is here you know) why I should consider it very natural and to be looked for and it would not begin to affect me as it would elsewhere. So in regard to my own life only for your sakes it is dear to me. It is marvelous how my health is holding out. I really do not know of another man in the Regt. who has not been sick. Every officer— surgeons and all, but I have not had an hour of illness. I eat everything, but regularly I sleep in all sorts of ways and places but look out for the flannel. My appetite and brown complexion are maters of joke. You perceive we have changed our camp. We are now at the mouth of the Antietam (pronounced an-tee-tam). I am placed in command of the grand outpost along the shore of Potomac, just a third post this time. We have a picket line of miles. I go out again tomorrow came in yesterday. I enjoy it. I occasionally witness a little skirmish. The other day Stuarts cavalry—a squadron or two came galloping up toward the ford I was guarding when bang and screech went our shell into them and there was a fine skedaddling. Col. Ames was in command of the Brigade for some time. So I had the good fortune to command the Regt. As he did the Brigade upon occasion of the grand Review by President Lincoln. My horse looked so finely that I was nobody. My position was in the very front of the Brigade and the horse knew it was a great occasion and did his part much better than his rider. We shall probably move again in a week or two. Give my love to all the dear friends. Be hospitable. Invite the young people in. You will not spend the winter there. Much love and sorry to close.

Your aff. Lawrence

JLC to Fannie, likely 11/20/1862
Two and a half months after leaving Maine, Chamberlain wrote another note from the field describing his diet and daily routine. This one, written in a much darker tone than those previous, offers a far more bleak assessment of his surroundings.

171

Warrenton/62 Thursday noon.

Our eating arrangements in moving about in this way are rather droll. The officers do not "draw" rations, we have to shift for ourselves; when we are not near any village and have no sutler we have to fare hard. Monday I had (begged!) a tip of salt tongue 3 inches long, and 2 pieces of hard-bread. Next day 3 cakes bought of a rebel I believe and eaten with grave apprehensions; as five or six Massachusetts men have been poisoned in this neighborhood of pounded glass in cake. Yesterday a few cakes and some cheese bought of a sutler for breakfast and nothing more till 9 P.M. when the Col. got hold of some peaches and he and I ate half a peck for supper, which repast as you may imagine, lasts us pretty well into the day this morning. The peaches were such as I just wish I could send you; but they would not keep. We are going to quit begging today and have some things sent us for our mess. I sleep on the ground a blanket under me and the shawl over. After we get a little more established I shall ride over the country a little, visit the picket line in front and more especially the Maine boys in this vicinity. The old 2d is within a mile about 150 left out of the 1000. Charlie Roberts[13], lucky fellow, instead of being killed is Brigadier Gen. I am going to see him as soon as I can. I wish I could send you something, but this country is perfectly desolate. Nothing seems to flourish here but graves. A few rods across the rifle pits in front of us is a little family burying ground under a group of locust trees. Some mother with her six children sleep there "in Jesus" as the inscription says. Sad enough! but sadder far, to think that in the attack that very spot will afford an evident shelter to the enemy from which to annoy us, and will not doubt be the theater of angry strife. Cannon shot will crush the head stones, and tear the mounds. But the dead are happy there, compared with those who live to see these cruel days. That mother and her little ones are no traitors and the storms of shot and shell that will rage around their resting place will not vex their ears. I declare it almost weakened me to think what this nation is now doing, wholly devoted to mutual destruction! But there is no other way and there are things worth more than life and peace. Nationality—the Law of Liberty, public and private honor are worth far more, and if the Rebels think they are fighting for all that men hold dear, as I suppose some of them really think they are, we are fighting for more, we

---

13 Charles W. Roberts, Bowdoin, Class of 1851, was the son of a Bangor lumber baron. He was appointed lieutenant colonel in the 2nd Maine in 1861.

fight for all the <u>guaranties</u> of what men should love, for the <u>protection</u> and <u>permanence</u> and <u>peace</u> of what is most dear and sacred to every true heart. That is what I am fighting for at any rate, and I could not live or die in a better cause.— You can tell Mr. Tenney[14] and others where we are situation and what our prospects are. Say we are well and cheerful. Write to me often.

Lawrence

~~~

JLC to Fannie, 11/22/1862
Written while the two armies were maneuvering near one another in Virginia, this letter to Fannie reveals the great enthusiasm that Chamberlain felt toward camp life despite uncomfortable living conditions. It also describes the origin of the iconic mustache he wore for the rest of his life.

Bivouac near Hartwood, VA
Nov. 22 1862

My dearest Fannie,
We have been sitting all of us—the Col., Major, Adjutant, Doctor and I around our tent fire which we have tonight in the middle of our big tent, telling ghost stories and other marvelous tales and have enjoyed ourselves very much. Innumerable bugles are sounding the "extinguish light," and the thought of how much you would enjoy the evening and still more the sight of this city of camp fires and the sound of the bugles, prompt me to write one word to you before I roll myself up in my blanket and go to my sound sleep. Not in the least am I disturbed now by the message which just came from the General "<u>Be vigilant tonight</u>." You know we are in the midst of the enemy's country now and have plenty of spies around us; and tonight it happens that we are rather a small body to be left alone so far from aid. But we can be just as vigilant without being nervous. N.B. I don't get "nervous" now. 12 or 15 hours daily in the saddle is going to <u>rejuvenate</u> me. How you would enjoy this camp—comfortable for once and these <u>bugles</u> again one answering another from all the hill tops around. I wish you could be here.

---

14 Samuel W. Tenney graduated from Bowdoin in 1856 and the Bangor Theological Seminary in 1861. He served with the U.S. Christian Commission during the war. He died at Camp Stoneman in Washington, D.C., on June 13, 1864.

But what should I do with you in the morning my little girl? On the march muddy, cold, and often rainy, you would not be comfortable. My clothes have not been dry for three or four days. All day to day we have been standing packed and saddled, waiting the usual signal "forward:" but at sunset the order came to camp, for some good reason we could not move. Mr. [Adjut. John Marshall] Brown took the opportunity today of cutting my beard to suit his notion of my face. He has left me with a ferocious mustache and my bit of an imperial only. The ends of the mustache he has waxed and twisted and they reach positively the angle of my jaw (you have no angle on yours) and would almost meet under my chin. Mr. B. thinks he has me now to suit him—especially for a profile. You would not know me.

We have had many changes in commanders in regard to which we soldiers having other things to do have not much to say.[15] We are now in Griffins Division, Hooker's Grand Division. The old corps of Porter is commanded by Butterfield, the brigade by the senior Colonel. You may address simply "20th Regt "Maine" Vols" "Washington D.C."

We are on for Richmond once more and finally we shall take it this time you may be sure. But we have got to fight all our way from Fredericksburg, I suppose.

Wednesday night

I think I must have been dreaming something very sweet about you all last night, my own darling love, for my thoughts dwelt so lovingly upon you the moment I awoke, and you have been such a delight to me all day. Lonely I cannot deny I have been, though indeed not for one moment this day alone until now, and such a day—soft Indian summer—and the night—the harvest moon—the roar of water—the frowning cannon—the camp—so many and such silence! How I have loved you to day! How longed for you. How dwelt every moment upon—I was going to say your love—your character!—but I say "upon you." How I have yearned all day to clasp that dear form to my heart—to gaze into those eyes—to touch my lips tenderly upon the marvelous softness of that loved cheek—to drain a kiss of love—like waters of life—from those lips—"more like me" will you say, to snatch it with a wild rush of passion and a flush as from ruby wine? Ah, well, something of that there may be in me too at times; for the blood in my veins: but earnestly,

---

15 In a fairly short span of time, President Lincoln had replaced George McClellan with Ambrose Burnside as commander of the Army of the Potomac. Burnside then reorganized the army into three "grand divisions," causing a shuffle in various command positions.

my darling, darling, and you do know it, I do love you as one breathes a pure, life-giving air—life is built up and renewed by such love, not exhausted and spent. My heart lives on you.

And, dearest, what do you think I think I do all this time I am clinging to you so? Do you think I am sitting solitary and musing? No! let me tell you. Busy, Busy. Official papers plunged into, masses of them—the camps of my Brigade visited and inspected—the conditions and quarters and food of the Men looked after—the cleanliness of camp—the least and the lowest things sometimes,—I am about, earnestly, impatiently, almost, as is my habit. Then, this done, if I return and there is still loneliness, that is, if I am myself—not wholly tired out—if my whole being, as to day, cries out for you—why—darling—there is my horse—my noble fellow—ready always to go with me—my own wild way. He looks at me and he knows—and with a snort and snuff of air away he goes and away I go after you and somehow— in some strange way, I find you. I find you, in doing good as I am able to men: but I find you most in my wild rides. So today—with my aides behind me trying to keep near—stopping at brooks and hedges which 1 leap without knowing it—wondering at me no doubt—have been riding after — and with you.

With you still to night, dearest, loving you with this passionate calmness which you know. You called me a "marble statue". I was, and I am; but— is that all? You know that too.

How sweet it is to think of you, my wife,—my darling, thrilling girl, calm and gentle mother of my children; twelve years ago, and tonight,— which is dearest, the rock of that river, or the banks of this? That where I stood a boy of passionate wishes, or this where I stand a man of thought and will, and deed? "Toujours"—"toujours à vous"[16]—. Write me, sweet one, though you have not the vast Silence, and solitude I have on such a night as this, to write in.

To his dearest, his loving blessed wife.
from Lawrence—her own...

---

16 "yours always" in French

JLC to Fannie, 11/27/1862
Chamberlain wrote of events in the field and began to discuss his ambitions and how they stretched beyond the Bowdoin faculty.

(No. 11)
Camp Near Falmouth VA
Opposite Fredericksburg
Nov. 27th 1862

My dear Fanny,

The major is going to Washington and I hasten to write a word. It is Thanksgiving day in Maine, I believe, and just now you are probably in church. How different my circumstances! In the midst of a great army making great preparations for battle. Still everything is beautiful today, and peaceful as child's play. These formidable battles are silent, and the bugles sound only the calls for the daily routine. How long things will continue so, we cannot tell. The women and children are moving from Fredericksburg which lies almost at the mercy of our guns. But the bridges are all destroyed and we shall not offer a crossing without a severe contest as the enemy are in great force opposite.

The skirmishing has been chiefly of artillery and cavalry during our march down through Virginia. There are no signs as yet of any great change of tactics or policy since Burnside assumed command. I am going to answer your inquiries. Drawers and shirts. Made or knit either. I wear out drawers fast being so much on horseback. The bill for Boston Journal was right. The express for the Door could not be adjusted. John tried it in Bangor. Double windows on the dining room I advised you to have some time ago. (Do you get all my letters?) The stable bill was right. I think I have not paid Gross. Will you? (Has any payment been made me at the bank from gov't?) Griffins bill must be very small, but will be correct. Yes, buy green wood. It is profitable. When wood is cheap you should have Mr. Booker perhaps buy about six cords for next summer's use. Let it lie out doors till May—sawed and split. I see Genl Howard and Mr. Whittlesey very often. Wm. Henry Owen is near captain or Gen. Birney's staff. I see all my friends often.[17]

---

17 Oliver Otis Howard, Bowdoin, Class of 1850, was Chamberlain's roommate in 1848. He graduated from West Point in the Class of 1854. Eliphalet Whittlesey was a pastor in Bath, Maine, who became professor of Rhetoric and Oratory at Bowdoin in 1861 before accepting a commission as captain in the U.S. Army in 1862. William Henry Owen graduated from Bowdoin in the Class of 1851.

General Whittlesey! It would mortify him much to be addressed in that way. I noticed Mr. Tenney with his usual air of finality refers to Gen. Whittlesey. No man who knew a particle of military affairs would make such a mistake. The Adjutant General of the army has the rank of Brigadier assistant adjt. Genl has the rank of captain no more. Mr. W. is called "General Whittlesey" of course. It is the same place offered me by Genl. Howard. It is a very honorable position however far better than that of a captain in the line. The work however is chiefly officer work. No special duties on the field, that is few. I like the field and the command of men. Mr. W's office does not furnish this. So much for that.

Please give my regards to the misses Weld and all those kind friends who mention me. I think of them much. Between you and me I do not think it at all certain that I shall reside in Brunswick after my return. I find that I can stretch my faculties to a somewhat larger place than even the field pronounced so extensive and rich by Profs Upham and Smith.[18] I feel cramped by the thought of going back but time will determine. I think I can work on a somewhat larger scale.

You do not know how much I think of you darling, and those precious little ones. My eyes are not dry in speaking of you. Thank Aunty for her love and prayers. I feel as if you were all praying for me and loving me. I will try to live worthy of both the love and the prayers.

Take a new token of my constant affection in this
Your own loving L.

JLC to Fannie, 12/17/1862
This is the first written account of Chamberlain's experiences at the Battle of Fredericksburg—his first experience in combat—taken largely from his battlefield notes. During his lifetime he would write of the battle many times but never from a memory this close to the actual events.

---

18 Thomas C. Upham was professor of Mental and Moral Philosophy from 1824–67. Egbert C. Smyth (Bowdoin, Class of 1848) was a graduate of the Bangor Theological Seminary (Class of 1853) and professor of Rhetoric and Oratory and then Natural and Revealed Religion from 1854–63, when he left to teach at Andover Theological Seminary.

Camp opposite Fredericksburg December 17th, 1862

My dear wife,

I know how much you must desire to hear what I have witnessed and experienced during this eventful week. Let me begin by a few extracts from my note book. "Dec. 11th. 10 A.M. In the saddle waiting the word to cross the Rappahannock in front of Fredericksburg. Hooker's Grand Division, closed in masses, covering the grounds around as far as the eye can see. Our batteries open upon the town—forty five or fifty shots a minute. We cannot see the river, but are told our engineers are trying to throw across the pontoon bridges, and rebel sharpshooters under cover of the town are picking them off as fast as they appear. Our cannonading is to shell the Rebels out of the city. Their formidable batteries in the rear of the town are plainly to be seen, but do not reply, or but rarely. I asked permission to ride to the front a short time ago, and with Mr. Brown for a companion (one would not wish for a better one); and, with some of the rashness of youth perhaps, we made quite a minute inspection of affairs. Advancing beyond our line of batteries we were fully within the circle of sharpshooting operations. But the result repaid the risk. From the famous Lacy House directly opposite Fredericksburg, and I should think almost within pistol range, the scene (let the word include sounds as well as sights) was grand beyond anything I ever witnessed or expect to witness. The flame and smoke, the thunder and scream of artillery—the shells bursting in the city— the bridge of boats half done—the Rebel sharpshooters running from the shells and rallying to the front again—here and there a huge pontoon whose weight had broken its carriage lying like a stranded whale—and on the other hand a train of ambulances full of wounded slowly winding its way to the rear—before us this beautiful city, on fire in a dozen places, columns of dense smoke streaming into the sky and lurid bursts where some enormous shell had lifted a brick building in the air ground to dust—behind us glittering in the sunlight our countless hosts—it was a scene not given to everyone to see. Antietam was not anywhere equal to it, because more spread; this is all gathered into one focus. —Dec 12. Not ready yet. Moved nearer however and waited yet another day. —Dec 13. The day opens with sharp musketry, followed by a spirited artillery fire. Griffin's Division is drawn up near the head of one of the pontoon bridges, in full view of the engagement, waiting the critical moment to 'go in.' Line after line advances to the very crest of the hill before the Rebel batteries and rifle pits, checked each time by the nature of the ground, and the strength of the entrenchments, no less than by the awful fire that seems to scorch them from the hillside. I see tears in the eyes of many a brave man looking on that sorrowful sight, yet all of us are eager to dash to the rescue." —

No more of note books now—other work now. Griffin is in motion—the hour is come! It was perhaps two or three o'clock. The Rebels could see us perfectly well, and had the range of the bridge and roads through which we had to pass. Shot and shell were plunging and bursting around us all the way. We kept under cover of the city as well as we could, though every street was raked by cannon shot—emerging at last in rear of the town, and in front of the fire.

We halted under the partial cover of a slightly rising ground, but precisely in range of the hottest fire, to form our line. The dead and wounded lay thick even here, and fragments of limbs were trampled underfoot. Some of our own men fell here. Suddenly two new batteries opened—it seemed as if the ground were bursting underfoot and the very sky were crashing down upon us—the bullets hissed like a seething sea. In the midst of the hellish din we heard the bugle call the "3rd Brigade." I was standing with the Col. in front of the colors. He glanced up at the Batteries.

"God help us now," said he. "Colonel, take care of the right wing! Forward the Twentieth!" and forward it did go, in line of battle smooth as a sunset parade, in face of that terrific cross-fire of cannon and rifle, and underneath the tempest of shell—its gallant commander in the van.

For some reason the two Regts. on the right of our Brigade did not advance with us, and our right wing consequently took the flank fire, as well the torrent it breasted in front. On we charged over fences and through hedges—over bodies of dead men and living ones—passed four lines that were lying on the ground to get out of fire—on, to that deadly edge where we had seen such desperate valor mown down in heaps. We moved in front of the line already engaged, and thus covered, it was enabled to retire. Then on the crest of the hill we exchanged swift and deadly volleys with the Rebel infantry before us. Darkness had now come on, and the firing slackened, but did not cease. We felt that we must hold that position, though it was a desperate thing to think of. For the Rebels knowing the ground might flank us in the darkness, and to be found under their very guns at daylight would be offering ourselves to destruction. To retire however was to expose the whole army to defeat. So we lay on the trampled and bloody field. Wet and cold it was too, and we had no blankets—the officers, I mean. Little sleep we had then and there, I assure you. Our eyes and ears were open. We could hear the voices of the Rebels in their lines, so near were they, and could see many of their movements. I did sleep though, strange as you may think it, in the very midst of a heap of dead—close beside one dead man—touching him, possibly—the living and dead were alike to me. I slept, though my ears were filled with the cries and groans of the wounded, and the ghastly faces of the dead almost made a wall around me. It was very cold in the night and we suffered. Mr. Brown and I wandered over the field hoping to find a blanket or an overcoat on some dead man, but others had been before us. Once, on such an errand perhaps, or it may be to find some friend, a man came and lifted our coat-capes from our faces, peering into our eyes thinking we were dead.

The morning broke—Sabbath morning—calm, silent, serene. There we lay, a little handful, in a slight hollow on the hillside, and only thus protected from the batteries and rifles that swept the crests before us and behind us too. No man could stand, without being shot down—troops ordered to our relief could not come up without being annihilated—the aides that sought to bring us orders riding at full speed had their horses shot from under them the instant they reached the crest behind us. The enemy tried to dislodge us by shell, but they did not succeed in bursting them exactly over us, and the shot that swept the two crests, just skimmed over our heads, if we kept down. Next they sent three or four hundred skirmishers to get a position on our flank under cover of a ravine, and we had to build a breastwork in the midst of their fire, and under this shelter we succeeded in driving them off with our rifles. We kept up the firing all day, in momentary expectation of some desperate attack but resolved not to flinch in that fiery ordeal.

At last, on the second midnight, having been in that hell of fire for thirty-six hours, an order came that we were to be relieved. But our dead lay around us, and we could not leave them thus. "We will give them a starlight burial," it was said; but Heaven ordained a more sublime illumination. As we bore them—the forms of our fallen heroes—on fragments of boards torn from the fences by shot and shell, to their honored graves, their own loved North lifted her glorious lights, and sent her triumphant procession along the arch that spanned her heavens. An Aurora Borealis, marvelous in beauty. Fiery lances, and banners of blood-red flame—columns of pearly light, garlands and wreaths of gold—all pointing and beckoning upward. Befitting scene! Who would die a nobler death or dream of more glorious burial? Dead for their country's honor, and lighted to burial by the meteor splendors of their Northern home!

Then making sure that our wounded had all been gathered, cold, wet, and battle-worn we entered the town, and bivouacked for a few hours on the pavements. Once then before morning we had to rally to repel a night attack. After so great labors, we expected a short relief, that we might be ready for another and victorious charge. But in the morning we were ordered to prepare immediately for action again, and had scarcely fallen asleep on the next night, when our Brigade was called to arms, and in darkness and silence we marched over that fatal field once more. Here among the thick-strewn dead and scarcely to be distinguished from them, we found a few of our troops lying flat on their faces, and fairly trembling with fearful apprehension. And indeed it was a more thrilling and harrowing business to be creeping around in that dark and dangerous place, where you could not see whether a man was friend or foe—only two hundred yards from the enemy's works, amidst all the ghastly relics of the slaughter, than anything we had experienced before. Our friends informed us in tones by no means calculated to reassure our feelings, that the Rebels were in plain sight extending their rifle-pits close up to us, that a whole Brigade had been "rushed off" from that spot a short time before, and that a new battery had been placed that night so as to sweep us from the ground at day break, and they bade us good bye, saying that we could not stay there two hours. But our order was simple and stern— "Hold that ground at all hazards!" Our regiment was here alone—the others were out of sight to the right and left. We felt that something was at stake, and creeping cautiously up to the very edge of the rifle-pits, we collected a few picks and spades that had been brought there, and used them with a will you may be sure. We protected ourselves as well as possible by throwing up little breast-works, and sinking pits, to hold only a few men each, so that a shell or cannon shot striking in one would kill only the few who were in it. Often we were interrupted by alarms, and were fired on whenever seen; but just as we had nearly completed our work, a hurried order came to retire in perfect silence and re-cross the river with all possible dispatch, as our forces had evacuated the city! We had been sent out to hold the front, while they retired. So we quietly withdrew, picking our way among the sharp bayonets, and stumbling over dead bodies that lay in heaps around, and wound our way back over the pontoon bridge which had been strewn with earth to deaden the sound of our march, once more north of the Rappahannock.

This was our part in the battle of Fredericksburg. Disastrous, as it proved, though we did not suspect that the battle was given up until the order came to retire, and we brought off our gallant little Regiment that had so nobly stood the trial, without having once retreated, or flinched or even hesitated in the face of a tempest of death—its ranks thinned, but still unbroken—its color still aloft, though the golden crest was shot away, and its blue field rent by many a ball. Nor did we murmur though drenched with rain and having no shelter obliged to lie on the ground, or lean against a tree (as I did) until the murky daylight showed us where we were. You notice that we passed some hours in Fredericksburg city. It was a strange sight for this age—so completely battered by shell—from both sides, remember—the inhabitants all gone—the houses, with scarcely an exception, broken open, and everything, left evidently in the greatest haste, perfectly exposed to our whole army. Yet it was far more the effect of the shot than of violent hands that everything was in such confusion and exposure. I saw no ruthless or malicious destruction. What our men wanted for use and could carry, they took with perfect freedom, but I assure you no wanton mischief was done there under my eyes. Of course many valuable things must have been taken away, but you must remember that the rebels were throwing shell into the town all the time we were there, and would undoubtedly have destroyed the place. I do not attempt to palliate the possible charge of pillage. I simply deny it, and think our men showed a great deal of forbearance, considering that the houses had been used as a cover for rebel sharpshooters and that they were shelling the town more or less all the time. We made our Regimental Head Quarters in a house, and did not displace or disturb anything, but rebel shell struck the house more than once during our stay and if any damage was done there, they did it.

I have given you not a brief, but a hasty account of our doings and sufferings—it is all I can find time to give and it may be of interest to you. Let me add that our men behaved gallantly, and we gained a good name both from our own companions and from the Rebels whom some of us afterwards conversed with. None of our officers were wounded. A rifle ball that had struck the crest of the hill and lost most of its momentum, grazed my right ear, but made no wound. Our loss was four killed, thirty-two wounded (two of them missing, perhaps dead) and one (Dr. Hersom[19]) taken prisoner on our hurried evacuation.

We are now in our old camp of a fortnight ago criticizing, all to ourselves, (you will not get anything in that line on paper) and preparing for

---

19 Dr. Nahum A. Hersom, a native of Lebanon, was commissioned assistant surgeon of the 20th Maine in 1862.

new adventures or for winter quarters or for anything to which we are ordered. Hoping much to hear from you, and with renewed love to all, I am ever yours—"toujours à toi"[20]

J. Lawrence C.

~~~

JLC to Fannie, nd/1862

Sunday morning

Dear Fanny,

I send some seeds of the Pawpaw—is that it? That is the way they pronounce it. The fruit is equal to the Banana. It grows in abundance here. I want you to have these planted in flowerpots. I want them to grow around the well by and by.

I find the "persimmon" around here. I am keeping some seeds of those too. We have just had a gale and storm. So we did not march last night as expected. It was a glorious storm. To be sure, I was not warm, but then the wind roared and the storms hissed against the tent—lulling me to sleep, and now others crashing me awake again. Goodly I am off again as Field officer on the day. A high gale blowing—now for a dash up hill and down. I hope you take rides this fall as usual. I am glad you have a "beau". Give my love to your father whom I think of with admiration. God bless you all and make you happy.

L

~~~

JLC to Fannie, 1/1/1863

Having had some time to think about his first experience in battle, Chamberlain wrote more to his wife about how it affected him. After suffering a horrendous defeat at Fredericksburg, Gen. Burnside was formulating a plan to attack Lee in more favorable circumstances. Meanwhile, portions of the

---

20 "yours always"

army made various reconnaissance movements to determine the status of Confederates in the area.

[note at top] I have to stop abruptly. I will try to write again tomorrow. Your own loving Lawrence

Camp opposite Fredericksburg
January 1st, 1863.

Where are you, my own darling, that I do not hear from you all this long while? May I love and wish you a <u>Happy New Year</u>, not knowing but some sickness or other calamity has come upon you? You cannot think how my heart yearns with love for you. I have just taken out your letters, which you know I always carry with me, and just it is more than a month that I have had a word from you. Possibly you do not appreciate how much your words are worth to me Dearest, and may think me very unreasonable, because I did look for a letter after the terrible fight, and the subsequent dangers and hardships I had to undergo. Then too I fancy you or the children are sick and that worried me, you know.

Our division has been on a Reconnaissance fifteen miles up the Rappahannock, to cut off if possible a Rebel force said to have crossed a ford there. We expected an exciting time, but after two or three days of constant hurried searching, in rain mud, we had only a little skirmish of pickets, and have come home rather tired and possibly not in the best of spirits. It is rather normal business to be creeping around in woods and rain and mist and darkness a dozen miles away from your friends not knowing but you are going bump into an ambuscade the next moment. And I assure you I can imagine a more comfortable lodging than to glide out of your saddle for an hour or two just after midnight in a mid winter rainstorm, and drop down on the soaked ground, lay your head on your arm, pull your dripping cape over your face and with no other covering, go to sleep till your horse pulls too hard at the rein, or the half-spoken "Forward" rouses you again. A little experience of that sort of late may not have tended to brighten my views of things. But, Darling, I did and do feel almost like a child in my disappointment at not finding a letter when I came back just now. It is such a pleasure to write to you that I do not feel quite so babyish; but you must indulge me, my dearest, if you are well in a <u>few</u> answers to my letters to you.

It is almost 12 now—midnight—but let me tell you how I cherish and love how I long and long for you, so that my heart aches to see your face. Such experiences as these of mine reveal to me the depths of my own being, all that is in a man, comes to his consciousness here, if he tries to be a man, noble and bright, and does not fall in with a trifling and coarse spirit that sometimes prevails. If you could look into my heart, you would be happy, I could almost believe men if I were with you woman; because love like this I bear you is stronger than Death and better than life even; and I know it would be a blessing to have such a love even as a last will and testament. I thought of it on the battle field the other day and I felt a thrill of pleasure in the midst of the awful uproar, when I thought that you must know how I loved you, if I fell. When the air was all ablaze above me with busting shell, it stopped itself sometimes with bright pictures of you and darling Daisy, my noble boy, and I smiled and said almost aloud "god bless those dear ones" and pressed on calmer and braver and purer than ever. God showed me that days and though I did not pray for it—but I thank Him since and shall always, for such trials are blessings, and a man is better and stronger for them. May God bless you, my own sweet wife, and may the peace of blessed spirits be yours till I come to you again with my stormy love and with perhaps a better heart. God bless keep you too, my Darlings and love your mother as well as God. Good night,

L.

JLC to Fannie 1/5/1863

Army of Potomac
Opposite Fredericksburg
January 5th 1863

My darling wife,
What a night! Wondrous beauty—balmy southern air—high calm flooding moonlight that silence so vast so deep, to me so exciting of thousands of armed even all hushed to peace—shadows of sentinels stalk ghostlike across the hill and in the woody rains. I step out, and is it the breeze of the moonlight that stirs my hair? I believe, and I will believe, it is the moonlight. Do you think I am satisfied and have no longing for a face and a voice and a hand I know of?

If you do, you are a foolish girl, which I know you are not. But what is this music that bursts out of the cavalry camp in the pines. Why must that Band make the night intolerable to me. Such rich music, entrancing, melting, dreary stirring—everything at once. I know how you won't like to hear this, and if you were with me I don't think I should be made so unhappy by it. But I can only wish, wish you were here, and try to be patient. One good thing that I shall be made absolutely stupid with emotion that can find no utterance nor object here. I am never much alone—never when I am writing—and you know my habit about solitude. This is a good thing for me I suppose. I shall not write you a love-letter tonight. I've one in my pocket for you—or to you I should say for on the whole I don't think I shall send that epistle—not, at any rate, till I hear from you and know whether you have forgotten me or not. Good night.

Your Stupid L

JLC to Capt. Badger, 1/6/1863
Captain Joseph Badger, a former sea captain, was president of the Pejepscot Bank in Brunswick and a financial benefactor of the Chamberlains.

Head Quarters 20th Me. Vols
Opposite Fredericksburg Va.
January 6th 1863

My dear sir
I am grieved to learn by the papers of the great loss you have experienced in the death of Mrs. Badger.

I am sure I can do more than offer you my heartfelt sympathy, for I feel that I, with very many more, must sorrow on my own account at the loss of one whom we also much respected and esteemed. Her kindness and generosity surely can never be forgotten by any one whom she has ever known, and for my own part I have every reason to cherish her memory.

I will not tell you that I can somewhat understand how desolate this great affliction must have left you, for no one can enter fully into another's sorrow—yet I know very well that a man can look death in the face for himself a thousand times far easier than he can bear to see even the littlest of those he loves taken from him forever.

May you be supported by those hopes which the world cannot give, nor death destroy.

I pray that we may all so live, so believe and so trust that we shall meet again the loving and faithful who have gone before us.

For myself I have been well, and have come out of another terrible battle unhurt. To night, however, I am not quite so bright as usual. Our Regiment went out on the late reconnaissance and we had a good deal of exposure and hardship. But I am tough and sound and am, I think, the <u>only</u> officer of this regiment who has not been off duty since we came into the field.

I am conducting a court martial now, which takes all my time. We do not have any leisure, even when the Army of the Potomac is not on the move.

I have not heard from my wife for six weeks at least, but your kind letter and her own assurance of your attention, set me at rest in regard to her business condition. We have been so much on the move that no Paymaster has reached us at all, but we are now, I am told, to be paid in a few days, when, if not already done, some four or five hundred dollars will be paid in at the Pejepscot Bank to my wife's credit. I shall attend to the matter as soon as it is possible. But I never ask a leave of absence to go to Washington, and so, I dare say, it may be two or three weeks before you will receive the money.

With much respect and
Sympathy
Yours Truly,
J. L. Chamberlain
Capt. Badger
Brunswick

~~~~~)

JLC to Fannie, 1/11/1863

Army of the Potomac
Jany 11th 1863

Your glorious little hero,
If it is 12 o'clock I shall not go to my pile of straw without thanking you for your letter received tonight. I ought to be willing to wait seven weeks

for such a letter as that. You published my letters I see, though I had not supposed it before, as we did not happen to get that number of the "Press" to which you plead guilty. I am only sorry because I did not dream of such a thing as the letter going into print—or I should have given you more completeness and finish to it. Two or three touches were much wanted. I had them noted down to give you, but something prevented me. I wrote the letter one midnight after the camp was still and I thought I could fill in the other parts afterwards—I was in a hurry as I am now. I can not adequately describe it now, but do you know what was one of the most thrilling sights to me on going in to the fight? It was the parks of ambulances by hundreds—all so orderly in line, horses harnessed, drivers seated, red flags all flying, ready to go on, and only to go on, when our mangled bodies lay writhing on the field. Thoughtful and with a certain hush of awe I can assure you we watched by them, and I said to Mr. Brown "when we shall see those again, it will be another sight for us". And I wish I could paint you the scene when they did come—stealthily—by night and in darkness gathering up the crying, bleeding, freezing bodies that lay around us. I only wish to note it now, to tell you sometime.

Then I did not tell you as I should of the birds, yes the peaceful swallows and doves that soared amidst the lurid clouds of battle, so startled in their serene and innocent haunts, what did they know of those voices of the pit, of those sulfurous flames that quenched the odor in blood? There they wheeled and skimmed over the bursting bombs. There they cut their wild racing on the pale blue clouds of death. Do you know how they spoke to me. Do you believe that I gazed at them, amidst all my stern and tasking duties, which I believe no one will say I did not keep in view. Then the musket— right in our faces! Talk of the Count of death!

Then too my noble girl, this for you. While we held that forward line— battling sharp and heavy and with men falling at my very side, do you suppose I did not see, I was going to say pray for, that dog—that tiny, timid dog—that had sought out his dear master, and crouched and cowered there amidst the hissing balls, licking the ghastly wound—looking love and almost life into that calm upturned face. "You will not waken him, poor watcher", we said aloud, and faced to the foe again. Just then a volley of balls, I can't believe aimed, but I hope unerring in their errand, crashed around that faithful head, and I saw the poor dog no more. I was going to say, I believe I shall see him in Heaven. Let me just tell you one thing more—you say you honor us—the foremost man that fell on that deadly front was a soldier of the 20th Maine. I know it, for it was my part that Saturday night to lead a line of <u>videttes</u> to the very walls of the rebel batteries, till we could hear their whispers, and I trod that whole front over, and the man who lay foremost was from the calm, cold state of Maine. True, true for once—"Dirigo"—"I lead"—empty boast no more! Not that I honored less the noble son of New Hampshire, who lay almost beside him, nor the sons of New Jersey, Pennsylvania, and Michigan—side by side in death, or patiently watching it. I spoke to dead men that night thinking they were alive, and I waked living men thinking they were dead.

Now for the questions. (1) My salary is actually $198.00 a month $2376. a year. But the war tax and various deductions leave only $165. a month or $1980. a year. That includes you understand the keeping of my horses for which the govt. charges me $24 a month, whether I have over two or three. Thus far I have had no money except the $90. I brought. I don't need any money except for my own being which I can manage very well. We expect to be paid off in a few days now, and I shall lose no time in sending you all but what I positively need. (2) All my college salary went to pay notes at Bank. The new notes are for the last payt. on the house which I hope has been properly deeded. (3) My new horse is not paid for yet[21]. I shall give about $100. (4) <u>No liability for any body</u>, and owe nothing except these bills. (5) I don't think I ever had any bill of Dr. Ellis. You can ask for one. (6) The rubber drinking cup was given me by the Major. Have never needed it at all. I am very sorry you are so troubled about money affairs. But it is the fault of the Govt. you shall soon have money enough, and I want you to use it. If you have any occasion for more before this comes to you speak to Capt. Badger about it in person. It is perfectly safe and secure—The only embarrassment is in the delay. It is rumored that the army is to move and that the 5th Army Corps is to go to <u>Baltimore</u> for the winter. If so then—I shall certainly see you, but nobody knows. I wish you could go to New York but maybe it would be well to wait a little.

Love to Aunty and all
yours_____

---

21 Prince, the very valuable dapple grey horse that local citizens presented to Chamberlain as a gift when he left Maine, was wounded in the head on May 4. What finally became of the horse is unknown.

JLC to Fannie, 3/30/1863
While the army was safely ensconced in winter camp in Virginia, Chamberlain received a furlough and returned to Maine for a visit. Fannie joined him on his return to camp and spent several weeks among the army. Her pass to the army expired near the end of March.

Monday Eve March 30th 1863

I have come back and have been waiting for you all this long day and evening, my dearest Fanny, sure you would come at last. Everything around here so speaks of you—the tent which I had made more comfortable to suit you—the little trifling things which no none would notice but which have so close and dear an association with you, darling, and this sighing wind and flapping canvas boding another mild storm which I know you would so enjoy with me. I never missed you so, darling; I can't bear to see everything the same and the best and brightest gone! It is dreary, desolate, blank. I would gladly have marched today. I want to change the whole aspect of things about my tent, yet it was your hand or your dear "sake" at least which put everything so, and I cannot touch it. My heart has been with you every instant. How I long and long for you. We have had a sweet sweet time together, dear one, were not those blessed nights when you first came, with the shadows of leaves dancing in the moonlight on the tent wall above us and we could not sleep for sweet waking dreams of youth and love? I knew how I was loving you and how hard the parting would be. When the cars moved away carrying my soul with them, I sprang on my grey horse "Prince" who gave a wild snort and away we flew like the wind. He knew, noble fellow, that it was a heart-breaking day for me, and that he and my sword were all that was left me now, and a right wild and camper we had of it—we three—we have been together on more awful mornings than that, but my eye was always dry before.

I await you still, I turn and look for you. Everything else is here and I am sure you are behind me. But no! no! darling, so I must bear it again—my heart with you, my trust in God.

Good night your own.

JLC to Fannie, 4/1/1863

Camp April 1st 1863

My dearest Fannie,
The order suspending leaves of absence for fifteen days has been revoked and we shall undoubtedly remain here for a considerable time yet. We are all anxious to have you come back and very sorry you went away. Now the only trouble will be to get a pass. Perhaps the old one will do. Find out through Mrs. Harris. Take the old one erase the other names and see if Col Conrad will not renew it. "Sick Husband" being just occasion of visits to the army of the Potomac. Try if you have time to prolong your visit here a little. The sooner the better.

By the way ladies came down today even from Washington. Now I shall expect you right off. Mr. [John Marshall] Brown has applied for leave of absence for fifteen days and will undoubtedly get it.

The major is here, and we are glad to see him. My new coat has come and is a beauty. Nichols[22] has escaped a court martial. The enemy were reported last night at 12 at Hartwood Church[23] and we were all put on the "gun vive" again.

Gen. Howard has the eleventh corps. Whittlesey will be Lieut. Col.

(Dated March 17th)
I have a letter for you from Rebecca Simpson. She is at Rev. Dr. Geo. W. Sampson's, College Hill 14th Street. Washington.

I had a letter today from Daisy and Auntie all well. I retain the letters because I hope to see you so soon. Auntie adds a postscript to her letter in these sad words "Capt Badger died last night." Poor man, he just grieved himself away, I suppose. What a loss to me! My friends are growing thin in number, I fear you will know how I miss the Capt.[24]

Fanny dear try to come if you can, and please get me a few things; viz. paper collars 15 inch or 15½ a box or less.

---

22 Lt. James H. Nichols was a brave soldier in the 20th Maine whose problem with alcohol caused him to get into trouble.

23 Hartwood Presbyterian Church is ten miles northwest of Fredericksburg, Virginia.

24 Captain Joseph Badger, president of the Pejepscot Bank in Brunswick, died March 23, 1863, at the age of seventy-two, just three months after the death of his wife.

A glass like the Cols—not so costly. also hair dressing and some perfume. Toilet you see. Give my love to Mrs. Harris and tell her I shall answer her kind letter in season to meet her wishes as to the vitality or vivacity of the Col.

Dearly thanks for the oranges and apples "for a good boy" and "for a bad boy."

There is a grand review here tomorrow. President Lincoln is to be here I am told.

Wishing you were here, I endorse a lone-letter I wrote the morning you went, and sending a great deal more love than I express.

Your own Lawrence.

The Col says "try first to get a new pass, and if you can't come on the old one. Mrs. H. Will manage it.

L.

JLC to Fannie, April/nd/1863
Having served duty sitting on courts martial in Washington, Chamberlain was back in camp alone since Fannie had left when her pass expired. As it turned out, passes were available for her to remain or return to camp, but she heard of this too late.

My darling wife,
You do not know how I have missed you this week, when everything has been in such gay and brilliant motion. I have rushed around when I could, like a frantic man; not in search of enjoyment, nor allured by bright colors and dark eyes, but because I was so lonely amidst all the festivities, that I could not keep still. I would not go to the Reviews and Soirees when I could help it, because you were not here, and it was only for you and with you (I mean more by that than words can tell) that I enjoy anything in this world. Where you are not, there is no joy for me. Nor do I desire anything without you and except you. This is not "lovers talk" because you know I am not in the foolish age now, nor can I have any motive to express to you a tenderness I do not feel. What I know and feel always is that you are a part

of all that is glorious and sweet and good and great. From every radiant height which I see with the eyes of my soul it is you that beckon me. Whatever I am it is you who are the best of me.

But I see I am not expressing anything at all. Let me tell you that I do not wear the hat with the cord which you wore. It hangs where you left it every dimple in it just as it came from your darling little head.

You don't know how hard it is to go without you. This spring weather brings all the old associations and makes me love you as I did when a boy— only so much the more now as I know you better.

How sorry I am you went away! No need of it at all. But that can't be helped now. I shall hope you can manage to come down, still, if only for a day or two. We are liable to move any moment. Still you may as well be here as in Washington and if we go suddenly you can manage perfectly well to get away. Perhaps it is providential while we have the small pox so near that you should not be exposed. So I will try to bear it though I assure you I am so lonesome I don't know what to do with myself. Be sure though that I love you with all my soul and be patient with me for telling you that old story.

Saturday P.M.

I was sure you would come today for Col. Allen was to take the matter up and he always succeeds. It would vex me a good deal if I had not learned patience in waiting and obeying military orders. I hope you are having a pleasant time with more to take up your attention than I have.

I went to a magnificent review yesterday, rather accidentally, of Gen. Howard's corps. I was in the midst of Generals and fine ladies and was just invited to go with them to some entertainment, when I thought possibly you might come that day, and I turned and rode like a shot from Stafford courthouse almost killing "Prince" and then not to find you spoiled that night for me.

Our court martial adjourned yesterday since and I have been like a bird without a mate all day. If I ever get through this we will have some sweet spring times, will we not, darling? Tomorrow is Sunday again, a long long day without you, but a blessed day if you were here. I send you a kiss, here my precious one.

Your loving Lawrence

JLC to Fannie, March/April 1863

Dearest, dearest one,

Do not be troubled. I love you and think of you all the time. We are having a wretched time of it just now—changing camp in a tearing rainstorm, but I have thought of you and it made me happy. Dearest, be happy too. I have only a moment to say it in.

I expect to go home the first of May to see to the will business. If I get on [Gen. O. O.] Howard's staff I can do it. That is why I wanted you to stay. But as it is, maybe you had better go to New Haven and let me meet you there, if I can go. Provided you have a proper escort.

I will let you know by telegraph (if you stay) when I shall leave, or you might let me know when you go by telegraph.

How sorry I am you are sad. If you knew how I love you you could not be very sad. I can't be, happen what may to me because I love you.

Thank you for the beautiful cross. I will wear it for your sake, more than as a common badge. It is perfect.

Forgive me, sweet wife, if I have done anything to grieve you. I would not, Heaven knows.

You pray for me, darling, I am sure; and don't be discouraged because you have not the immediate comfort you wish. I know you and know that your prayers are heard, and that you are a true Christian.

My precious darling don't, don't be sad. It makes my heart heavy to think of it.

A thousand kisses for you sweetest wife, and may Heaven bless you with peace and joy. I never can stop writing to you, but must.

With eternal love, L.

JLC to Fannie, 5/20/1863

Chamberlain continued to hope that Fannie would get another pass and return to see him in camp. In this letter to her, he briefly described his part in the Battle of Chancellorsville. His regiment was kept out of the battle because of a widespread outbreak of smallpox in the unit.

Camp 20 Maine
N[ea]r. Falmouth VA
May 20th 1863

So my darling found it better to send word to me thro' Mrs. Harris where she was here just to tell me herself! Well meantime I had not the least idea where the young lady was, but was writing all the time to my supposed home and not yet having "had time" to answer Mrs. H's first letter, she has not given me to understand that you were all this time in New York. A very foolish girl is my darling to be worried to sickness on account of me. Far better to come and see me, as I have been writing for her to do for some days. That is if you want to come for a few weeks you can.

I have sent money enough home to pay all the bills you owe there, and pray tell me if Mr. French has sent you two $100 US 5-20 bonds?[25]

You have not said a word about them and I fear they are lost.

Send home for Cousin D to pay up the bills, and come yourself and see me in this "new camp" if you think it worth while.

Oh! I had to give up all the will business. Just at the critical moment for deciding to go or stay came an order from Gen. Butterfield direct, to go to the battle field and take possession of the signal line from U.S. Ford where the battle was to H. Q. of the Army. No one will say that I did not have as honorable and responsible a part as anybody in the affair at Chancellorsville— though the Regt. was not engaged. I had the pleasure of seeing a great deal and of being in a situation to improve myself in standing fire.

No Regt. of our Brigade was engaged.

I write in this haste today that you can authorize Aunty to pay your bills wh. must be done and turn about and come to see me in this new camp where we have just come to day.

It is fresh and sweet and beautiful a fit place for my darling wife. Big cherry tree just before my door! Seats to be made around it! New moon! Green slopes! Whippoorwills! Frogs! Would you forgive me for adding by way of climax that only you are wanting! I shall not undertake to get away. I want to be here. Everything is going well. I send another letter to Boston for you (Katie's) have sent to Brunswick.

L.

---

25 Luther French was the chaplain of the 20th Maine.

JLC to Fannie, 5/nd/1863

Monday noon,

What would you think, Fanny, of my obtaining the colonelcy of one of the new Regiments to be raised in Maine under the recent Law—the "conscript" or "drafted" Regts.

Would you leave the <u>old</u> <u>20th</u>? I declare it makes my heart heavy to think of it. But the Col. says if he does not get his appointment, I ought to go in for another Regt. The colonels are to be apptd. by the President Col. Ames thinks We've been Lieut. Col. long enough. We have been through two memorable campaigns and very likely shall be into another one before any change can be made.

I can imagine there would be the least difficulty in obtaining the place if desired.

The only thing is I have an affection for this <u>20th</u>. That <u>color</u> somehow has wound my heart up in it—especially since certain fingers that I know of, and was bold enough to kiss, by stealth, some twelve years ago, have consecrated it anew for me.

I'll see it through one more battle, anyway.

Just tell me what you think of my plan or proposal rather. I have not argued the affirmative side. But there are some wonderful advantages in the new Regt.

Think of it for me. You will know a woman's wit—against man's cogitations.

JLC to Fannie May/June 1863

Chamberlain wrote to Fannie about financial matters and the Battle of Chancellorsville, where he had hoped to serve under Gen. Howard while the 20th Maine was quarantined. Howard's 11th Corps was badly routed at the battle by a flank attack led by Confederate general Stonewall Jackson.

Monday eve.

These beautiful summer nights! How I would love to have you with me now to sit out beneath the stars—the air so soft and sweet and everything so full of poetry. How soon after the battle, all becomes quiet again. I am lonely often now-a-days. I long to be with you. I have hardly got rested yet—you see I did not go with Howard. Perhaps it is well. I should have been ashamed to death of that disgraceful rout, and should have thrown away my life perhaps in trying to stop the rush. It was disastrous to us—changed our whole plan from the offensive to the defensive nothing went well after that. It was not the fault of our gallant Howard however. We all know how nobly brave he is. Nobody here says anything reproachful to him.

Maj. Whittlesey, fortunately, was not in the fight.[26]

You will find $200 at the Pejepscot Bank, over. French will send you two Govt. 5–20 bonds of $100 each.[27] That is said to be the best stock one can have, and I thought I would invest a little for you. It pays six per cent in <u>gold</u> or the equivalent in currency. Now for instance six dollars are worth $9.

The $200 at the Bank (from the state Treasurer) will last you some time with what little you may have with you. I will send more as you wish.

Do write me and give my love particularly to all my friends. The Regt. is in fine condition now. We shall go with our Brigade in the coming advance.

Love to Aunty and to the dear little ones. Be happy all of you.

L.

Blood and Fire at Gettysburg

During the hard marching of June 1863, the men of the 20th Maine suffered greatly in the oppressive Virginia heat, marching twenty to thirty miles each day in unusually hot, humid weather for that season. Making matters worse, malaria and dysentery infected many of the soldiers, including Chamberlain. In late May, Colonel Ames had taken a promotion to command a brigade in General Howard's 11th Corps, leaving Chamberlain to command the 20th. His official promotion reached him on June 30, the night before the Battle of Gettysburg began.

On the second day of fighting, the 20th Maine was placed as the last regiment on the left of the Union line and held off repeated attacks by troops from Alabama on a hill that later became known as "Little Round Top." After

---

26 For more on Whittlesey, see JLC to Fannie, 11/27/1862.

27 So-called "5–20 bonds" were worth 6 percent payable in five years and had to be paid within twenty. Because they were linked to gold, they could be worth far more if the price of gold rose.

fighting for more than an hour, the 20th Maine charged down the hill, sending the Alabamians running to the rear.

Later that evening, Chamberlain volunteered to take his badly damaged unit up the adjacent hill, known to locals as "Round Top." The men carefully ascended the hill in darkness without the support of any other units, fully expecting they would be attacked by a large Confederate force at any moment. As it turned out, the enemy was as unsure of the surroundings as they were and did not attack, though Chamberlain's men captured more than two dozen lost Texans during the tense night, and the Mainers held the hill until daylight when fresh units were sent to relieve them.

This was the first battle in which the regiment had been fully engaged with the enemy, and Chamberlain's calm, deliberate actions, while suffering the effects of malaria, probably dysentery, and wounds in his left leg and right foot, drew the attention of officers throughout the army. Many of them marveled that a man who trained to be a minister and college professor had performed so well in combat during his first battle as commander of a regiment.

~~~~~~

JLC to Brig. Gen. James Barnes, 7/6/1863[28]
Chamberlain wrote this unofficial report of the 20th Maine's part in the Battle of Gettysburg to the commander of his division, Gen. James Barnes. Drafted just three days after the fighting ended, it is his first written account of the battle.

General Barnes
Comd 1st Div. 5th Corps

General,
In accordance with your permission I beg leave to submit, unofficially, the following memoranda (which I have hardly had time to condense as I could wish) of the part taken by the 20th Maine Vols. on the left of your Div. in the action of July 2d at Gettysburg.

This Regt. was on the extreme left of our line of battle, & its original front was very nearly that of the rest of the Brigade. At the general assault of the enemy on our lines, my Regt. from the first received its full share.

---

28 Courtesy of Maine State Archives

While we were warmly engaged with this line, as I stood on a high rock by my colors I perceived a heavy body of the enemy moving by the right flank in the direction of our left & rear. They were close upon me, & I had but a moment in which to act. The head of their column was already coming to a front, in direction only a little oblique to that of the rest of our Brigade. Keeping this movement of the enemy from the knowledge of my men, I immediately had my right wing take intervals by the left flank at 3 to 5 paces according to the shelter afforded by the rocks & trees, thus covering the whole front then engaged; & moved my left wing to the left & rear making nearly a right angle at the color.

This movement was so admirably executed by my men, that our fire was not materially slackened in front, while the left wing was taking its new position. Not more than two minutes elapsed before the enemy came up in column of Regiments with an impetuosity which betrayed their anticipation of an easy triumph. Their astonishment was great as they emerged from their cover, & found instead of an unprotected <u>rear</u>, a <u>solid</u> <u>front</u>. They advanced however within <u>ten</u> <u>paces</u> of my line, making what they call a "charge"—that is, advancing & firing rapidly. Our volleys were so steady & telling that the enemy were checked here, & broken. Their second line then advanced, with the same ardor & the same fate, & so too a third & fourth. This struggle of an hour & a half, was desperate in the extreme: four times did we lose & win that space of ten yards between the contending lines, which was strewn with dying & dead. I repeatedly sent to the rear reports of my condition, that my ammunition was exhausted, & that I could hold the position but a few minutes longer. In the mean time I seized the opportunity of a momentary repulse of the enemy, to gather the contents of every cartridge box of the dead & dying, friend & foe, & with these we met the enemy on their last & most desperate assault. In the midst of this, our ammunition utterly failed, our fire, as it was too terribly evident, had slackened, half my left wing lay on the ground, & although I had brought two companies from the right to strengthen it, the left wing was reduced to a mere skirmish line. Officers came to me, shouting that we were "annihilated", & men were beginning to face to the rear. I saw that the <u>defensive</u> could be maintained not an instant longer, & with a few gallant officers rallied a line, ordered "bayonets fixed," & "forward" on the run. My men went down upon the enemy with a wild shout, the two wings were brought into one line again. I directed the whole Regiment to take intervals at 5 paces by the left flank, & change direction to the right, all this without checking our speed, thus keeping my right connected with the 83rd Penna, while the left swept around to the distance of half a mile. In this charge the bayonet only was used on our part, & the rebels seemed so petrified with astonishment that their front line scarcely offered to run or to fire—they threw down their arms & begged "not to be killed", & we captured them by whole companies. We took in this charge 368 prisoners, among them a Colonel, Lieut. Col. & a dozen other officers who were known. I had no time to inquire the rank of the prisoners, but sent them at once to the rear.

The prisoners were amazed & chagrinned to see the smallness of our numbers, for there were only one hundred & ninety eight men who made this charge, & the prisoners admitted that they had a full Brigade.

I reported at once to Col. Rice, who immediately came up, & who with the greatest promptitude brought up a Brigade as a support, & a supply of ammunition. We then threw up a small breastwork of rocks, & began to gather up the wounded of both parties. 21 of my men lay dead on the field, & more than 100 wounded. 50 of the enemy dead were counted in our front, their wounded we could not count. What is most surprising is that often as our line was forced back & even pierced by the enemy, not one of my men was taken prisoner, & not one was "missing".

It was now nearly dark, & Col. Rice ordered me to take the high & difficult hill on the left of our general line of battle, (but more nearly in front of my own line) where the enemy appeared to have taken refuge on their repulse. My men were exhausted with toil & thirst, & had fallen asleep, many of them, the moment the fighting was over, but the order was given, & the little handful of men went up the hill with fixed bayonets, the enemy retiring before us, & giving only an occasional volley. Not wishing to disclose my numbers, & in order to avoid if possible bringing on an engagement in which we should certainly have been overpowered, I went on silently with only the bayonet. We carried the hill, taking twenty five prisoners, including some of the staff of Gen. Laws comm[an]d[in]g the Brigade. From these I learned that Hoods Division was massed in a ravine two or three hundred yards in front of me, & that he had sent them out to ascertain our numbers, preparatory to taking possession of the hill with his Division. Fortunately I was able to secure all this party, by sending out one of my own more cautious than they, so that Gen. Hood never received the reports of his scouts. My men stood in line that night, & received the volleys of the enemy without replying, & the enemy apparently puzzled, desisted from their attempts. In this movement I lost one officer mortally wounded,

& one man taken prisoner in the darkness. The prisoners in all amounted to 393 who were known; 300 stand of arms were taken from the enemy. We went into the fight with 380 officers & men, cooks & pioneers & even musicians fighting in the ranks, my total loss was 136 as more fully appears in the tabular report already sent you.

We were engaged with Laws' Brigade, of Hood's Division, Longstreets Corps, —the 15th & 47th Alabama 4th & 5th Texas: our prisoners were from all these Regts.

My authority for some of my statements are Col. Powell 15th Ala. Lt. Col. Bulger, comdg the 47th Ala. Capt. Johnson of the 5th Texas, & Lt. Christian, Inspector Genl. Laws' Brigade who were among our prisoners.

The Hill carried in the evening is said to be Round Top, or Sugar Loaf, reported by Col Rice as "Wolf Hill."

Justice required me to express my gratitude for the admirable support I received from the 83d Penna. Capt. Woodward comdg.

I am, General,
Very respectfully
Your obdt servt.
J. L. Chamberlain Col.
20th Maine Vols.

———

JLC to Fannie, 7/18/1863
More than two weeks after commanding his regiment to victory and praise at the Battle of Gettysburg, Chamberlain wrote to update Fannie as to his whereabouts and activities. He had written a few other letters to her since the battle, but did not realize at the time that she was not at home. He finally learned, to his dismay, that she was in New York City while Cousin Deb watched the children back in Brunswick.

Head Qts. 3d Brigade
Camp in Blue Mountains, Va. July 18th 1863

My dear Fanny.
We are on the pursuit—5th corps in the advance—Griffin's Division leading of course—and the casualties of the service have brought me in command

of the famous old "Third Brigade" now more famous still from its heroic conduct at Gettysburg.

You saw perhaps in the Times[29] of the manner in which the "20th" carried the formidable heights of "Wolf Hill";[30] but as I do not employ reporters, our most gallant fighting will not appear to the eyes of people at home. I see the "Telegraphic" reports me as "probably not in the battle" "being sick" etc. That is not altogether the record of my whereabouts that day, which is recorded in the army. I think most people here know where I was that day and the day following. Never mind—all will come out at last. I shall write you a "private letter" about it when we have a moment's halt.

You know the 5th corps has been for a long time separated from the main army, and cut off from mails and baggage so we have been living a savage and desert life for a month at least. Still I have continued to send you now and then a slip written in pencil on my knee on saddle—but thinking you were in Brunswick I directed there.

I had not recovered [from illness] and the surgeons absolutely refused to let me go on when the army pushed for <u>Penna</u>. But I <u>went</u>, and think I did good duty there, and afterwards at Sharpsburg ...

You are witnessing some rather unpleasant scenes in the city now I judge.[31] I am sorry you happened to be there. Don't you think you are staying away rather too long from home. I should imagine you should wish to see the children. It would be impossible for you to reach me if anything would happen. For instance I came very near dying at Gum Spring Va. a month ago, from an attack brought on by a forced march in a broiling sun when my men were falling as if shot down, and I had no surgeon and was worried half to death.[32]

How sad about poor Vincent[33]—noble fellow—He sent for me a little time before the battle and we sat till midnight talking of our dearest things. I saw in Him a noble <u>ambition</u> just balancing with the tenderest love <u>for his</u>

29 The July 9 edition of the *New York Times* included a large, front-page report from its chief correspondent, L. L. Crounse, which briefly described the actions of Chamberlain's brigade and the taking of "Wolf Hill" (meaning Big Round Top) by the 20th Maine.

30 Neither soldiers nor local residents began to refer to the hill where the 20th Maine fought as "Little Round Top" until 1867. Wolf's Hill was actually on the opposite end of the Union battle line at Gettysburg.

31 Fannie was in New York City while riots erupted over plans for a draft.

32 In June, Chamberlain suffered greatly from malarial fever. Many of his men also suffered from dysentery around that time, and this may have been part of his illness as well. He was so ill that he was forced to leave the army for ten days, returning to his regiment the night before the Battle of Gettysburg.

33 Col. Strong Vincent commanded the 3rd Brigade at Gettysburg and was thus Chamberlain's immediate commander. He was mortally wounded July 2 in fighting on Little Round Top.

wife, which made him doubt whether to stay in the army or resign. He felt that he had done his share of duty—so far as patriotism went. He lingered a day or two after his wound; but was most of the time, unconscious. His wife was too feeble to go to him, and so he died alone except one or two of his staff were with him. My own poor fellows went down like rain—it seemed to me the very best men of all. What heroes they were! Some of them with big gashes in their head, tied their handkerchief about it, and were in the foremost line again, in ten minutes, fighting like tigers.

You can do as you choose about going home. I had a note from my father saying that Cousin D. was failing and that you had better go home. But do as you wish. What in the world can you have been doing in New York? Not writing me letters surely. I doubt if I am able to go home at commencement. I send $100 a month to Penobscot Bank for you.

L.

~~~

JLC to Fannie, 7/30/1863
The illness that had overtaken Chamberlain in the weeks leading up to the Battle of Gettysburg finally rendered him unable to continue in the field, and he was sent to the rear for medical treatment and given a fifteen-day pass to go home.

Warrenton July 30th 1863

My darling
I am ordered to Washington for medical treatment shall try to be sent to Baltimore where the air is better and society too. But you may come at once. I will send you a despatch if I go to Baltimore so that you will know how to find me. I leave here tomorrow. The army moved the same day but we shall have no fighting unless Lee attacks.

You will come. I send a similar card to Brunswick. I think I shall have to be away about twenty days unless there is fighting.

On the whole you had better go at once to Baltimore stop at the Eutaw House. Lieut. Col Rice is boarding at Mrs. Hewes, 49 Lexington St Baltimore Md.

I would be delighted to see you. Could you send me a despatch to care of Mrs. Harris, 468 Sixth St. If you have left for Baltimore.

When you leave for Baltimore send me a telegram or else be sure and write so that I shall know where to address you—

JLC to Fannie, 8/1/1863
Still unable to locate his wife and get word to her of his whereabouts, Chamberlain wrote this letter to their home in Brunswick. In it he mentioned his connection to Bowdoin from which his current leave of absence was approaching one year.

Washington DC Aug 1 1863

My dear Fanny
Everything works wrong. I have been telegraphing and writing to you at New York all the week. I am ordered here for medical treatment—don't know for how long a time. I can't get sent north—nor even to Baltimore, nor anywhere that is comfortable. I have been sending for you to come here. I telegraphed the hotel this morning to know where you are and I find that you are at home at last. Well, let it go so then. It will be right I suppose. I expect to be kept in this detestable place for two weeks if I live that time here. You don't think it worth while I suppose to come here now, is it. I am trying to get sent north or even to Baltimore, I will write every day.

How vexed and lonesome I am. I send to Pres. Woods[34] my explanation of absence with request for further leave while the exigency of the public service may require I offer to resign my professorship. I am sorry you did not write—you were leaving New York.

How everything plagues me and I am worn out with the awful hardships and toils and vexations of the last campaign.

Not hoping to see you very soon (unless I am sick unto death) or I go part way north.

Yours L.

I send check for $200.

---

34 Leonard Woods, president of Bowdoin College.

JLC to Fannie, 8/25/1863
When Chamberlain returned to Washington, he learned that Colonel Rice had been promoted and that General Griffin had appointed him to replace Rice as commander of the brigade.

Head Quarters Brigade
1st Div. 5th corps
Beverly Ford, VA
Aug 25th 1863

My darling,
How lonely it is! Here I am in a new place—a new tent—new surroundings—new duties—I feel like one making his debut. I have left the noble "20th" having been assigned by Gen. Griffin to the command of this Brigade which he says is a "permanency" for a long time, that is.

This makes me virtually a Brigadier General, but I feel badly to leave the 20th and shall be glad when I can return to it. I have a pleasant staff and shall get routed in a few days.

When I got here my Regts were on Battalion drill. I went down to look at them and if you thought there was any noise in the church that Thanksgiving evening you should have been within a mile or two of this uproar and judge of that.

Your spearhead glitters above our battle-torn flag and your big little heart would swell to see it. The Rebs stand and look at it with admiration I dare say; for they are just across the river only a stone's throw from us and we are all in full view. Right over our heads are a goodly number of Rodman Guns, not quite so formidable as those opposite Fredericksburg which you saw, but very good friends and quite as good enemies.

We do not think Lee means to attack, but we are ready for him though our numbers are so reduced.

This evening we had some of the sweet pickles, and it was universally agreed that they were beau ideal of soldier's sweet meals. Many thanks went forth to Aunty. But, oh, Fan, the big jar—the square bottle—was smashed into 10,000,000 pieces and the contents! And the spectacle! One side of my valise was mashed into a medley never before seen. A "sweet pickle" surely was there. Buy paper collars, books, clothing (but that will wash) the packages sent to men in the Regt all in the "dye pot".

I went to call on a certain lady friend two or three times very late in the evening two successive eves and found a certain financial general there and though he was very polite, I could not fail to see that they were waiting for me to go. My opinion is not favorably modified. You will not hear any boasts of conquest over me, I can tell you.

How the rain falls on the tent roof! Like the glorious nights before. Only now you can hear the roar of water at the falls close by and in full night by day. The spot is too lovely for war, and for me alone. Do you want to see me? Was I "good" enough to suit you, this time? Ah, you little rogue you are glad I am off, I know. When you were peering into the cars with that queer hat, although it was a familiar face, "By George" I said, "that is a pretty face a little faded (owing wholly probably to this dim window pane) but mighty bold, I fancy. I'll just step out and take a look at that girl." When, lo!—I have much to say but will write again soon.

Your own loving one.

JLC to Fannie, 8/30/1863

3rd Brigade 1st Div. 5th Corps
Aug 30 1863

My dearest,

I pleased myself with thinking, all the morning after I awoke, what a fine quiet time I should have today to write you. But with the day began a tedious round of duties and don't tell! Callers. Besides I have not been well today just a temporary derangement brought on possibly after an unquiet night in consequence of having taken my Brigade out (yesterday) to assist in the execution of 5 deserters. Anxiety to handle the Brigade well in the presence of so many spectators, and the painful strains on my nerves at being obliged to assist at so awful a spectacle no doubt overtaxed my not yet restored powers.

I didn't get the letter I expected today and I wouldn't write you if I could help it. Donnell came today and didn't bring me any port wine! Now you must get two bottles of that for me and two of Madeira if you can and send by the ladies boxes or barrels: they will come straight to me in that way.

Col. [Charles] Gilmore is here and [Ellis] Spear is Major. [William] Donnell I shall detail on my staff for the present.[35] We are in a beautiful camp, in full view of the enemies picket and are on the opposite slope. We are at Beverly Ford at the junction of Tin Pot Run(!) and Hegemann's River which here form the north of branch of the Rappahannock.

Dr. Benson has resigned on account of ill health. Lieut. Twitchell is very sick and is to leave tomorrow. I have just written the Governor recommending him for promotion in the Artillery.[36]

I wrote Mrs. Whittlesey last evening saying that it would cause too great an inconvenience to rent the house for a short time, and would be very embarrassing to rent it for a long time in the event of my return. But I renewed my proposal to sell the house. I think that would be better. It shall be as you say though. I am not anxious to see it go but simply think it would be well to change our locality. We have had that house about long enough. If it would give you too much trouble to remove without me, don't try it. It is your house and nobody shall disturb you in it.

My army friends are urging me to allow them to move for my promotion. I am almost persuaded to let them begin. Some stupid fellow I suppose is going to be promoted and it may as well be me. It is however a hundred fold harder and more honorable to be made a Genl now than it was a year ago. I find that I have recd honorable mention in the official reports which have gone from the HdQrs of the army to Washington.

Now everything will bend I imagine on Pitt Fessenden. He doubtless means for Frank to be made a Genl and Frank is a good soldier and deserves it, but he need not prevent me.[37] He has not seen the hard fighting I have, but then he was wounded at Shiloh. Now I want to find out discreetly through Dr. Lincoln whether I could count on Mr. Fessenden's support. My military recommendations will be ample. But it needs a politician. If Mr. F. will be induced (by Dr. L.) to do this good, if not I shall take hold else where and strong and get it without him. Do what you can discretely for me as a friend. Don't supplicate any favors. If I deserve this, I shall have it. Loving you as ever, Lawrence.

---

35 Gilmore had continued his usual habit of avoiding battles, while Ellis Spear, Bowdoin, Class of 1858, and a close friend of the Chamberlains, especially Horace, had proven a good soldier and officer. William E. Donnell graduated from Bowdoin in September 1862 and then joined the army. Chamberlain made him his adjutant.

36 Lt. Adelbert B. Twitchell of the 5th Maine Battery was a graduate of Bowdoin, Class of 1860. He was promoted to captain of the 7th Maine Battery.

37 William Pitt Fessenden was a powerful Republican senator from Maine. The senator's son, Francis, was colonel of the 25th Maine and later the 30th Maine.

James Rice to William P. Fessenden, 9/8/1863
General Rice, who took command of the brigade that included the 20th Maine when Col. Vincent, his predecessor was mortally wounded on Little Round Top at Gettysburg, wrote to Maine's powerful Republican senator on Chamberlain's behalf.

Army of the Potomac
HdQtrs. 1" Div. 1" Corps
Sept 8th 1863
Hon. Wm P. Fessenden
Washington D.C.

Dear Sir,

I am advised that the friends of Col. Chamberlain of the 20th Maine Vols., now commanding the 3d Brigade l't Division 5th Corps have presented his application to the President for the position of Brigadier General.

My personal knowledge of this gallant officer's skill and bravery upon the battle field, his ability in drill and discipline, and his fidelity to duty in camp, added to a just admiration for his scholarship, respect for his Christian character, induces me to ask your influence on his behalf.

Col. Chamberlain joined the Brigade of which he is now the commanding officer, about a year ago. At all the severe conflicts of this army since, he has greatly distinguished himself for the skillful disposition of his command and for his personal bravery. Not a battle has been fought in which the 20th Maine under his command has not added luster to our arms, and a brighter page to our history. At the battle of Gettysburg he held the extreme left of our entire line of battle; and for the brilliant success of the conflict upon the second day of the struggle, History will give credit to the bravery and unflinching fortitude of the 20th Maine volunteers, more than to any other equal body of men upon the field. A copy of the official report of the commanding officer of the Brigade of which their Regiment formed a part is on file in the War Department and I desire to call your attention to the same.

The conduct of this regiment at the battle of Gettysburg has rendered, for all time, the prowess of the arms of your state, imperishable—conduct which, as an eye-witness I do not hesitate to say, had its inspiration and great success from the moral power and personal heroism of Col. Chamberlain. Nor do I state the case too strongly when I say that the State of Maine but partially rewards the distinguished services of this officer, when her influence at Washington shall make him a General, for his magnificent gallantry upon the hard-won field of Gettysburg.

But beyond and above all these considerations, I would urge the promotion of this officer since the service, more than ever before, demands that high-toned, moral, patriotic Christian men shall lead its forces to victory.

Pardon, Sir, the apparent warmth of this letter of commendation. My excuse is the respect and admiration which a soldier feels for the bravery and fidelity of another.

I am most respectfully
Your obedient servant
James C. Rice
Brig. Genl. Comdg. 1" Div. 1" Corps

JLC to Fannie, 9/22/1863

Chamberlain wrote to Fannie about his circumstances, including his decision to abandon his efforts to get a promotion to brigadier general.

Beyond Culpepper Court House
Sept 22 1863

My sweet girl how is she this morning? Well and happy I hope. She does not write to me much, so I wrote a saucy letter one morning wh. I think I will send hoping no evil consequences will result. If apprehended they may be checked by sundry precautions almanacks, antidotes, subterfuges, sleights or ex-post facto expedients so well known to the mission of this world. By all means often ready, take a slight infusion of "cold water." Write me, you darling; what are you doing? Getting deep into coal and wood? I'm afraid you are not enjoying yourself. You are going to live in that horrid uncomfortable way, again, I fear. Now be happy and let me think of you as without a care. Don't sew and stitch and bend over old clothes. Romp and play with the children, and have some pleasant people (your girls now I am saying) and don't criticize them too much. Nobody is very pretty or very good and always excepting you for the first quality and me for the second!

I'm not going to do anything about the promotion. I have won it in the field and if Napoleon had seen it he would have made me a Genl. on the spot. Here everything is mean. You can't expect much personal heroism in this country. So let me stay where I am—only I wish I was back with my Regt. Don't think everything is not well, and going easy with me <u>here</u>. It is. And my service is acknowledged here. Promotions, however, are managed strangely in Washington. All will be right—Providence will direct. I sent that little bloody testament to the family today. It is the <u>only trace</u> they have of their son. They had searched the awful field over and over but not a trace of their son.

Please answer—or write rather. You may <u>answer</u> the pencil letter if you dare. I shall send $100 tomorrow. We are under orders to move <u>on the Rebs</u> I suppose.

Evening

I knew I should have a letter from you tonight, my beautiful. You notice that you do not answer my letters. If it happens that you do <u>not</u> receive any from me, why then you sit down and write always reporting that you have had one (a letter I mean) in the mean time. You are a "funny fellow" more like. Here is a statement and accompanying reflection "I rec'd a letter from you yesterday. You are a funny fellow, I think. Your expressions and ways of looking at things are so droll." Now you see I can't recollect which of a dozen letters I have written you of late is referred to in that. Moreover there was <u>something</u> in my letter you did not quite like. Was I scolding you, Darling? Well I will not do so any more.

The fight of the day before the 7th (you <u>must not</u> make 7's like 9's so "7") was chiefly a cavalry fight. We have them nearly every day—cav'ly and artillery.

I appreciate your dear letter and <u>love you</u>. A grey-headed man out here sends you a little poem "Equinoctial." He is just there being <u>half</u> of three score years and ten of age. The second stanza he does not adopt. He thanks God that "youths glowing hopes" were short of manhood's strong and calm successes. He has all and more than all he ever hoped for.— Moreover the first line of the sixth I <u>breast</u> the "gale". A <u>woman</u> wrote that I'll wager. That is all woman.

I wonder if you get all my letters. If you would refer to something in item, I could tell. Especially if you would author each one! Where is the photograph of you? One more kiss and my love to all the Darlings. <u>Write to me</u>. For my darling.

210

JLC to Fannie, 9/23/1863
Chamberlain wrote this fanciful note to Fannie during a lull in activity in the army.

3rd Brigade Sept. 23rd 1863

Good morning my splendid little Plant-a-genet or Viking's daughter or whatever else your pride prefers; what a morning is this! I should like to lead you on a race over the hills this morning. If not literally on account of your pretty little neck—figuratively perhaps though all things considered you would not like that any better.

But I will not press you any further on that subject. I dare say you will not care to ask after my <u>health</u> now. It's <u>not bad</u>, I assure you. At present take my <u>word</u> for it!

It is one of those humid summer days. A fine band is playing some exquisite music in a grove close by my quarters—music such as nobody here appreciates or in the least comprehends. How happy you would be here under these broad oaks sitting in the sunshine (with your big brown eyes shaded by just a branch of hanging vine) listening lazily like me now to that ravishing music! To be sure this has been the scene of a fierce struggle only a week ago—and pieces of shell and half buried bullets and the torn trees and the recent graves are sadly suggestive but after all, how charming such a day is now and then amidst the rude scenes of such a life! But the <u>music</u>— the <u>music</u>—why it can make a man do just what it will. Strength, courage, hope, aspiration, all with me blended into a great current of <u>love</u>— boundless, ceaseless, inexplicable love! All that make me strong and brave, all that makes me calm in the storm of battle, and restless in the moonlit solitude all this is music, and it is love. It is all one. I believe I am fit only to love. That's the only thing I can do <u>thoroughly</u>.

Fan how is your piano? Have it where you live. Do you want me to order some fine pieces of music sent you. Shall I have somebody in New York send you all the best music whenever it comes along? Why will you not let me do something for you? Let "sir Benny" sew and scrub; you can be at something better.

Have that piano out, or do you <u>go in</u>.

Write and tell me everything you do—unless you are making a drudge of yourself in that case don't say a word about it. I shall try <u>to forget you</u>. If you are happy, I shall love you; if you are unhappy I shall <u>not</u>! That is, I shall try. Generous fellow, am I not? Yes, if anything vexes you, you <u>may</u> tell me—if your roosters do not lay well or if people say one thing and do another, or things persist in standing on their heads, tell me and I'll help you out of them perhaps once—after that leave those things to others.

Don't you see that I could have married a maid of all work or a washerwoman, if I had wished, but I didn't or at any rate didn't intend to—send me that picture of yours but don't delay writing till you can conveniently get a photo. Are you pretty now? Who are your lovers? Give them my compliments.

Please acknowledge the $100

JLC to Fannie, 9/28/1863
Chamberlain sent another update for his family at home on life in the army on campaign during a respite.

Sept 28th 1863

How are you today, all my sunny-faced darlings? Do these soft autumn days make you happy or sad, or both? I suppose you miss me, and I miss you more than I would like to tell. But darlings do not miss me too much; for I am where I would choose to be although I love you so far, far beyond anything in this world, that love inspires me to be good and true and brave.

So if I long to see you and be with you in these balmy radius summer days I check myself with thinking that I am where it becomes a man to be and where you shall never hear that I bore myself otherwise than because the object of your trusting love.

I love all your shining heads—whether they have the deep moonlight sheer of the sweet mother or are little sunny heads glancing like thistledown in the light. May God bless and keep you all.

How lovely such days are! And the music—music around me by day or the deep music of moon and star light by night how glorious it is here among the oaks on this thrice fought ground. The bands have been playing the druids march in normal and many such to noting minor strains from operas and I have had to hear it without you! And you my sweet love interpreter of this to the rest how is that bearing face and the regal forehead of the "daughter of sea-kings"? do things plague you or do you live happy and bright? Do you have music and light laughter around you as I wish you to? Do you play to the little ones such music as will instruct and cultivate as well as entertain them?

Your piano is doubtless in the sitting room—the only obligation being the dust or smoke from the fire.

Shall I get my friend Christian of New York to send you all the genius of press masters that come to him? Does anything annoy you? You have leisure and means now to do anything you wish. Now write and tell me how happy you are.

As for me, I am in the right place. I was born for this. We are now awaiting orders to move again (probably to the rear). You will hear soon how things are going here. This army is getting broken up a little, which fits my ideas perfectly. The 11th and 12th corps under Gen Hooker have gone west.

Possibly the 5th [corps] will go somewhere! Explicit isn't it? With a thousand kisses of love, Love passionate as boyhood, strong as manhood, and deep as life.

"Toujours"

JLC to Cousin Deb, 10/17/1863
Chamberlain wrote to Cousin Deb, who was at home caring for his children, to express his frustration at not getting any letters from Fannie.

(Monday 3 a/m. The bugle sounds forward!)
Hd. Qrs. 3d Brigade
Centreville, VA Oct 17th 1863

Dear Aunty—
Can you tell me where Fannie is? It is agonizing to receive no letters day after day when I have every reason to expect them. I sent a check for $100 from Culpepper three weeks ago and more and I have had no acknowledgement of it. Mr. French has also been in great anxiety about bonds for $200 which he sent Fanny asking an acknowledgement. It seems neither love nore money can attract any notice from that lady. I have a good mind to go to Illinois and get divorced.[38]

---

38 Chamberlain probably meant to write "Indiana" rather than "Illinois" since the former was renowned for having among the most liberal divorce laws in the nation.

We had some very exciting times for the last ten days, I assure you. It has been a race for Bull Run. We marched 30 miles a day with the enemy on our flank and rear and three times formed line of battle and went back double quick on the enemy who were cannonading our rear and drove them from their position. We are now massed on the old Bull Run field and are going to attack probably. All depends on Lee's movements.

I wish you would tell me how things are getting on. I utterly and almost bitterly despair of hearing from Fanny.

I remember the childrens birthdays. But they were hard days for us soldiers.

I had the post of honor again in an attack on the enemy this side of Culpepper. Had a strong position of theirs to carry with my brigade but the rebs ran before us and my own brigade color was on their heights before a single one of my regiments could reach the position.[39] I more fully expected never to see any of you again on that day than ever before. It was considered a desperate affair. But the Rebs ran and se we all escaped harm. I think we shall go forward tomorrow morning towards the Rappahannock again.

We have mails every day but no opportunity to write.

I have become so sick at not getting any letters from Fanny that I am afraid I shall not welcome one much when it does come.

However you can give my love to her and tell her I have given up writing and shall await some recognition of my scores of letters before I make any more demonstrations in that direction.

With much love to you all, and hoping you are happy.
Yours Lawrence

—

JLC to Fannie, 10/19/1863
Camped near the site of the two Battles of Bull Run, near Manassas, Virginia, Chamberlain wrote of the scene of those battles and other news.

Bull Run Battle Field
Oct. 19 1863

---

39 By "color" he means the brigade commander's flag and thus he reached the heights before his men did.

My dearest girl

I have just rec'd your letter dated Oct 7th delayed on the way I suppose. I hasten to answer it from my fire light bivouac on the field. I have been pained and vexed and sick at not hearing from you all this long time during which we have been through with all sorts of exciting and dangerous scenes and this is now the fourth time we have gone back to check and drive the enemy since we abandoned the Culpepper position. We knew all the time that we should have to leave that position the moment Lee announced his flank movements. Well, after having been within 15 miles of Washington here we are out at Bull Run again on the very ground where this Brigade fought and lost so fearfully a year ago last August. I have been looking over the ground this evening (we came in about sunset) and I saw in less than a quarter of a minute where our mistake was in Bull Run second and exactly how it could have been successfully managed on our part. I never would sacrifice even so—it is that same stupidity which you know I call the worst of crimes.

I believe this field is more awful than a recent battlefield. Skeletons, skulls, and bones strew the ground. I stepped out toward my horses just now and stumbled on three skulls ghastly grinning in the moonlight—the hands and feet sticking out of the little heap of brush and earth that was thrown on the bodies as they lay. Right where I am sitting I picked up three bullets and fragments of shell. This is a memorable shot. It is the field of Bull Run second, which was probably the most desperate and inexcusable of the two.

If we have a third let me tell you it will not come out like those. I shall study their ground in the morning and when the 3rd Brigade is put in next time you will not hear that it was murdered at whole sale for no possible good: but that it did its full share in winning an overwhelming victory.

Do you know that every bit of my experience in former life and studies is of the utmost value to me here. Habits of perception quick judgment, reflection, of self-control—and of command too—everything helps me. I feel it and others see it. I am rapidly improving now—not as a tactician I am past that having drilled my brigade through the whole course of evolutions till they are in the finest condition—but in the better broader and more congenial sphere of strategy and handling preparatory to an engagement a few days ago I had confided to me one of the most responsible and desperate undertakings we have made. It was trying to one's nerves, but the preparation handling of the books was such that the enemy did not wait for us in their strong position, but ran before we got in rifle range.

I enjoy this life. It is hard, hard, but glorious! These marches in night and storm through woods and fields, through flood and mud, wet, hungry, cold and tired and sore, but our hearts as stout and true and brave as you could wish. I honor the stout fellows who will march with their heavy loads from midnight to midnight—thirty miles to fight the enemy two hours on the way.

I suppose we may be off at about 3 in the morning, if the enemy are not here for if he does not fight us we shall certainly fight him.

I carry a pen and ink-hand in my pocket now-a-days, so as to write you whenever I get a moment. Our baggage cannot be with us you know—so I will write again soon, if possible.

Now good night, darling I have to say it now. The wine I suppose is safe with Mrs. Fogg.[40] I have not the slightest notion as to her whereabouts.

I rec'd a "telegraph" today making three I think since I came back in August. I have rec'd some very kind and warm letters from several Generals. I wish you could see them. I haven't time to copy if I had them. I enclose a little piece of John heads and some flowers for Daisy from the battlefield in return for her bird.

Good night my dear love and do write me
your own Lawrence

JLC to Fannie, 10/21/1863
In autumn 1863, Chamberlain wrote home telling of his frustration with haphazard military movements.

Field near New Baltimore
Halt Oct. 21st 1863

My dearest girl
We are so exhausted with the heavy night marches that we halt a while from sheer inability to move further without rest. We have not slept a single night since we left the Rapidan [River] ten or eleven days ago. We have suffered more, I think, than on any march yet. Do let me tell you how things are

---

40 Isabella Fogg was a Maine woman who established a line of supplies from Maine to soldiers in the field, which was unprecedented in American warfare. She helped found the Maine Camp Hospital Association, which, as the war ended, boasted that not a single package from Maine had failed to reach its addressee.

done and why opportunities are missed and battles lost. It is unmilitary, I believe, to refer to such things but I can't help it.

I will "suppose" that we have just got into camp after a hard days work—say at 10 or 11 at night and after witchedly scrambling over some bog or muddy ditch for mates to make coffee to give a relish or a soaking to our hard bread, have given it up and gone to sleep with a rubber blanket spread over each of us as if we were corpses and this to keep the heavy dews off.

Then will come a mounted orderly post haste waking you up to read an order to have your command at such a place by daylight. "Reveille will sound at 1 a.m. move promptly at 2." It is of the utmost importance that your command be on the designated spot precisely at the time specified.

A whole division will thus be roused up after two hours sleep and put their heavy burdens on and stand waiting for the roads to be cleared for maybe an hour or two, and then start to find twenty rods ahead a creek which is impossible to cross only one at a time and in consequence the movement is so checked that the rear of the column does not cross till sunrise and has been standing still or creeping up by inches all the four or five hours in the heavy drenching dews and half-dead already before their days work is begun.

This because some lazy wagon master or quartermaster has not got his teams out at the hour appointed to us to leave the way clear and because twenty pioneers have not been sent forward to bridge the creek by a few rails—an hour's work but nobody seems to think it his business particularly.

This way of doing things worries me—you know how much I wish I could have the ordering of things.

Well enough of this. We have grand sights here every day. Imagine this army moving in four parallel columns—artillery, infantry, cavalry, and wagons winding along by the roads or over hillsides and valleys fording and climbing.

You would enjoy seeing this very much. We are pushing on the enemy. He is falling back to his old position, I believe. Meade is determined to give battle wherever he can find Lee.

I love you very much my darling, and always think of you. If you are fresh and fat why don't you have your picture taken and send me?

Please direct.
Comdy. 3rd Brigade
1st Div. 5th Corps
As H Qr. mails sometimes comes when the regular ones don't

JLC to Fannie, 11/4/1863

Nov. 4 1863

My love,

I just write you now to tell you that you are my own sweet love and that I think of you with fervent and passionate affection every moment. When I am leading (as I have been) solid battalions into the deadly eye of mortal conflict, if I do it well it is because I love you well. It is you who do it, through a person dressed in a colonel's uniform who fears no foe and betrays no friend. As I tell you so often (though you never answer me) what is life or death to love—or music which is the same, for you must know music is swelling the very air with love tonight. Am I well? Why, yes. You would think me well.

Well my darling how do all things go with you?

The cheeks are round, are they? Are the breasts so too? I did not know I had written that till the music struck a new strain and took away my common (place) sense.

I have been trying to write a military report tonight and in fact I am a little tired of it though I glory in it. My sweet girl—how sweet you are!

Well darling wife perhaps you can come to see me again soon. I think we shall advance shortly, and then for the autumn fight and following winter camp. Be ready. Get those naughty teeth all right.

I send you a funny note from a pretty woman, who had a couple of Union men taken by Mosby near our camp a night or two ago.[41] I had just left the place which was my head qurs. In haste,

Lawrence

~~~

JLC to Fannie, 11/8/1863

Chamberlain wrote about a small battle near Rappahannock Station in Virginia on November 6, 1863, where two army corps attacked a Confederate position on the Rappahannock River and drove the Rebels across it.

---

41 Colonel John Mosby led an independent cavalry command known as Mosby's Rangers.

Rappahannock Station
Nov. 8 1863

Dear Fanny,
We had a brilliant little fight here yesterday. 5th and 6th Corps. drove the
enemy over the river and took their redoubts and guns. I lost in my Brigade
about 4 killed and wounded. 20th Maine 1 killed and 7 wounded. My brigade
took 70 prisoners—Louisiana 8th and 6th. I was a little impudent, I believe;
but my little horse took the consequences. Shot in the leg. You ought to have
seen the little hero plunge. The conduct of the men was splendid. Gen. Griffin
was away sick and Gen. [Joseph J] Bartlett commanded us. He is a gallant
officer. I believe people are satisfied with the way the brigade was handled. We
are pushing in so this morning. I can't tell you more. The man killed in the
20th is Kinsell Co. E. You will hear by the papers what the army is doing and
where we are.[42]

I wish you could have seen the splendid charges yesterday. The 6th
Maine lost terribly—They were on our right. 9th [Corps] crossed the
Rappahannock at Kelley's Ford and are pushing for the Rapidan.

L

JLC to Fannie, 12/nd/1863

Saturday evening

Abed, if I may so speak
The Drs. say I have a malarial fever, darling, and I shall be several days
getting over it. While I was lying tossing and burning last night, some body
came and said a letter for you and from your wife they say. You may be sure
I had a candle brought and read my fever to sleep. Don't be worried, dearest.
If the army moves within a few days, I shall have to be sent to Washington.
Everybody is kind to me and I shall not be very long sick. I think the fever is
much abated even today. But I am in much pain and very restless. It is
lonesome, but I suffer too much to mind it a great deal.

---

42 Private Fred Kinsel died November 7. He is buried at Arlington National Cemetery.

You should direct letters to me now as "Comdg. 3rd Brig. 1st Div. 5th corps" I would get them sooner. Head Qr. mails come when others don't.

Do you want me to send you another $100 now or put it all in 5–20s

Please answer love to the precious little ones, and to all. L

JLC to Fannie, 12/14/1863
In December 1863, Chamberlain suffered a severe attack of malaria and was ordered to Washington for medical treatment. From there, he was furloughed home to recuperate.

Monday Eve Dec 14th

Still gaining fast my own precious darling. I went down two pairs of stairs today. It makes my muscles a little sore now, but it will help me to gain strength. I'll tell you what I am trying so hard for. I want to see my blessed darling and have her dear smile to grow strong under.

I told my surgeons this morning that I was going to start for home Thursday night so as to get home Saturday p.m. He shook his head, but I told him I had the strength of a magnet he did not think of perhaps, to draw me and to strengthen me for the journey. He laughed, and with his usual kindness sent up an application for a leave of absence for me to date from Thursday. I hope I shall not disappoint my dearest love and does she want to come to Boston to go down with me Saturday or will she await me in her and my own dear little home. She might come to Boston Thursday and stay Friday to rest or be sure and take the Saturday morn train for Portland and she will see a languid looking officer leaning up in one corner of a seat. Just as my sweet little wife thinks best. I shall not probably need her, for I shall have come all the way thus far in sleeping cars.

My strong constitution has saved me, so I am told, but you won't care to hear much about that. You thought I was a little too well a few weeks ago.

I shall be a very mild and brotherly guest now. If you don't get me well too long before my leave expires!

Bless you I am so happy at the thought of seeing you that weak as I am I feel as well as ever while I write.

I should have grieved sorely at your last dear letter, precious, had I not known that you understood all now and every thing is right. Not a soldier has been to see me today. Gen. Ames yesterday sends love. So does Somebody.

I will write everyday.

~

James H. Rice to JLC, 12/15/1863
General Rice wrote that he continued to work to get a promotion for Chamberlain.

HO of Representatives
Washington DC Dec 15 1863

My Dear: Col:
I really must gladly do all in my power to effect the promotion which you do well deserve. I have today been to the department to have all the testimonies collected and hope to have it done. I think I may present the entire case to the President within a few days. When may I expect you down? Please come to my rooms as I suggested.

You must not trouble yourself about the movements of your Reg't in the field if you would speedily rejoin the Corps.

Very truly
Brig General
James H. Rice

~

JLC to Fannie, 1/2/1864
Chamberlain wrote from Washington to apologize to Fannie for his demeanor when they were recently together during his furlough home.

January 2nd 1864

My own Love,
Everything makes me miss you so! My chamber—our chamber is too full of tender, loving thoughts for me to be quite happy without you.

I see that neither time, nor danger, nor the stern strife's of later years have made me any less capable of loving, or made you any less dear to me. How I long to see you now, here where without a disturbing care we might live over again our earlier days (if indeed they were any better than these) and at least experience some of that calm, sweet, deep communion we could not, somehow, enjoy at home.

Did I break my darling's heart with my impatience? Do not, dearest, take it too deeply to heart that I said those unkind things to you. Yet it was absolutely impossible to avoid doing so, I can't tell why and I came away in shame and vexation to think how miserably I was spoiling the few brief hours we had to spend together. I could not, weak as I was, bear the way things went. Can you forgive me my dearest, dearest one?

You know how I love you. You know how I can love—more like a romance of passionate poetry than anything I ever saw or knew in others. And, darling, darling love, that is the way I love you. But I know how the words of cruel discontent, such as I uttered in my impatience, sink deep into the memory and heart and will not easily be forgiven or forgotten.

And will my precious one forgive and forget all this for the love I bear her evermore? For the love that treasures every memory every look every token of her—which makes the places she has been in hallowed and the places where she is not empty and drear?

The cup of happiness has not been drained dearest, and all that was best in youth is still with us. You are a joy to me now, and never in my boyish days so dear.

Jan 3rd

I am expecting to be at home on Saturday—possibly before if you should happen to come, not till Tuesday or Wednesday of next week. But just as my darling wishes and when she says.

I am feeling much better, and I think improving fast. Lonely, but then I rest. Mother and Sae are very cheerful and Father in good spirits.

The children will have great sliding now, after the rain (which was hard for me to bear alone) and the subsequent cold of which (in a roguish way) I might say the same!

How Happy and thankful and proud I am in my darling wife! From your own.

JLC to Fannie, 1/20/1864
Chamberlain wrote to Fannie from Georgetown, where he had reported after returning from furlough.

Washington Jan. 20th 1863 [misdated, actually 1864]

My darling girl,

I miss you so much everywhere that I find myself whispering as I walk about the hotel or hospital "my loved darling" "my dearest, dearest girl" and other boyish phrases. No matter what I may be thinking about intensely as I have things I think of that may here the loved heart seems to be at with my own with just enough individual consciousness left to maintain personal identity.

I hope my love is well. She must let me know at once. If not, take the most vigorous measures to make herself so. I believe however, she must be free from solicitation by this time. Need I tell you again how sweet beyond telling you were to me and how I love to think of you? Shall I say a word of myself ...

Reported to hospital Monday morning. Dr. Ducachet[43] said he did not expect me for a week. But it was better to come as I did. I shall get discharged in a day or two and go to my command.

I found things very "quiet" about my promotion. I went to Senator [William Pitt] Fessenden and told him that I wished very much that before any promotion was recommended the authorities would just look at my record at the military history of my last year. He said he presumed that would be done. He was however frank enough to tell me he did not think I deserved immediate promotion—that another colonel—Colonel Burnham did deserve it and he should be the next man. So it seems to be settled. Col. B. is a gallant officer. He commanded the storming party that took Fredericksburg, Heights last May. Col McGilvery I spoke of will not probably be a serious competitor.[44]

Everything will be right, I know. Men may not do right towards me, but Providence will. I don't feel at all disturbed about anything but you darling.

---

43 Dr. Henry W. Ducachet was surgeon in chief of Seminary Hospital in Georgetown.

44 Col. Hiram Burnham commanded the 6th Maine infantry regiment. He was promoted to brigadier general on April 26, 1864. Freeman McGilvery of Searsport, Maine, was a captain in the Sixth Maine artillery battery. He was promoted to chief of artillery of the 10th Corps in August 1864, but was wounded in the finger a week later and died of a chloroform overdose during surgery.

I will tell you more next time, soon. Let me hear from you, dearest love as soon as you can the old address

Remember to all your own love

JLC to Fannie, 1/29/1864

Chamberlain wrote from back in Washington, where he had again been detailed to serve on a court martial.

273 "F." St. Washington
Jan. 29 1864

Dear Fanny,

I am very anxious to hear from you. In fact I am becoming nervous about it

Please write me at this address until I notify you of some change. At present I am in the Hospital at Georgetown but shall probably soon be transferred to this city. I want to know if you mean or wish to come and spend a month or two with me. I think I shall be here that length of time as the court I am on is ordered by the Sec. of War and I cannot easily be relieved even after I fully recover.

I would like more than I can tell to have you with me and do not you think of <u>expense</u> for I am sure I can afford to have my own darling with me. And you know I have now over $100 a month extra pay.

At all events do let me hear from you. If you come the sooner the better. The weather is marvelous. How you would enjoy it. If you wish you could bring Daisy.

I can find some good healthy place for you no doubt. But Washington I confess is not particularly distinguished for such places.

But I miss you and could be well content to be here if you were here.

Please write and tell me about it

In haste
your loving
Lawrence

Do not think you must be a month getting ready. Stop in N.Y. a day or two and then come here and finish your preparations. L.

Please go and see if Mrs. Pieser is doing those copies of Daisy and Willys photographs well and get them if done and send one of each to me.

Have you sent the shawl and boots to John C. Chamberlain, Bangor Maine Get Stanwood to call for the package.

Do write me

L

~~~

JLC to Fannie, 2/2/1864

Send telegram to
273 "F" st
Court Martial 205 Pa. Ave.
Washington D.C.
Feb. 2 1864

Your letter was rec'd by me after long wandering on its part—more on mine understand. You need not be afraid I shall do that so long as you are the weak little wife you are now. Well for "business."

no shirts bought by me.

Glad to hear of the "immunity" I shall take courage and confidence here after from that mind you.

The $10 not taken by me, nor any recollection of it existing on my part.

The $400 bond was taken by me—the proper form to have it, my lady. That's for business.

What on earth are these hieroglyphics—"$ b and ½ a yard"

You mean $6.50 I suppose.

I want you to come this week without fail. Don't wait for anything I'm in a great hurry for you.

I can't think of you without a big heartbeat, nor even see your name on one of my envelopes without a warm thrill.

I am afraid this will not be a very strong inducement for you to come.

Do come, right off. You can start without waiting to hear from me again. I am sure to be here. Send me a letter or a telegram if you stop in N.Y. a day.

You can do so (stop I mean) on this <u>through ticket</u> which you will get in Boston. You know how to manage it. But don't stop if you can help it.

Mrs. Sampson's address is simply <u>Washington D.C.</u> Oh, can't you get me some dearer little thing for $5.00 or so for a present for her. No time to write more or better now.

Only to say that I have been trying to find a pleasant room for you, and succeed well enough—but when a man has a lady in hand people think him a fair game for prices especially in this city.

But I am sure I can afford to have a wife here, as well as other people can a mistress.

Come at all events and soon as you can, letting me know by telegraph when you leave N.Y. city and I can meet you or else some other man will get you.

L

A Severe Wound at Petersburg

On June 18, 1864, during the first few days of fighting near Petersburg, Virginia, which eventually led to a nine-month siege of the place by Union forces, Chamberlain was dangerously wounded while leading his brigade in a charge on the enemy works. In the midst of the charge, a bullet passed laterally through both of his hips, damaging bone and tissue in its path. He was barely saved by a battlefield surgery and carried to the U.S. Hospital at Annapolis, Maryland. Fearing he was mortally wounded, General Ulysses S. Grant awarded him a battlefield promotion to brigadier general. Remarkably, Chamberlain was well enough to return home to Maine on furlough within four months and was back at the head of his brigade by November.

Though he survived the wound, the damage caused him great pain and difficulty, particularly from a hole or "fistula" it caused where his urethra joined his bladder. This led to repeated and dangerous infections, and the effects of the wound plagued him for the rest of his life. In fact, the effects of the wound may have contributed to his death fifty years later.

JLC to Fannie, 10/18/1864
Chamberlain wrote to Fannie from his parents' home in Brewer during a leave from the army, passing along the happenings among friends and family there.

He took his young son Wyllys along on this trip. On October 16, the Bangor branch of the U.S. Christian Commission held a meeting at the large meeting hall in downtown Bangor known as Norumbega Hall.

Brewer Oct. 18th 1864

Dear Fanny,

I have the honor to report that I arrived safely here with my staff-officer, your much respected son. I found him a real hero. His conduct, and I judge, his appearance, too, made him a conspicuous object of interest and attention all along our route. Of course I found "Missy" Libby at the depot waiting for me. Mr. and Mrs. Libby were away, but Miss Katie made a beautiful hostess. She and her friend Miss Stelle seemed very much devoted to Wyllys. Also John Brown and Phil[45] who called in the evening. He called on Mrs. Bacon and Wyllys became perfectly absorbed over their magnificent <u>parrot</u>. He had her out of the cage in short order, and seemed more amazed at the parrot's performances, scolding, crying, singing, laughing, whistling, and then he was at the antics of William Eaton's dog. Wyllys behaved like a perfect gentleman at all places, and made the wonder of every body in the steamer. "He looked like a little prince," says John C. by the way he kept me out on the deck till after midnight looking at the ships and ports and lighthouses we passed, and by that time the sea became pretty bright. He looked rather pale and I put him to bed. He said he wasn't sick resenting the intimation with expression of contempt, but admitted that the "drinking" of the boat "hurt" his stomach. Pretty soon he turned over in his berth and deposited his supper and dinner too I should think upon the pillow and bed. I came to his assistance with a bowl. He then lay down quietly (after I had adjusted the bedding) and to my frequent inquiries the little hen answered "no, dear, I feel pretty well" and so he lay like a lamb or a hero; just as you please! till he woke me at dawn banging open the state room window to look at the sea. We have a great many callers and his behavior and <u>dress</u> call forth much praise. Today he is not to be seen. Having devoted himself to helping his grandpa gather turnips so that he can drive the horse, he excuses himself to all visitors. Mother is suffering

---

45 John Marshall Brown and his brother Phillip, both sons of prominent Portland merchant John Bundy Brown. John Marshall began his military service with the 20th Maine but transferred out to accept a promotion to the staff of General Adelbert Ames, first commander of the 20th Maine. Brown went on to become lieutenant colonel of the 32nd Maine. He was severely wounded at Petersburg on June 12 and discharged September 23, 1864.

from neuralgia. She and Sae send much love, and regret that you did not come. Everybody enquires for you most kindly. Daisy is much loved in this region I find. Dr. Harris thinks she behaved wonderfully.

I was dragged into a great meeting of the Christian Commission at Norembega Hall on Sunday evening. I sat till I didn't know whether I had any brains or not and then had to get up and say something. Don't you pity me? My cold troubles me—irritates my wounds and spoils my appetite, but I am having a pleasant visit. Expect to be home Friday but may not come till Saturday don't expect us till then.

Lawrence

Petersburg to Appomattox

After he had become barely well enough to return to the army, which was still at Petersburg, Chamberlain resumed command of his old brigade, despite being unable to walk more than a hundred feet. Despite his illness, he led several reckless and memorable charges into Confederate lines during the last few weeks of the war.

On April 2, 1865, Gen. Robert E. Lee made a desperate dash out of his Petersburg defenses in hopes of eluding the enemy by escaping to the west. As the closest army corps in that direction, the 5th Corps, including Chamberlain's brigade, took up the chase. Seven days later, with the 5th Corps having cut off his retreat, Lee sent word to his Union counterpart, Gen. Ulysses S. Grant, that he wished to discuss terms for surrender. The following morning, April 9, 1865, Lee and Grant signed the formal surrender document.

JLC to Col. Gustavus Sniper, 4/10/1865
Despite the surrender of Lee's Army at Appomattox, Chamberlain wanted to be sure that those who had earned promotions were properly recommended for them.

Head Quarters 1t Brigade 1st Div. 5th Corps
Appomattox Court House Va.
April 10th 1865

Colonel:

I would respectfully recommend to you for promotion to the rank, if possible, of First Lieutenant, of Henry A. Kelsey of your Regiment for his conspicuous good conduct during all the engagements of this campaign. At the battle of "Lewis Farm" on the 29th of March he was constantly on the line rallying the men, though only acting as my orderly, and I was an eye witness to his capturing an officer and five men out of the very line of battle in the enemy's ranks. At the battle of "White Oak Road" March 31st he really acted as aide de camp. At the battle of "Five Forks" his behavior was heroic. And at the battle of Appomattox Court-House April 9th he advanced into the town in advance of the skirmish line, and captured several officers and men, besides rendering me important service in conveying orders to different parts of the field.

I am very desirous that such a distinguished instance of gallantry would be suitably rewarded.

I am, Colonel,
Very respectfully
Your obt. Servt.
J.L. Chamberlain Brig. Genl Comdg Colonel
Gustavus Sniper Comdg. 185 New York Vols.

JLC to Col. Sniper, 5/30/1865
More than six weeks after the surrender, Chamberlain wrote to one of the officers who served under his command in the last months of the war to express his appreciation for his service.

Head Quarters 1" Div. 5th A.C.
May 30, 1865

Colonel

As you are about to leave the military service of the United States with your Regt. I desire to tender to you this expression of my high appreciation of your character and services while you have been under my command.

In every engagement with the enemy since your Regiment has been in the service, you have acquitted yourself with distinguished honor. At Watkin's

Farm March 25th, at the Quaker Road March 29th, the White Oak road March 31st, at Five Forks April 1st, and at Church Road Crossing on the river April 2d, your conduct and that of your command was in the highest-degree commendable. At Appomattox Court House April 9th your regt. was in the advance line when the flag of truce came in, and you lost the last man killed in this war, before the surrender of Lee's Army. You may have the proud satisfaction of knowing that you have done your duty to your Regiment, to the service, and to the whole country.

I part with you with regret, and shall ever take pleasure in the recollection of the noble men of the 185 New York and its commander in this closing campaign.

> I am Colonel,
> Your friend and servt.
> J.L. Chamberlain
> Brig. Genl.
> Comdg. 1" Div.
> 5th A.C.
> *Colonel Gustavus Sniper*
> *Comdg. 185 N.Y.V.*

~~~

Tom Chamberlain to Col. Sniper, 6/26/1865
Two months after the surrender, there was still no avoiding army paperwork.

Head Quarters, 20'h ME
June 26. 1865

My Dear Col.
I have just returned from Washington and found your letter on my desk. I thought we put your discharge paper in with the rest. I am quite positive of it only it was not signed by the General. It will do no particular harm though for me to sign another only I am liable to be dismissed from the service for furnishing duplicate discharges, so if you find the other please tear it up. Hoping this will prove all right.

I remain Colonel Very respectfully
Your obt. servt.
T. D. Chamberlain To
Col. G. Sniper 185'h N.Y.Vols

~

JLC to Col. Sniper, 9/5/1865
Chamberlain wrote to offer to recommend Col. Sniper for promotion.

Brunswick Sept 5 1865

My dear Colonel,
On my return home yesterday I found your application which I endorse and
forward to you.

I should be pleased to hear from you, and if it would meet your wishes
would like to forward a recommendation for your Brevet of Brig. Genl.
Your name was not on our original list simply because you were too young
in comparison, but you deserve that appointment better than nine tenths of
those who have it. If you care for it say so.

I am out of service now, the fighting being over the Govt. has no occasion
for my services. It is the politicians turn now.

Very truly your obt. Servt.
J.L. Chamberlain
Col. Sniper

CHAPTER FIVE

The Postwar Years

With the war ended, Chamberlain was not officially discharged from the army until March 1866 so that he could continue to receive medical care at the government's expense. Additional surgery helped alleviate some of the effects of the wound he received at Petersburg, but it also became clear that a complete and permanent repair of the damage caused by the Confederate Minié ball was beyond the reach of the medical technology of the time.

When his military discharge became final, Chamberlain faced a decision about whether to return to his career as a professor. Before this decision became necessary, however, the Maine Republican Party nominated him for governor. In autumn 1866, he was elected with the most votes and by the largest margin in the state's history. He was sworn in on January 2, 1867.

JLC to Fannie, 1/17/1867
With his brother John seriously ill in New York, Chamberlain traveled to New York City to consult with his doctors about sending him to Florida. John died several months later.

5th Avenue Hotel
New York Sunday
Jan 17 1867

My darling love

I want to let you hear from me because you may be anxious. Axle broke on train last night which delayed us eight hours. So I <u>had</u> to stay till tonight. I was very stupid on the way to Boston. <u>E.G.</u> and <u>N.B.</u> a charming young lady took the vacant seat beside me, and was very willing to enter into conversation but after a feeble attempt I had to excuse myself and sat like a sick monkey till she pretended to espy some acquaintance in another part of the car and <u>left the seat</u>! <u>I was relieved</u> would you think it? *

I called on Mrs. Lefforts; but did not see her she has a sick grand daughter to wait on today. Mrs. Graham and Miss ____ and Mr. and Mrs. Dobb are out of town. I will perhaps call again. <u>I leave tonight at 7:30</u>

* I don't think it agrees with me very well to "<u>husband my strength</u>" as said and not so far as my disposition towards pretty young ladies goes!

Dr. Peaslee is out.[1]

I did not feel well on the journey, as I said but a good driver today makes amends.

I thought of you and loved you [and] longed to be with you and grieved at leaving you all night long but all will be well for us my own precious love. How sweetly I shall remember my little visit home. How <u>dear</u> and <u>loving</u> and <u>sweet</u> you were. (I have to underscore words because I can't stop to write right.)

Don't be sorrowful love—dear, dear, one

I think of you always and I believe God will spare us to meet again and be happy.

May he bless you my own
Love to all
your <u>lover</u>
Lawrence

Break fasted at "Tontine" New Haven this morning waiting for cars. L.

---

1 Dr. Edmund Randolph Peaslee was a medical doctor and professor of medicine in New York.

Arthur Folsom to JLC, 7/9/1867

Arthur Folsom's sisters included Fannie Chamberlain's stepmother, Sara Ann Adams, and "Cousin Deb" Folsom. He was the Commercial Agent of the United States at Cape Haytien (now Haiti). As his closest family in the United States, Chamberlain helped to manage his finances back home.

Cape Haytien July 9, 1867
Gen. Chamberlain
Brunswick Maine

My Dear Friend
I had the pleasure a few days ago since via Boston, enclosing a receipt for $300 in gold to be sent to you by Adam. I pray, by same conveyance Sch[ooner] Twisden I sent about $600 gold drafts to Richard Thackray, Esq 44 Exchange Place N[ew] York for collection to be remitted in gold or currency as you may direct. I also directed you to purchase another set of furs that Mrs. C and Mrs. A[dams] should have each a set, I have written to our good Br. Baker in regard to my dear children's board, and wished him to let you know if he would be willing to take $400 a year, which I learn is even higher than other small towns in New England, I do not by any means wish them taken from Mr. Baker, and hope at some future day to be able to raise the price again, he no doubt will communicate to you what I wrote him.

I beg you to give me a full statement of the finances you have in hand for my children, that I may be able to govern myself accordingly, their educational expenses will soon become an item which added to their clothes will run their income very hard.

With my kindest regards to Mrs. C[hamberlain], Br. [Rev. George] Adams and Family I

Remain Dear Sir most Respectfully
Your obt st.
Arthur Folsom

Arthur Folsom to JLC, 5/20/1868
Sylvain Salnave was the political leader of Haiti from May 1867 to December 1869. In April 1868, he suspended the national constitution and made himself president for life. The Cacos were peasants in the north of Haiti, who frequently attacked the cities and the capital, demanding social and political rights.

Cape Haytien May 20/68
Gov. J. L. Chamberlain
Brunswick Maine

My dear friend
I had this pleasure a few days before I rec'd your esteemed and kind favor of 16th Ult[imo], which informed me of the ending position of my children which I trust will have been only transient still I feel a little anxious to hear from you again.

I wrote you my prospects of a visit have been cut off by the revocation of my leave of absence in consequence of our intestine troubles, so far, or rather at present they are confined principally to the capital Port au Prince, there things are in a dreadful state, all business is suspended, the foreign consulates are full of refugees and are threatened to be violated by the mob, which are excited by the President Salnave, who was drawn there by a flash movement of the "Cacos" he near could have got there before them, had he not had the steamers at his command, but he is now hemmed in there on every side, except by Sea, he evidently cannot hold out long there but we hope the affair will be settled there, for if he returns then he knows he can hold out for an indefinite period, as the town is surrounded by inaccessible mountains, and can be easily defended, but he threatens to burn and destroy, and kill every one he can. before he gives up, send there is no doubt of his purpose and capability if some stray shot does not give us peace, he is the only obstacle, the "Cacos" say put in another President, and they will lay down their arms unconditionally, and i think they will, all respectable women are leaving Port au Prince for Jamaica no one consider themselves safe, even foreigners are threatened, we may look for a solution at any moment.

Very Truly Yours
A. Folsom

Since writing the above it is reported the contending parties have come to an agreement, and the "Cacos" agree to retire, no doubt if true he is to give up the Presidency, and I suppose a good indemnity, for money had always been his motive of action.

~

Mother to JLC, 2/18/1870
Mother Chamberlain wrote to update her son on the schooling of Wyllys, who was with her in Brewer. As governor, Chamberlain had to deal with two major issues in 1870. One was the Maine Law, which was a model of prohibition for other states. The other involved the highly controversial issue of capital punishment, which was raised when a black man killed a white woman and was sentenced to death.
Mrs. Chamberlain was thrifty with her use of punctuation.

Brewer 18 Feb 1870

My Dear Sir
I hope you are all well and happy. We are keeping now quite comfortably. Wyllys is pretty well and happy—much interested in his school and worried because Daisy is not going to school, regrets that he had not been sent to school sooner, but means to improve his time and have an education yet but shall never be a <u>Governor too hard</u> he is a boy of correct principles and will be useful in some place. I hope Daisy will never be a <u>foolish Miss</u> but a <u>whole woman</u> taking the right view of life, calmly meeting all the adverse changes to which we are all subject for I think such ladies are of infinite importance in the world. I see what they are doing in Augusta in regard to capital punishment am surprised, but have not a word to say, let them have it as they will. But on the liquor question I have much—the <u>terrible</u>, <u>dreadful</u> evil of <u>drunkenness</u> and I leave you to supply the language—for I cannot express one half that I feel, language fails me and do all in your power to prevent this cruel evil and save poor unfortunate men from becoming fiends. Who is so dangerous in community as a <u>drunken man</u>? I dare not trust myself where they are. I shall not write any more for you must know the danger as well as I beseeching you to do your whole duty to God and Man in this respect I leave the subject.

Father is now feeling rather poorly. He went to Otis about 20 miles distant. Rode home in the night. When he got home was almost insensible. Froze both hands one pretty badly. They seem to be doing well now so that he attends to business.

Sae's babe has been very sick (and is still but some better with the same cold cough that Wyllys had). Poor Sae has a hard time with her children, Wish I could be with her to help her. I hope you will all come home soon. I think we could entertain you at the old homestead now. Hadn't Daisy better come here and go to school in the city?

With much love to your wife and daughter
Your affectionate Mother

Dear Papa,
I hope you are as well as I am. I have just come home from school and have been running and my hand trembles so I can not write good. I am having a splendid time here in Brewer, and going to school and trying to learn as much as I can, and trying to be a good boy.

I can't write any more now because it is time to eat my dinner and go to school. So good by.

from your loving son,
Wyllys

~~~~~

Arthur Folsom to JLC, 2/21/1870

New York Feby 21/70
Gov. J. L. Chamberlain
Brunswick Maine

My dear friend
I had this pleasure a few days since,

I regret exceedingly to be compelled to importune you so often, but my necessities compel me, as the House is near being finished. Them are about $1500 now due, and hope you have been enabled to negotiate a loan on mortgage as I cannot get along without it, I did not collect a cent in Hayti because they had no funds yet but shall get it later and shall not want the loan long.

I am Dear Sir
your obdt st
A. Folsom

From Governor of Maine to President of Bowdoin

After serving four terms as Maine's governor (from 1867 to 1871) and choosing not to run for a fifth, the trustees of Bowdoin College asked Chamberlain that he again return to his alma mater, this time as its president. Though the vote was unanimous, it was a departure for Bowdoin since it meant that it would be led, for the first time, by a man who was not an ordained minister. Chamberlain accepted and was inaugurated at the commencement exercises of 1872.

JLC to Governor Coburn, 10/15/1872
Abner Coburn was governor of Maine in 1863–64 and then president of Skowhegan Savings Bank and the Maine Central Railroad. He was among the first people Chamberlain turned to when he began raising money to expand the role and curriculum of Bowdoin.

Brunswick, Oct. 15 1872

Dear Governor:
I rejoice at the good news of your recovering health.

May I not now use the privilege of a constant friend to advert to the great honor you can confer upon your name and the infinite blessing upon the state by establishing the school of higher scientific learning which I once proposed to you.

I will not weary you with my warmest regard and earnest prayers for your recovery.

Your friend J L C

The Great Count-Out Crisis of 1880

In September 1879, Mainers went to the polls in record numbers and overwhelmingly voted to give Republicans the governorship and three-fifths majorities in both houses of the state legislature. Daniel F. Davis, the Republican candidate for governor, had garnered nearly 69,000 votes, 49.6 percent of those cast, just 437 votes shy of a majority. His nearest competitor, the Democrat and incumbent governor Alonzo Garcelon, had received just 34.3 percent.

At the time, gubernatorial elections in which no candidate received a majority of votes became the responsibility of the legislature, with the House choosing two of the top four candidates and the Senate then choosing from these two.

Through a complicated and barely disguised scheme to reverse these results, Democrats "counted out" votes from towns where Republicans had held sway so that their reconfigured results showed that Democrats had won majorities in both houses of the state legislature, giving them control over the election of the governor.

The plan did not fare well among the people of Maine, and Governor Garcelon felt their wrath, receiving daily threats against his life. In fear of his life, he wrote to Chamberlain as the official head of the state militia, asking him to come to the capital at Augusta to "protect the public property and institutions of the state until my successor is duly qualified."

The arrival of the constitutional end of the term of office for the governor and legislature meant that Maine had no government and the state capital was under the military jurisdiction of the state militia, with Chamberlain as de facto military governor. These circumstances created a dangerous and volatile vacuum as both major parties sought to effectively seize power by any means they could conceive. James G. Blaine, the Republican U.S. senator considered the strong favorite to become U.S. President in 1882, called for "A great and popular uprising."[2] The arsenal at Bangor was loaded onto a train bound for Augusta while the Auburn Light Artillery brought a Gatlin gun.

Despite the open bribery by both major parties of offering Chamberlain a seat in the U.S. Senate if he should choose their side, he held fast, refusing to allow any governor to be sworn in until the state's Supreme Court could be seated and rule on the matter. His actions brought the ire of both sides, and many threats were made to kill or at least kidnap him.

Through it all, Chamberlain refused to use the militia in a show of force, fearing it would only exacerbate the situation, and he held to the rule of law throughout. Meanwhile, newspapers across the nation reported daily on the events as they transpired.

---

2 Bangor *Whig and Courier*, 12/20/1879.

In the end, the Supreme Court ruled in favor of the Republicans as the largest vote getters and the whole episode went down in the history books as the "Great Count-Out Crisis." Though it did some harm to his political standing in both parties, Chamberlain's actions in the crisis led to great praise from citizens across the country.

~~~

James H. Goodsell to JLC, 1/9/1880

Goodsell, president of the National Associated Press, wrote to Chamberlain to inquire about the crisis.

New York office Natl Assd Press Jan 9
145 Broadway New York

Maj Gen Chamberlain
Sir, great interest centers in Maine in order to allay apprehensions exposed by our editors throughout the country will you kindly delegate some one to telegraph me this morning statement of situation and prospects for publication if possible over your signature in order that public may know it is official.

Jas. H. Goodsell
Prest.

~~~

Edward H. Knight to JLC, 1/10/1880

Edward Henry Knight was the U.S. Commissioner General to the Universal Exposition of 1878 in Paris. Chamberlain served as the Commissioner for Education to the exposition. In the midst of the Count-Out Crisis, Knight was busy completing his report in an effort to get it to the publisher.

Washington, January 10 1880

My dear President and Major General,
I cry you mercy for bothering you with a matter which seems very small in 'comparison' with your present duties which go to the preservation of our

very form of government. Each fellow however to his duty and the "Report" is the main question with me.

I thank you for your letter of Dec 25th Glad you remembered me on Christmas Day.

Mr. W. W. Story's[3] report is all in type and yours goes next to the compositor. I send what I have today. I put in the interpolated sheets without difficulty, following your indicators in blue pencil as the head of each.

It bids fair to be very valuable, and is certainly very interesting.

When will the remainder come? What is the question and it really looks like "cheek" to interpose such a question in the turmoil of Augusta and Nevertheless I think you will forgive me the question if you can overlook my pen's so long undid about it.

I hope to send you proofs. Shall I direct to the armory, the president of the committee of Public Safety, or let us as peaceable citizens hope, the classic shades of Bowdoin?

Forgive me I pray and consider this all strictly unofficial as it is no joking matter.

My desire is to meet your wishes in the most direct manner and to testify that

I am as ever
Yours very truly
Edward H. Knight

~~~

Calvin Leavey to JLC, 1/11/1880

Bangor Jan. 11.1880

Dear General:

Let me congratulate you upon the proud position which you now occupy. You are a native citizen of M[ain]e and no man ever lived within her borders who possessed the power that you do today. You hold the keys of her noble institutions in your own right hand and by a word from your lips or a turn of your hand, those institutions may flourish and live, or they may fade and

---

3 William Story was the Commissioner for Fine Arts.

die. It is for you to say whether the will of the people shall be respected or not. I am a native citizen of Maine and I love her people and her institutions and every inch of soil within her precious. I know your history, and I rejoice in the belief that all will receive justice at your hands. By a divine command Moses led his people out of Egypt from the house of bondage, passed the Red Sea, and within sight of the promised land, when in consequence of the transgression of his people, they were turned back into the wilderness and there wandered about until the whole generation of offenders had died, and poor Moses was not allowed to enter the land of promise but merely to stand upon Mount Pisgah and view the rich and beautiful vales beyond. Well, you will not pass the Red Sea with your people. There will be no crimson waves to roll back that you may walk upon dry land, by no means. This matter will be settled in harmony and peace under your command. Joshua of old was a good commander, the sun in the heavens obeyed him and I have full faith in the modern Joshua as a commander.

Now my dear sir, you are aware that all eyes are upon you, not only of this state but everywhere throughout this broad land of ours, and though you seek no promised land as did Moses. Yes we all believe that you will seek the best manner possible to defend the land of your birth, and the rights of the people.

Yours with every sent of respect
Calvin Leavey

~~~~~~~

L. T. Forrest to JLC, 1/11/1880
A Bangor resident wrote his thoughts about the crisis in the form of a poem.

Prayer
For R. P. and G. [Ross, Pillsbury and Garcelon]
Descend and bring thy minstrelsy divine,
Misnamed, in ancient myth, the 'muses nine';
Instill mellifluous verse, indulgent skies;
Dispel the misty cloud before our eyes;
Insure a sweetly solemn Sabbath rest;
Imbue with tender love the aching beast;
With tears of sorrow, penitently shed,

We bow before the Lord reverent head.
Taunted with evil mocking, we forgive;
Implore the spirit holy let them live;
The arms secure that meant us cruel wrong
Epeaud the mischief hunts birds of song
Pour out on Freedom's air their loudest lay,
Remember Ross and Pillsbury when they pray,
O Lord thou knowest best what most they need,
Thy blessings on those Publishers we plead;
O Grant them grace not on discordant note
An honest motive when they count the vote
Give them a clearer sight a finer sense
That they may not defy Omnipotence
A gentle patient sweet believing heart
To each our fathers graciously impart
Stir warm affection for their brothers' good
And substitute for that a pleasant mood
Hear us O Lord we further wait on thee
Boundless in mercies vast and full and free
O condescend, through thy Beloved Son
Sprinkle the head of Doctor Garcelon
He needs thy smile seraphim as he
Chew him with hope of immortality;
Forgive his sins, his follies full atone,
His errors well confessed help us condone;
Correct his thoughts, conduct him safely through
The old returning board plane over new.
These favors Lord in pity on us pour
And we will sing thy praises forevermore

　　Theophilus
　　Bangor Jan 11, 1880

I shall not be at all disappointed if I you do not find time or patience to bear
with my instruction enough to give these introductions any notice whatever,
your time is so precious and duties now so ho—I'll fill it out as I begun it—
norous. Though I meant onerous; but I hope they will soon be by then. The
skies indeed are brighter. Peace, sweet blessed peace shall come again, and

we behold the glory of God wonderfully manifest, it seems to me, following this disturbance. I bid you good night

Truly yours
L. T. Forrest

~

Mary P. Clark to JLC, 1/11/1880
Mary P. Clark was a nurse who cared for Chamberlain at the U.S. Hospital at Annapolis after he was wounded at Petersburg. They remained friends after the war.

South Framingham
Jan 11th

My dear General,
With no small degree of mingled interest and anxiety have I contemplated the state of affairs with you—Now, new thoughts, new hopes and in as much as you have command and surely the people will take heed and trust in you, as they have before—you have always led them by the right way, a better than Moses, for he spoke 'unadvisedly' and this reminded me of what I read in the newspaper, that you would make no promise, not you, but they may be sure of the performance.

Now my dear General, while I deeply lament the cause of the strife for no one can love the dear old state or her dearer hero better than I do and for this I deplore to see her plunged even for the moment into such a vortex, yet in the midst of all, I thank God there is a man with head and heart, equal and reach for the unlooked for emergency.

God bless and prosper you in the undertaking and in blessing you, he blesses those where you are leading

Why not come to see us when matters are settle to your winch

With much love to Mrs. Chamberlain and to Miss Grace and Wyllys in which I am your loving friend

Mary P. Clark

~

G. T . Packard to JLC, 1/12/1880

George Thomas Packard was at Bowdoin, Class of 1866. He was an assistant minister in Brooklyn, New York, and a rector in Jersey City, New Jersey, before returning to Maine in 1875. In failing health, he took up newspaper work with the Boston Advertiser.

Brunswick, Maine Jan 12 1880

Dear General,

Can you take five minutes, from your time and write me the note to Mr. Evarts? I go to New York tomorrow when my address will be 937 4th Avenue—I am sorry to intrude upon you with a personal matter, which in the hurry of your departure you overlooked. If you could get me the letter by Sat and by night in N.Y. it would be entirely in season. The Boston Herald took up what I said about you in the "Nation" and says "Why not have both sides unite and make him Governor"! I put doctor of Laws on the envelope seeing you are showing yourself the good "Doctor" in not favoring bleeding for the patient, but rather rest and quiet. How Capt B. of the "Whig" and others have waked up to see you as you are![4] The "boom" for you is about the liveliest one ever in operation.

Forgive me for bothering you again.

Yours truly,
G. T. Packard-

Mr. Tenney's stationery ought to be counted out.[5]

S. S. Bright to JLC, 1/12/1880

Stevens Harris Maine
Jan 12th 80
To.
Maj. Genl. Chamberlain.

---

4 Charles A. Boutelle, originally from Brunswick, served in the Navy during the Civil War. In 1874, he and his partner B. A. Burr purchased the *Bangor Whig and Courier* newspaper. He later served in the U.S. Congress from 1882–1901.

5 A. G. Tenney was the proprietor of the *Brunswick Telegraph* newspaper.

My dear sir,

As an ex soldier and citizen of this common march, in view of the present situation of our state politically allow me to extend to you my hearty congratulations and gratitude also; for the able and patriotic manner in which you are performing the delicate duties of the important position you now occupy. I have had the extreme pleasure of meeting you a number of times socially. Being upon the occasion of the reunions of the Grand Army. An organization I am proud to be a member of. Though not a member of your immediate command during the dark days of the civil strife I followed well your course from my position in the 10 and 29 Maine regiments and do not hesitate to say that your whole military record is such as one as might well be the outgrowth of so true a life as yours has ever been. You can but feel assured that the people are with you and will aid your every effort to maintain the noble name of our dear old State. May God bless and protect you.

> Yours truly,
> S. S. Bright

W. S. Howe to JLC, 1/12/1880

Howe was a former captain in the 1st Maine Cavalry and a doctor in Pittsfield, Maine, who, in 1877, was charged with practicing homeopathy.

Pittsfield. Jan 12th 1880
Gen. J. L. Chamberlain

Dear Sir,

Pardon me Gen. for intruding on your time, but I wish to say when you took command as Governor and commander in chief there was heart felt joy went up from all true and loyal citizens of Maine and the country— all say we have confidence in Gen Chamberlain and he will bring us out of this difficulty. They must surrender and do and be right or be punished. As a party, we believe and know we are right then no <u>compromise</u> but stand firm to the front—God and truth has just such men as you to lead us up and out of trouble.

Mrs. Howe and family joins me in kind regards to you and she hopes you may get good rations and have more time to eat it than you had when at Pittsfield.

I am respectfully yours
W. S. Howe

~)

J. R. Libby to JLC, 1/13/1880

Biddeford Jan 13th 1880
Maj. Gen. Joshua L. Chamberlain
Augusta Me.

Dear Sir;

Permit me to take the liberty to show you my appreciation of your noble conduct and mark of true Stability, and pure manhood, you have thus far displayed in your present trying position in endeavoring to bring our State out of—not only a degraded but very dangerous condition, and I as a citizen subscribe myself ready and willing to abide by and help support the decision of the court be it for or against my party

Very Respectfully yours
J. R. Libby

~)

L. T. Carleton to JLC, 1/13/1880

Carleton was a lawyer in Winthrop, Maine, and county attorney for Kennebec County, which included Augusta.

Jan 13 1880

Dear General—

Permit me to hastily thank you for the noble and patriotic stand you take in this trying ordeal—it does my heart good to again read words of commendation of you in the public press. You have too long hidden yourself away from public gaze—let me assure you that the old time enthusiasm for you has not abated in the least

The people wait only for an opportunity to prove their love and respect for you—keep the conspirators against popular suffrage in check until such time as the courts shall determine this matter and your triumph will be complete

Very sincerely yours
L. T. Carleton

~~~~~

Samuel Harris to JLC, 1/13/1880
Harris was a graduate of Bowdoin, Class of 1833, and its president from 1867 to 1871. He left Bowdoin to become the chair of Systematic Theology at Yale University and was replaced by Chamberlain.

New Haven Ct Jan 13 1880

My dear General,
When I saw your appointment a year or more ago as Major General of the Maine Militia I was amused at the thought of your taking command of 8 or 10 scattered militia companies after commanding great bodies of soldiers in actual service. But to some men small positions are great opportunities; and so it seems to be in your case. I have greatly rejoiced that your position has called you to "see that the republican received no detriment" and that you have seen and used the opportunity for rendering this service. It must be gratifying to you, as indicating the confidence which people have in you to note the feeling of relief which your action has given to honest people of all classes—I have been hoping you would refuse to recognize the President of the Senate (so called) as governor and thus keeps the way open for an appeal to the court and am very glad this morning to see that you do not intend to recognize him. And I hope the issue will be the entire frustration of the plans of these usurpers. I have obtained all the information from all quarters that I could and the more I look into it, the more I am convinced that it is a monstrous usurpation. It rises above all interests and questions of political partisanship. It is one of the deadliest blows ever struck in this country at the life of republican institutions—it is a crime against civilization and human improvement. It seems to me to have been deliberately planned and carried through by unprincipled and unscrupulous men with the deliberate intent to frustrate the growing voice of the people under a hypocritical pretense of a

sacred regard to the constitution and laws. If the scheme can be thoroughly defeated it will be a warning against such attempts in the future but that cannot undo the immense evil which the recklessness of those selfish and ambitious men has already caused. I hope for the honor of my native state and I confidently believe that the honest and honorable men of all parties will depart the scheme—wishing great success in all your important and responsible positions, I am, with cordial regard sincerely yours,

Samuel Harris

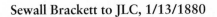

Sewall Brackett to JLC, 1/13/1880

Jan 13/80

Dear General
Thank God he we have a Moses and Joshua combined. Stand firm the morning light is breaking

Sewall Brackett

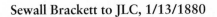

Cyrus Agustus Bartol to JLC, 1/15/1880
Bartol graduated from Bowdoin in 1832 and the Harvard Divinity School in 1835 and became pastor of the West Church in Boston.

Boston: 15. Jan. 1880

Dear General:
Let me express my deep and lively honor to you for your moral and intellectual as well as military mastery of the situation. May the good and great one keep you and my mother the state of Maine, and prays cordially yours

C. A. Bartol

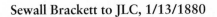

D. M. Shapleigh to JLC, 1/15/1880
Dennis M. Shapleigh was a lieutenant in the 27th Maine Infantry.

Kittery Me
Jan 15th 1880
Gen. Chamberlain

Dear Sir:
Permit me to say that the thinking portion of our town irrespective of party, congratulate themselves on having a safe man at the helm—one who places the honor of our staid old state of Maine above party lines—whose aim it is to "prove all things and hold fast that which is good" whose orders have no equivocal scope and whom sophistry or threats will not turn from his course one already crowned by fame.

Gen. Chamberlain we were never so proud of you as now—not even when you stood upon the boundary lines and received the surrender of our vanquished but brave foe. We are also fortunate in the man who represents us—who has the entire confidence of his constituents we hope for the best, and wait the decision of the Supreme Court with the honest determination to abide by it on whichever side it may turn, otherwise we should be wanting in the elements of an enlightened manhood as in the respect due the precedents of a noble ancestry.

That you may soon be able to return to your scholarly pursuits and that God will bless and prosper you is the sincere wish of your most

Obt. Servt.
D. M. Shapleigh

George M. Bodge to JLC, 1/15/1880
Rev. Bodge was a Unitarian minister in Dorchester from 1878 to 1884.

Dorchester Mass Jan'y 15th 1880

My dear General,

In this trying time we are all proud to know that in all the disgrace that is brought upon dear old Maine she has <u>one son loyal</u> and brave and true, to stand as a strong shield of her honor.

Be your own <u>best self</u> you <u>dear</u>, <u>splendid man</u>, I <u>can't help</u> writing this letter in token of my great thankfulness that <u>you</u> are <u>there</u> with your strong will and prepared to save and restore from the scoundrels who are bound to "rule or ruin the State"

God bless you,
I love you,
George M. Bodge

~~~

J. W. Chadwick to JLC, 1/15/1880

John White Chadwick graduated from Phillips Academy and Harvard Divinity School before becoming a Unitarian minister and educator.

Latin School
Boston, Jan 15, 1880
Gen. Chamberlain:

My Dear Sir:

At this time of severe trial, perhaps it may afford you some satisfaction to know how your acts are regarded in Boston. Permit me to say that having carefully observed the opinions of many of Boston's representative men, I have failed to find a single one who does not equally sympathize with you in your trying responsibilities, and fully support your position thus far taken. Without regard to party, or sympathy in other matters, all agree in commending the noble conduct of Gen. Chamberlain, and many a "thank God" is heard that there is in Augusta at the present time, a "man for the emergency." There is very little sympathy in Boston for the confusionists. Allow me to offer my personal congratulations that you have been thus far successful in keeping at bay the minions of anarchy and disorder. That God will spare your life till justice and order reigns in our beloved state, and reward your noble sacrifices, is the proffer of

Yours Very Truly,
J. W. Chadwick

~~~~

Solomon Payson Fay to JLC, 1/15/1880
Rev. Fay was a Congregational minister and missionary. He was a trustee of the
Bangor Theological Seminary from 1872 to 1901.

Calais Me Jan 15, 1880
Gen. J. L. Chamberlain

Dear Sir

Do not think it strange that so humble an individual as myself without even
a D. D.[6] should presume to write to one so loaded with titles of honor as
yourself, but I can't hold my pen fr[om]. letting you know how glad I am at
the course you have taken in this time of disgrace and danger to our dear
old commonwealth. Had you thrown the great shield put into your hand
just now over the men who are so wickedly trying to overthrow our republic
and tremble to think what blood shed might have been the result I am so
thankful. God has put power into the hand of one whose head is so clear
and strong and whose heart is so good.

I am down here for only a few days but I am here long enough to hear
praises enough of your course to satisfy the most extravagant lover of a
good name. I feel sure, my dear general, you will stand closely by the
decision of the Supreme Court. Every other path will certainly lead to
anarchy and bloodshed. I look upon it as a kind providence that put the
reins of power into your hand just at this critical time. God bless you my
dear sir and keep you true to the promises of liberty and of popular gov't.

Yours respectfully S. P. Fay

~~~~

---

6 Doctor of Divinity degree.

Walter M. Moses & Charles Moody to JLC, 1/15/1880
Moses was chairman of the Republican committee of Biddeford, Maine. Moody was president of the First National Bank of Biddeford.

Republican Headquarters
Biddeford Jan 15th 1880
Hon. Joshua L. Chamberlain

My dear Sir:
At a large meeting of the Citizens of Biddeford this evening we were instructed to express to you their approbation of your past course in your efforts to maintain the peace and good order within our state under the laws and constitution thereof and urge upon you the necessity of a "standing firm while standing well" and we hereby pledge ourselves to support you in every effort to secure the rights of the people as declared by the highest tribunal of our state, The Supreme Court. We also pledge ourselves to render all possible aid and assistance in executing the law as it may be declared by the said court.

Walt M. Moses Chairman
Chas A. Moody Sec'y

A. L. Pearson to JLC, 1/16/1880
Maj. Gen. Alfred L. Pearson commanded a brigade in the same division as Chamberlain during the last few weeks of the Civil War. Pearson was awarded the Medal of Honor for his actions at the Battle of Lewis's Farm, March 29, 1865. He understood what Chamberlain was dealing with. He had commanded a division of state guards during Pittsburgh's portion of the multistate "Great Railroad Strike" of 1877.

Pittsburgh, Jany 16, 1880
Maj Gen J. L. Chamberlain

My Dear Genl,
Allow an old army friend to compliment you on your course in the late and continued troubles in Maine.

The people of this end of Pennsylvania are high in their praise and I sincerely hope the result will be all you could wish for.

With many wishes for your continued success I am

Now as of old

Yours most truly

A. L. Pearson

~~~

Grenville Mellen Thurlow & B. D. Metcalf to JLC, 1/16/1880

Thurlow graduated from Bowdoin in 1861 and was principal of Lincoln Academy in Newcastle, Maine. He was married to Metcalf's daughter. B. D. Metcalf owned a shipbuilding business in Damariscotta and was a member of the Maine State Senate.

Damariscotta, Jan. 16. 1880

Gen. J. L. Chamberlain

Augusta, Me

My Dear Sir

The undersigning desire to express to you their high appreciation of the noble work you are so fearlessly doing for our state and assure you that the people will sustain you in enforcing the decision of the supreme court; whatever it may be.

Very respectfully yours

G. M. Thurlow

B.D Metcalf

Cut from the Boston Herald and endorsed by all honest loyal citizens. BDM

~~~

Horace Chandler to JLC, 1/16/1880[7]

Horace P. Chandler was the son of Peleg Whitman Chandler, Bowdoin, Class of 1834.

---

7 Harrisburg 1995.459.5.22

Jan 16 1880

Gen'l J L Chamberlain
My dear Sir: Allow me to add to what others are saying in unqualified praise
of your course in the present condition of affairs in Maine. You are right and
you know it and therein is your strength. They are wrong and they know it
and therein is their weakness. They wanted a casus belli and they developed
a casus juderis. The manner in which all decent people and most papers in
this State stand up for the position you have taken must be gratifying
indeed—and yet you have simply done your duty.

> Believe me
> Yours very truly
> Horace P. ChandlerM

~~~

J. C. Harris to JLC, 1/16/1880
*Harris was a member of another regiment in the same brigade as the 20th
Maine during the Civil War.*

> Gen'l J. L. Chamberlain
> Augusta, Maine
> Venango, PA Jan 16, '80

Dr Gen'l,
As a member of your old Brigade, and having had the pleasure of meeting
you in times "that try men's souls", and knowing of your efficiency and
bravery in every emergency allow me now to congratulate you on the
patriotism and finesse you have shown and to trust that you will yield to no
conspiracy now as then against the ballot box, or the expressed will of the
people.

> Yours & c.
> J. C. Harris
> (formerly of 83d P.V.)

~~~

J. H. Jordan to JLC, 1/16/1880

Portland Jan. 16th 1880
Hon. J. L. Chamberlain
Augusta Maine

Dear Sir
Stand firm the party will back you is it true that the militia is ordered out
by you as stated on 16th inst. D.H. Darius is the only true Governor of State
of Maine and the only one that we want. Hold the front.

Answer what you think of the prospect in regard to the settlement of
this trouble as soon as possible your faithful servant

General J. H. Jordan # 28 Cleaves St. Portland Maine

Francis Southworth to JLC, 1/16/1880

Rev. Southworth graduated from the Bangor Theological Seminary in 1856.
He was pastor of the Seamen's Bethel Church in Portland.

Portland Jan 16 1880

Dear Brother Chamberlain:
The reason that I have not written you is not that I am indifferent to your
trying situation and the most important position which has been assigned
you, at this perilous crisis by Him who loves us.

I see once more why you have been kept.

I have known that your every moment is occupied, and you had no time
to read letters, and all the points in the case that I could see are better seen
by you. But I could look up, with ten thousands, who are more with you
then any armed men, or insane men, who rush to the capital to help. I have
done what little I could to keep men quiet and at home. Have given them
one good text. "He that ruleth his spirit is better than he that taketh a city."

But I will not take your precious time, every moment of which is needed
for concerns, and for use. Take good care of yourself. Rest. The will of the
people are resting on you. May the blessings of the Omniscient be with you.

Truly yours
F. Southworth

~~~

N. Spofford to JLC, 1/16/880
Spofford was an engineer in Haverhill, Massachusetts.

Haverhill Jan 16 1880
Gen Chamberlain

Dear Sir

The thanks of every loyal citizen of this country are do to you for the courage and fealty to principle, that has characterized your conduct of the affairs of your state during the week past, but the great question to be decided will remain unanswered. Then to re-establish a Republican form of government for the state of Maine.

The present emergency of course has never been contemplated by your law makers, consequently you have no laws to meet it the supreme court cannot enact laws, therefore that is powerless in your care at this time. Please allow an outsider to suggest what you refer the matter to the only power that has authority to deal with it the Legal voters of the state of Maine

The supreme court of your state says "the right of self government is inherent in the people," consequently they can alter, amend, or totally abolish their government at any time when they choose.

The papers cause them trouble seem to be for the legal voters of your state to call town meetings throughout the state and elect delegates to a constitutional convention.

The convention meets organizes forms a new constitution, submits it to the people when ratified they choose a new governor and elect senators and representatives and all the votes are returned to the convention, and thus you will have a legally elected governor one grateful to call on the president of the United States for all military force necessary to protest the interest of your citizens from all green bank mobs.

If the people are not competent to deal with this question in this manner than Republican institutions are a myth, free government is a miserable farce, and the shortest road to despotism is the best one we can take.

Most respectfully yours
N. Spofford

~~~

R. W. Soule to JLC, 1/16/1880
Soule was a merchant in Augusta and treasurer of the Maine Insane Hospital.

Kent's Hill, Me. Jan 16 1880
Hon. Joshua L. Chamberlain
Augusta, Me.

Dear Sir—
I expect to visit Augusta tomorrow and several of our teachers will accompany me. I trust I shall not be asking too much of you to allow us passes to the House and Senate. I now hold a pass which you granted me last week but which is of no use now.

Very Truly yours,
R. W. Soule

~~~

J. F. Kingsbury to JLC, 1/17/1880
Kingsbury was assistant adjutant general in another brigade of the same division of the 5th Corps as Chamberlain during the Civil War.

Boston Jan 17 1880

My dear General
Your old comrades of the "Red Cross" Division of the 5th Corps[8] cannot fail to participate in the anxiety felt for your trying position in the Crisis which it seems possible will be reached today. Be assured for one of sympathy and encouragement and renewed administration for the course you have answered so nobly.

---

8 The symbol of the 5th Corps was a Maltese Cross, and the 1st Division used red as its color.

Yours truly
J. F. Kingsbury
a.a.g.
Maj'r Genl
Joshua L. Chamberlain
Augusta Me

~~~

J. Warren Brown to JLC, 1/17/1880

Brown was born in the tiny Downeast town of Kennebec, Maine, in 1832.
Raised in New York, he organized the Lebanon Mining Company and ran it for
its investors. He also managed the Cascade Mining Company, the Clear Creek
Mining and Improvement Company, and the Dunderberg Mining Company.

Washington, Jan 17th, 1880

General:

The events of this day in Maine must ever be memorable in its history. The
entire country is listening with great anxiety to catch from the electric wires
information of a peaceable settlement, in behalf of the right—of the
conflict—between an intellectual and nearly equally divided people of a State
heretofore noted for sobriety and wisdom in political management; and in
this unusual excitement it gives me great pleasure to hear the general and
unreserved expression of our public men and citizens generally that the
orders and papers recently issued by you could emanate only from a
statesman in whom the people may well rely for a proper and successful
termination of the conflict.

I am certainly very glad that Gov. Garcelon either in his blunder or
wisdom, designated you to perform so great a duty as that he committed to
your charge. I am also glad that you have the ability to demonstrate the fact
that the qualities of a great soldier and a great statesman can be combined
in one man.

It also pleases me to believe that the recent and present events in the state
will add to the chances of your political advancement to the U.S. Senate, in
relation to which I wrote to you a few months ago.

I hope that by this time entire success in the matter of a proper
adjustment of the contest is fully established.

Very respectfully,
J. Warren Brown
Gen. J. L. Chamberlain
Augusta,
Maine

~~⁀

Wm. Lester to JLC, 1/17/1880

Portland Jan 17, 1880
Gen'l Chamberlain

Dear Sir
In common with loyal Portland, my heart has been with you, and I have daily felt to write to you in your commendation.

Being fully satisfied that the acts of Gov. Garcelon in usurping the offices of the legislative and judicial were wrong, and that those of the fusionists were equally so, under their assumptions—was equally convinced that they and their acts would all fuse and come to dress in the judicial crucible.

There was left but one thing more for them to trust to the military. But with the right man in the right place, this, there last hope is gone.

With best wishes for you present and future well being

Most truly yours
Lester

~~⁀

Mary P. Clark to JLC, 1/17/1880[9]

South Framingham
Jan 17th

My dear General,
If, as in the olden time, that you and I remember so well, the sacred song of Praise "Glory to God in the highest" and on earth peace good will toward

---

9 See letter of 1/11/1880.

men took possession of our very hearts, what shall be said or sung at this crisis—for the glad teachings, the verdict of the court, has just reached me—how I would like to take you by the hand and very sure of the heart, say all I am prompted to, if your proceedings, which I have watched with clap indeed.

By your wisdom and prudence you have held the people in check until the hoped for result has come and it is indeed subject for thanksgiving and to you that have borne the burden of responsibility the judgment comes with deep meaning—you have maintained a royal firmness; a policy none purer or nobler exercising justice to all and acting in fear of one what more can man do for his troubled fellow men?

But I am writing more dear friend than you can need for I realize how strained body and brain must be. The tension has been a severe one and now do come for your dear self, and come to see us as soon as you can.

With earnest wishes for a continuation of 'peace' and 'good will.' I wish God bless you as always yours in loyalty and love,

Mary P. Clark

Nathaniel Waldo Emerson to JLC, 1/17/1880
Emerson graduated from and became an instructor at Boston University Medical School.

Boston, Jan 17, 1880
Pres. J. La. Chamberlain

Dear Sir,
As I am about to apply for a position as house physician in one of the Boston hospitals, it is necessary that I should present letters showing my moral fitness for the place. A letter from you, stating my standing in the class and college, would render me valuable assistance. You may have forgotten me, but I was a member of the present Senior class, and left at the latter part of the Sophomore year, to enter the Boston University School of Medicine, where I am still a student. My application is to be entered before the 25th inst.

I hesitate to address you, as I fully appreciate the value of your time, occupying the critical position which you do. A reply would greatly oblige,

Yours Very truly,
N. W. Emerson

Nelson A. Miles to JLC, 1/17/1880
Nelson A. Miles was colonel of the 61st New York during the Civil War. He was awarded the Medal of Honor for his gallantry at Chancellorsville in May 1863, where he was shot in the neck and abdomen.

Boston Mass
January 17 1880

Dear General
I congratulate you most heartily on your most important achievement. It has been accomplished without bloodshed and is most valuable in its results. It adds another honor and star to your splendid record.

The enclosed extracts will show you how your services and eminent abilities are appreciated by distant admirers and friends. I expect to return to the west very soon.

Very truly
Your friend
Nelson A. Miles

R. M. Jones to JLC, 1/17/1880
Jones was principal of the Oak Grove Seminary, a Quaker school in Vassalboro, Maine.

Philadelphia, PA
Jan 17, 1880

My Dear Sir,
I have watched your course through this crisis with intense interest, and last evening I could not forbear to touch the wire to assure you that my wife and brother have hearts to <u>feel</u>, and we can control our primaries. Our leading

morning paper "The Philadelphia Times" and our leading evening paper "The Evening Telegraph" both uphold your statesmanlike course. I look forward with dread to the future and think I can feel that our solutions politically must eventually be worked out, if worked out at all, by the cool heads. I have you in my mind as a man who has resolved to do his duty for God and country and leave the results to take care of themselves. In this course I believe Heaven will guide you and bless you. The scene on the opening day of the Maine Legislature dumfounded us all where partisans will lead us. God only knows what will become of us in a close Presidential Election. But I will write no more as I merely wanted to give you the assurance of my prayers and best wishes. With best regards to you and yours in which message my wife heartily join.

I remain yours faithfully,
R. M. Jones

~~~

Ellis Spear to JLC, 1/17/1880
Spear was a close friend of the Chamberlain family and a student of Chamberlain's at Bowdoin, and he commanded the 20th Maine during the Civil War longer than any other officer.

Washington, D.C. Jan 17th 1880

My dear General:
I must write you to add my word of congratulation, and my testimony as it what all good men send here are saying.

Your will and firm action has saved the state of Maine from anarchy, and I think will save it today. All the hope of the friends of good order and good government have been and are centered in you and find rest there. Although I know that the situation must be one which brings you great anxiety and a great burden of responsibility, I congratulate you. Such an opportunity does not come to every wise good and brave man, and does such a crisis find always such a man. I laughed when I saw and heard the threats against you.

The men who made them did not see you in the hell-fire of Petersburg. The country will not soon forget there new service. History will add them to the old and make the turn complete and such as you have paved yourself. "Every man in arms would wish to be"

Your friend
Ellis Spear

~~~

Whiting S. Clark to JLC, 1/17/1880
Clark was captain of Company E, 18th Maine Infantry Regiment, who later became a judge in Bangor before moving to Des Moines, Iowa, where he died in 1891.

Bangor Jan 17. 1880
Gen J. L. Chamberlain

Dear Gen'l,
I desire to congratulate you on the grand manner in which you have for the past ten days of tremendous public excitement done with the highest success the difficult and arduous duty devolving on you until we have again reached the solid ground of a constitutional and legal government. Today is a general holiday and day of jubilee here and your name is on the lips of every body equally with the court for services by which the peaceful result has been so well accomplished and everybody is according to you with the artful praise the highest credit

yours sincerely and truly
Whiting S. Clark

~~~

William A. Blossom to JLC, 1/17/1880[10]
Blossom was a court clerk who was prominent in the Order of the Eastern Star, a fraternal and charitable organization founded in 1860 by Dr. Rob Morris, the "poet laureate of masonry."

---

10 Harrisburg 1995.459.5.39

Boston, Jan 17th 1880
Maj. Gen. J L. Chamberlain

Dear Sir

Please accept the sincere thanks of a son of Maine for your manly and patriotic action during the few weeks just past.

Although a resident of Massachusetts for several years I cherish a feeling of deep regard for my nation state and take a lively interest in her affairs.

I feel that a bloodless solution of the difficulty which has existed in Maine is due to your ability, foresight, firmness, and integrity.

I am Sir
Very respectfully and truly yours
William A. Blossom

Helen E. Kilham to JLC, 1/18/1880
Kilham was a significant figure in the so-called "Woman's Club Movement" in Massachusetts in the latter part of the nineteenth century.

Huckins Avenue
Roxbury, Jan 18th 1880
Gen Chamberlain

Dear Sir

The good news we received this morning from Maine has put me in such high spirits that I cannot forbear congratulating you, who are indeed a worthy namesake of Joshua of old and like him selected to overcome all obstacles and lead the chosen ones into the promised land. I must indeed be fatally destitute of the power of making myself understood. If the homage I render to your merit and nobility does not occupy a prominent place among the things which you do not put at liberty to doubt. I have never wavered in this article of my faith since I had the honor to meet you at Brunswick during the years the class of '33 had their reunion. At which class I am a descendant. It must gratify you extremely to know of the admiration in which you are held by all classes at home and abroad. You have by your strength, delicacy and finesse, saved your Rome. A noble man is always ambitious to be great by doing right. Noblesse oblige! And I know you only feel that you have done your duty and would find aside from your bow the laurel crown with which a grateful people should act on you. His appreciation is sweet, and you ought to know that we who are the children of Maine, glory in you. I trust that all petty jealousies and quarrels will be laid aside, that nothing may paralyze your wonderful resources and betray such a brilliant termination you are already raised above other men by the victories you have won. But you rely on will lift you above yourself. We see it is possible for a man to be at once a statesman, a soldier, a scholar, a gentleman and a Christian. To have the gentlest and most thrilling pursuits, and to execute them with the loftiest equity and the most vivid like modesty. Pray do not think me wanting in the letter sweet quality. Rare deeds call for unusual recognition.

With sentiments of the highest consideration
I am sir
Yours sincerely
Helen E. Kilham
Gen J. L. Chamberlain

~

James B. Hayes to JLC, 1/18/1880
Chamberlain was a member of Alpha Delta Phi fraternity while a student at Bowdoin.

Cambridge Mass 1880
Brunswick Jan 18

Gen J. L. Chamberlain
We count upon your presence at the Alpha Delta Phi dinner on Thursday are we right in doing so? Pray come if it be possible

James B Hayes
President

~

Mrs. Wetshire A. Burr Baker to JLC, 1/18/1880

Gen. Chamberlain,

Dear Sir,
Please accept our congratulations for the Laurels recently won in our Native State at Augusta.

You are invited to Concord the 21st of this month. We hope you will come and we would be most happy to entertain you at the Phenix Hotel, <u>our home</u> in New Hampshire.

Yours, truly,
Mrs. Wetshire A. Burr Baker
Concord, Jan 18, 1880

Owen W. Davison to JLC, 1/18/1880
O. W. Davis, Jr. was the treasurer and manager of the Katahdin Iron Company, a charcoal, pig-iron producing operation in the center of Maine. He was Bowdoin, Class of 1864.

Bangor, Me., Jan 18th 1880
Hon J. L. Chamberlain

Dear Sir
Few men in history have had the opportunity of demonstrating the worth of personal certitude and independence of character like this that has fallen to you and I trust you will give me the privilege of writing that I sincerely believe that few men have ever proved more worthy of the occasion.

Yours Respectfully
O. W. Davis, Jr.

Richard C. McCormick to JLC, 1/18/1880
McCormick was governor of Arizona Territory from 1866 to 1868 and a member of the U.S. House of Representatives from 1895 to 1897. He was U. S. Commissioner General to the Paris Exposition in 1877, the year before Chamberlain served on the same commission.

New York, Jan 18 1880

My dear sir—I wish to add my congratulations to those of your many friends upon your most judicious and successful management in the very important, and critical position you have held in the tale of Maine for several weeks past. Beyond all dispute you have proven yourself "the right man in the right place," and the friends of law and order owe you a debt of gratitude

    Very truly yours
    Richard McCormick
    Gen J. L. Chamberlain

W. L. Putnam to JLC, 1/18/1880
W. L. Putnam was a judge on the Circuit Court of the United States.

Washington, D. C. Jan 18 1880

My dear sir
I am not willing to let the [Bowdoin] reunion pass without congratulating you although briefly upon the honorable stand in which you have carried yourself through the crisis in Maine. You have preserved the peace and yet have carefully at all times shown an intention to raise the law above force and have strictly and according to laws carried out the orders of it.
Late governor
be you

    W. L. Putnam
    Gen. J. L. Chamberlain

Lewis Pierce to JLC 1/19/1880
Pierce was a classmate of Chamberlain's at Bowdoin before graduating from Harvard Law School in 1855. He served in the Maine legislature and was a fellow in the Maine Historical Society.

Boston Jan 19 1880

My Dear Genl,
Just a word to tell you how glad we all are that you had the reins at the critical moment. Looking at it from this distance it seems to us that no other man could have prevented bloodshed—I congratulate you most heartily—Mrs. Pierce—who is still confined to the bed reads all the papers and rejoices that Maine has such a son.
    With sentiments of the highest esteem and regard

    Very truly yours
    Lewis Pierce

Charles Nason to JLC, 1/19/1880
Nason was a Methodist Episcopal clergyman who served as the chaplain of the 2nd Maine Cavalry during the Civil War.

Woonsocket, R.I. Jan 19th 1880
Hon J. L. Chamberlain

My Dear Sir:
My heart and mind have been drawn toward you for many days, but did not feel at liberty to ask for one moment of your valuable time and attention. Now the great anxiety has passed I want to thank you, and to thank our Heavenly Father for sustaining you in the discharge of your difficult and responsible duties. Although I am a stranger to you I am a native of Maine and have watched with intense anxiety the conflict through which you have passed. This mornings news allays my serious fears. My mind has been many times turned to the follow words within these anxious days whenever I thought of you. You may smile at my application of them, but they have been strongly impressed up on me.

"If thou altogether holdest thy peace (or failest to do thy duty) at this time then shall there enlargement and deliverance arise to the Jews (citizens of Maine) from another place, but thou and thy fathers house shall be destroyed: and who knoweth whether thou art come to the kingdom (the command) for such a time as this?" Esther 4:14

Although I am an Armenian yet I have an unwavering faith that all the ultimate purposes of God will be accomplished whether with or without the cooperation and sympathy of any particular individual. Further, that if we withhold our cooperation in the accomplishment of the Divine purpose it will bring upon us the Divine displeasure. It seems to me that yours, has in a marked manner, for a few weeks past been a wonderfully Providential position, which I call Divine whether the Fusionists will call it Divine or give it some other name I will not say. Time will give them better views than they have been recently entertaining

Very truly yours,
Chas. Nason

P.S. I have the pleasure of an acquaintance with your old chaplain Luther P. French, and had the honor of serving as chaplain in the 2 M[ain]e Cav[alry] under Col. Woodman.
C.N.

~~~

Geo. Sumner to JLC, 1/19/1880
George True Sumner was Bowdoin, Class of 1866. A veteran of the 26th Maine Infantry, he was later a lawyer and district attorney in Wisconsin.

Sheboygan, Wis Jan 19 1880
Gen. Joshua L. Chamberlain
Brunswick Maine

Dear Sir,
I have spoiled some paper in trying to express in something like an adequate shape, the thanks, which, in common with everybody else worth counting, I feel, that a benign Providence lately placed you at the helm in Maine. The view of the occasion even those loose fibered men whom no touch of hero

worship ever makes foolish might be pardoned for confessing to an electric thrill or two. Those who have never read of a brave and modest deed without wet eyes, in addressing you now, are in danger of saying more than you will consider becoming. But I will merely say that you have done what any honest man, built right for it, would have done under the circumstances. You could have done not otherwise. Therefore we sons of Bowdoin and of Maine will thank God only, and but love thee.

Yours truly
Geo. Sumner

~~~~

John H. Jarvis to JLC, 1/19/1880

John H. Jarvis was the father of Delia Jarvis, who married John Chamberlain and, after she was widowed, married his brother Tom Chamberlain.

69 Essex St
Bangor January 19th, '80
Genl Joshua Chamberlain

My Dear Sir,
I congratulate you on being so successfully relieved from the arduous duties which have devolved upon you as settlement to our Ship of State under such trying circumstances. The impartiality, firmness, and prompt decision which have been so prominent in your last official capacity have won for you hosts of friends, and not one dissenting voice have I heard from the separated expression. God bless you. Our good pastor Dr. Field[11] pronounced a most delighting, complimentary eulogy (in his yesterday morning discourse before his people) on you, for the exemplary manner in which you had performed your duty in your recent trying situation, and all the people in their hearts said,

Amen.
Yours very truly,
John H. Jarvis

~~~~

---

11 Rev. George W. Field.

John W. Atwell to JLC, 1/19/1880

John W. Atwell was a veteran of the First Maine Heavy Artillery and a state senator of Maine in 1880. Just after the crisis ended, he resigned from the state militia staff of General Chamberlain.

> Augusta Jan, 19th 1880
> Maj Gen Joshua L Chamberlain
>
> Dr Sir
> Complications having arisen since accepting the honor of an appointment on your staff not at that time anticipated.
>   I hereby resign that position. To take effect on rec't of this communication. With much res. for you personally
>
> I have the honor
> Yr. most obt, Rt hon Servt
> To remain John W. Atwell

Lewis A. Parker to JLC, 1/19/1880

Parker was a lifelong resident of Brunswick.

> Brunswick Jan 19/80
>
> Dear General
> I hope you will pardon me, if I weary you with a few lines. But feeling anxious for you as well as the Republican Party. I thought, I would drop you a line to let you know that we stand ready to help you in case you need anymore men, and I know that you will rule in this case as wisely as you have Governed in the past, and I stand ready to lend you my service at a moment. Notice even in the very jaws of death I would stick by you. When I know you are engaged in the cause of the right and if there is anything I can do, I should be pleased to serve you and I have no doubt but we could raise a company here in two hours notice, should you need them. I am to work for Mr. Greene this winter in the mill and I feel proud that I always voted the republican ticket and now may God bless you and guide you in the future as he has in the past.

I am nothing but a poor mechanic but I want to see justice executed—and now Dear Gen'l you have my best wishes and I would cheerfully do all I could to help the right cause and may He who doeth all things well guide and direct you now and forever.

Your most humble, and obed't serv't
Lewis A. Parker
Brunswick, Maine

~~~

George E. B. Jackson to JLC, 1/20/1880
George E. B. Jackson was the president of the Maine Central Railroad.

Portland, Me., Jan. 20 1880

My dear sir,
Please accept the enclosed annual[pass] over this [rail]road, as a slight recognition of what seems to me as valuable services to the State as it has ever fallen to the lot of any one citizen to render, and believe me

very faithfully yours
Geo. E. B. Jackson
Prest.
Maj. Gen. Chamberlain
Brunswick

~~~

Edward H. Knight to JLC, 1/20/1880
Commissioner Knight reiterated his request for Chamberlain to submit his report of the Exposition (see letter of 1/10/1880).

Washington January 20, 1880

Dear General:

I am glad and the whole country—all that is decent in it—is glad, so I am in good company at the result of your masterly activity in Maine. My voice does not go for much however.

Your report is now going into type and I am anxiously looking for the remainder. As you are reported as having gone home to Brunswick I have hopes that like Cincinnatus you will plow to the end of the furrow.[12]

My modest sense of propriety bids me add that I could hardly annoy with reminders but that Gov McCormick spurs me on to ask questions.

Yours very truly
Edward H. Knight
Maj. Gen. Chamberlain
Brunswick, Me.

George Parsons, Jr. to JLC, 1/20/1880
George Parsons, Jr., Class of 1876 and a banker, wrote to invite Chamberlain to a Bowdoin reunion in New York.

New York, 20th Jan. 1880

My dear General,

I desire to congratulate you upon the success of your management during the past few weeks of excitement in Maine. I could hardly believe we had so many ill-bred men in the State as have turned up at this time; but thanks to you they have received their just deserts.

I have had two objects in view in watching these proceedings—the good of the State and the success of our Annual Reunion which takes place soon.

We hail the adjustment of the State affairs with the greatest possible satisfaction; and now count on the pleasure of your presence at our dinner. I have written to Prof. [Alpheus] Packard urging him to join us and wish it

---

12 Cincinnatus was a Roman hero who left his farm to become dictator of Rome when it was under threat by invasion and then abandoned his title and absolute power at the conclusion of the crisis.

might be prudent for him to come on. However, that is a matter for him and his friends to decide. You know how much pleasure it would give us all to have him with us. Dr. Goodwin and Dr. Allen will be present.[13]

I enclose two invitations and would ask you to hand them to any of your associates on the faculty who may be able to come. We would be glad to have more of them come but feel sure that they could not be spared during term time.

We have made arrangements for you to stop at the West Minster Hotel. With kindest regards to your family

I remain
Sincerely yours
George Parsons Jr
P.O. Box 79

~~~

Hiram K. Morrell to JLC, 1/20/1880

Morrell was a member of the Maine Historical Society and editor of a temperance journal. He was also publisher of the Gardiner Home Journal.

Gardiner, Me., Jan 20 1880
Gen J. L. Chamberlain

Brunswick
Dear Sir—We shall be pleased to be honored with the attendance of yourself and lady at our reception of the Maine Press Association on the evening of Thursday, the 29th.

Yours Truly,
Mr. and Mrs. H. K. Morrell

~~~

---

13 Daniel Raynes Goodwin was librarian and professor at Bowdoin College before he became president of Trinity College in 1853. Stephen Allen, Bowdoin, Class of 1835, was a teacher and Methodist minister in several Maine towns and an overseer of the college from 1860 to 1888.

Jotham B. Sewall to JLC, 1/20/1880

Jotham Bradbury Sewall was in Bowdoin's Class of 1848 and was professor of Rhetoric and Oratory, then Greek and Latin at Bowdoin from 1865 to 1877. He was teaching at Thayer Academy in Braintree, Massachusetts, in 1880 (see JLC to Fannie, 2/21/1853).

South Braintree, Mass., Jan 20, 1880

My dear Mr. President

I should do wrong both to my own impulse and your high desert if I did not communicate in a mood to you, now that we all breathe freer, my warmest congratulations upon the manner in which, by the grace of God, you were able to carry through affairs in the interrogate between Garcelon and Davis. It was a very critical time, and a very responsible position, but, thank God, you carried it through with firmness, even handed justice, self-forgetfulness and dignity. You have gained to yourself great honor, and deserve and have, I am sure, the heartfelt gratitude of every son of Maine and lover of his country.

>   Most truly
>   yours
>   J. B. Sewall
>   Gov. J. L. Chamberlain
>   Brunswick, Maine

J. H. Ecob to JLC, 1/20/1880

James Henry Ecob was a pastor in Augusta in 1880 and an overseer of Bowdoin College.

Augusta, Maine
Jan. 20th 1880
Pres. Chamberlain,

My Dear Sir,

Allow me to do myself the pleasure of joining with the thousands of your fellow citizens in the state and country in thanking you for the noble services which you have rendered us. The church, the college, the state, are one in their grateful acknowledgements, and will hold in lasting remembrance that steadfast courage and prudence and skill which held us in the hour of our perilous crisis.

Hoping the best things for both state and college in the future. I am very sincerely yours

J. H. Ecob

~~~~~

J. W. Dresser to JLC, 1/20/1880

John W. Dresser was a merchant in Castine, Maine, dealing in "Chandlery and Naval Stores."

Castine, Jan 20 1880

Dear General

I cannot refrain from saying, that our best citizens express most strongly their appreciation of the wisdom that which have charactering your every act during the events of the past few weeks.

There is more than an abiding desire in all our hearts that you should fill a high place in the councils of the nation—that that day may not be very far distant prays also.

Yours faithfully
J. W. Dresser

~~~~~

Franklin M. Drew to JLC, 1/20/1880

Drew was an attorney in Lewiston, Maine. A veteran of the 15th Maine Regiment, he achieved the rank of brevet colonel.

Lewiston, Me., Jan 20th 1880

Dear Governor:

The papers report you at home once more. I congratulate you upon having been able to conquer a peace and make it safe and proper for you to leave the capitol. I think it is in the hearts of many people to believe that it was a providence of God that you was just in command at Augusta when Gov. Garcelon retired. If no provision had been made or a weak man had been put in command I fear the state would at this time be involved in civil war. I do not see how you could have done better. Your acting has been so far above mere partisanship that it commands the admiration and commendation of the best men of all parties. Your many friends here are enthusiastic over your conduct—they say you must be made Senator next winter. If that question could be determined now it would only require your assent to make it certain. How much the ring politicians can do to defeat this popular feeling time only can share. I hope and trust the people will prove the stronger.

The Department of Maine Grand Army of the Republic will hold its annual session here Thursday the 29th inst—the post here proposes to give a banquet in City Hall in the evening of that day to the inviting commandery and we desire very much for you to be present and respond to the toast "our country" "our state" or any toast you may prefer to raise to. If you can come I think you will receive a reception from the army boys, and the people of Lewiston which will be grateful to you. We, Mrs. Drew, Mrs. Record and I shall be delighted to have you take Mrs. Chamberlain and come to our house. We all want to see you. I hope you will be able to come.

In haste
F. M. Drew
Gen. JL Chamberlain

John D. Philbrick to JLC, 1/20/1880
Philbrick was superintendent of Boston Schools and a member of the Massachusetts Board of Education.

Asylum Station
Danvers [Massachusetts]
Jan 20 1880
Gen. J. L. Chamberlain

My dear sir,

I beg to tender you my most congratulations on your good fortune. Others by thousands will congratulate you on your great success in the conspicuous part you have acted in saving your State from anarchy and bloodshed, and the whole country from political disgrace. But I congratulate you on the possession of the qualifications adequate to the occasion and this is what I mean by good fortune. Without any personal knowledge of your character, this remarkable performance would have led me, or it must lead the whole country to infer your superior cast of mind. But knowing something of your characteristics when I saw that you were in command, I knew that there was a master at the helm, and I had confidence that the ship would weather the storm. Knowing the character, I had no doubt about the conduct. The whole nation has now seen the conduct and knows how to appreciate the character behind it. Others as politicians and jurists, no doubt, did well, but you did supremely well in the gravest situation, which demanded something more than political or judicial ability.

Should the people come to the conclusion that there is a college president in this Pine Tree State who would make a first rate President of the Federal Union my confidence in their sagacity would be considerably increased.

I should be more inclined to accept the democratic matter. Vox populi vox dei.

Knowing how very much esteemed friend Bussier looked upon you as a model representative American, I have sent him newspaper clips giving an account of your Dictatorship of Twelve Days and it's happy issue.

Yours very truly
John D. Philbrick

~~~

L. S. Metcalf to JLC, 1/20/1880
Metcalf was editor of the North American Review.

Boston 20 1880
Brunswick Jan 20th

Gen Joshua L. Chamberlain
Where can I see you a moment tomorrow or where Thursday. [telegraph]
Answer [will be] paid Youngs Hotel Boston.

L.S. Metcalf
North American Review

⌒⟩

Stephen M. Allen, 1/20/1880
Allen was Bowdoin, Class of 1835, and an overseer of the college for twenty years. He was a close friend of Fannie prior to her marriage to Chamberlain, and his son Horace married the Chamberlains' daughter Daisy in April 1881.

Niagara Falls
Jan 20 1880

My dear sir
I have been here and in Wisconsin during your troubles in Maine. I have of course heard and read much. I have heard nothing but in your favor from all true patriots. I congratulate you and your success in keeping the peace, establishing order and the right rule. You have certainly been entitled to the gratitude of the whole country, and the people will no doubt remember your service. Hoping that you and the family are well and that you are feeling happy in this additive service to your country. I am sincerely and proud

Stephen M. Allen
Gen J L Chamberlain

⌒⟩

Thomas P. Burnham to JLC, 1/21/1880

Biddeford Jan 21st 1880
Maj. General Chamberlain

My dear sir
It was suggested by one of our senators during the executive of last week that several of the republicans of this city express their feelings to you by brief letters. With other I did so render of the 13th but by neglect it was not mailed. But to make amends for the same and remembering proverb "better

late than never" my thoughts to you though on the subject will by found in the element *Union and Journal*.[14]

Yours in the highest esteem
Thomas P. Burnham
a Private Citizen

~~~

John T. Hostler to JLC, 1/21/1880
Hostler was a veteran of the regiments that served under Chamberlain's command during the last year of the Civil War.

Lawton Mich
Jan 21st 1880
Major Gen Joshua L. Chamberlain
Brunswick Me

Dear General
I have read with great satisfaction of the admirable manner in which you administered affairs during the recent troubles in your state. I send you greetings.

Yyours with the highest regard
J. Hostler late Capt. 185 NYV 1st Brig 1 Div
5 A.C. A.of P

~~~

James Henry Taylor to JLC, 1/21/1880
Taylor was Bowdoin, Class of 1856, and Union Theological Seminary, Class of 1859. He was a professor at several colleges in his home state of New York.

Rome, N. Y.
Jan. 21. 1880

---

14 The *Union and Journal* was published from 1877 to 1930.

My dear sir;

Allow me to congratulate you on the impartiality equanimity courage and success with which you have controlled affairs at Augusta. Your course has commanded universal respect. If I could control the Chicago[Republican National] convention I know well what I should do.

> Very truly yours
> James H. Taylor
> Class of 56

~~~

Kenny C. Bowens to JLC, 1/21/1880

An inquiry from the Independent, *a weekly newspaper based in New York City, which advertised itself as "The ablest religious, literary and family newspaper in the world." Despite the crisis in Augusta, Chamberlain's role as president of Bowdoin College did not allow him to sit idle.*

New York January 21 1880
J. L. Chamberlain L. L. D.
Brunswick Me

Dear Sir,

It will be seen by the enclosed that our club rates for give new subscribers is now $2.00 per annum. The success of a spontaneous movement in another institution started without our knowledge has resulted so well that it has occurred to me that the mere mention of these low terms to your students would induce them to subscribe in large numbers. If you will kindly place this matter in the hands of some trusty young man we will agree to give him one copy of the paper free for one year for every ten subscribers sent us. We will supply circulars and sample copies of The Independent without any charge. Pardon me this liberty and believe me very respectfully

> Yours,
> Kenny C. Bowens

~~~

Peter E. Vose to JLC, 1/21/1880
Vose was a Deacon in the Congregational Church in Dennysville in easternmost Maine.

Dennysville Me Jan 21 1880
Hon. J. L. Chamberlain

Dear Sir
From your many titles I select that of "honorable" as being perhaps as befitting as any.

It was my good fortune to meet you a few years ago at the house of a friend in this place. I should be most happy to see you again and give you my hand, with my heart in it. I express as a citizen of Maine as I do now gladly—joyfully—my profoundest thanks for the steadfast, constant, courageous, honorable and judicious course you have pursued in carrying out the powers and responsibilities conferred upon you by a recent governor of Maine. I cannot help the belief (I rejoice to believe so) that the Providence of God had to do with placing you in the "gap" which, perhaps, no other man in the state can fill so well, and I doubt not that many a prayer has gone up to him from the hearts of the good men and women of the state that you might receive all needful divine aid in the performance of the arduous responsible duties devolving upon you in these darkest and most critical days of the state's history.

The consciousness of duty well-performed gives satisfaction, but I trust the grateful words and acts of the people whom your strong hand and single purpose and earnest endeavor under God preserved from harm and loss will add largely thereto.

Pardon this epistle, but I wished at least to say, "God bless the State of Maine" and God bless and keep Gen. Chamberlain

Very respectfully yours
Peter E. Vose

Truman A. Merrill to JLC, 1/21/1880
Merrill was a classmate of Chamberlain's at the Bangor Theological Seminary and a Congregational minister in Massachusetts.

Wayland Mass.
Jan 21, 1880
Joshua L. Chamberlain,

Dear Sir,
Permit one who had the honor of being born in the State of Maine, (though a resident for 16 years in Mass[achusetts]) to express to you his high appreciation of your services in the exceedingly critical and trying times through which the good state of Maine has just past. I have been watching the events which have there occurred these 60 days past with profound interest. I have expected a bloody collision. Believing that this has really been prevented by your firmness, sagacity and wisdom and that to you more than to anyone else the people of Maine are indebted for the preservation of their liberties; and the lovers of law and order everywhere for the prevention of anarchy. I cannot refrain from troubling you with this note of thanks. I believe that every word of this slip which I clipped from the Journal is <u>true</u>. So I need say no more with reference to the obligations of the public to one who in a time of great public emergency and excitement came to the rescue and secured order and safety.

I do not suppose the <u>end</u> is yet. It is a <u>deep laid plot</u>. It is a thing in which not alone the state of <u>Maine</u> is interested. We wait the developments of the future with anxiety. I wonder what the Republicans of Maine have been about that for their punishment the people would vote the power out of their hands as they did in 1878? What sins have the leaders been committing that they deserve such a penalty? I hope the leaders will learn a lesson and show a little more wisdom and common sense in the future.

It is a rebuke to the spoils system of rewarding men for mere party services by important offices irrespective of their qualifications or character. All honor to Geo. William Curtis and such as he.

Now my Dear Sir, you may have forgotten me, in the important public affairs in which you have been engaged since our graduation from the Seminary in Bangor in <u>1855</u>. So I will only say that since that time my poor services have been given to the church and through it to the moral and religious imprisonment of the world.

But so little have I accomplished that I feel that my life has been a failure. And yet I am living very contentedly among kind and pleasant parsonages who are at least very forbearing. From my quiet nook I send hearty greetings to the man who <u>conquers rebels</u> in Virginia; preserves the power in Maine and teaches the boys in Brunswick to talk English and walk Spanish.

Truman A. Merrill—Pastor

～)

Alpheus S. Packard, Jr. to JLC, 1/22/1880
The son of Professor Alpheus Packard, Sr., of Bowdoin College, wrote to congratulate Chamberlain on his handling of the crisis.

Providence Jan. 22. 80.

My dear Sir,
Allow me to congratulate you on the successful result of what is generally believed to be largely due to your moderation firmness and moral courage. It is to be hoped that we shall have men of the scholar in state and national affairs. I send a rather bright speech of Prof. Diman's learning on this point.

With best wishes
Yours most truly,
A. S. Packard, Jr.

～)

G. K. Warren to JLC, 1/22/1880
Chamberlain's former commander wrote to express his congratulations and ask for information that he needed for a military court of inquiry to clear his name and restore his reputation (see letter of 1/2/1880).

Newport, R. I., January 22 1880
Maj. Gen. J. L. Chamberlain
Brunswick Me.

My dearest General
I have been in common with others watching with much interest your responsible position in your state, and now congratulate you for the success

which has attended your guardianship of the public property and your relief from its trying responsibilities.

I could not help feeling all the time however that you were a man that could be safely trusted for intelligence fearfulness and good judgment.

My Court of Inquiry has adjourned to await the return of Gen Sheridan who has gone southward on a sick leave.

Can you tell me approximately what the strength of 198th Pa and the 185th N.Y vols of your brigade was at the Five Forks, and that of the 187th 188th and 189th NY vols of Gregory's Brig[ade]. were. I want to know about the front they would cover in line of battle.

Yours truly
G. K. Warren

Isaiah Trufant to JLC, 1/22/1880
Trufant was Bowdoin, Class of 1863, and the principal of the Miami Classical and Scientific School for Boys, which later became Miami University in Ohio.

Oxford, Ohio. Jan. 22. 1880

My Dear Sir:
I have followed, from day to day, the changing scenes in my native state, with great interest; in which scenes you have been the chief actor. I wish now to express my high appreciation of your services in the trying situation in which you have been placed. Yours has been the hand which stilled the storm. The attention of the whole country has been upon you, and all honest men feel that you have done your whole duty without fear or favor. Here in Ohio we have watched your course with ever increasing admiration; and at times, it seemed to us, at this distance, that it would be impossible for you to avoid anarchy or bloodshed; but thanks to your wisdom, we have seen the dark clouds dispelled; and law and constitutional government again established in Maine. I have heard many highly complimentary things said of you personally here in the West. You have surely come to the front as one of the most prominent men, if not the prominent man in the "Pine Tree State." I have heard men of prominence here declare their preference for you as a candidate for the

Presidency of the nation, while all feel you have deserved well of your country. From the time you appeared on the scene at Augusta, I felt the destiny of Maine was in safe hands and I have not been disappointed.

That you may receive the appreciation due you patriotic services is the wish of your friends.

Isaiah Trufant
Maj. Gen. J. L. Chamberlain
Brunswick
Maine

~

M. A. Farwell to JLC, 1/22/1880

New Orleans, Jan 22nd 1880
Hon J L Chamberlain

My Dear Sir
As a citizen of Maine absent from the state I wish to express to you my thanks and congratulations upon your impartial and judicious management of the time of the mutiny of the Legislature I think to your skilful management we are indebted for a peaceful settlement of the trouble growing out of the fraudulent conduct of our late Gov and his council.

Yours truly
M A Farwell

~

Stephen Allen, 1/22/1880
Bowdoin colleague Allen wrote to Chamberlain about arranging a meeting with the governor of New York (see also letter from Allen to JLC, 1/20/1880).

Private
Niagara Falls
Jan 22 1880

My dear Sir

I expect to be in Boston on Monday and Tuesday next unless I am called to New Hampshire by a sick friend, of which I could telegraph you—of change of time. Could you not happen up there now? If I could introduce you to our Governor (a Maine boy) the speaker of the House and the Senate in a private way, at this time I am confident it would not hurt your future in the political field. We must not let the hour get cold again; now that they are hot. Please write me at Boston Box 56, on receipt of this and then I can telegraph you if need be I merely yours

Stephen Allen
Gen JL Chamberlain

Stephen Allen to JLC, 1/22/1880

Wainship Jan 22, 80
Pres. Chamberlain

Dear Sir

I take the liberty to serve you my congratulations upon the successful and admirable discharge of the different duties assigned to you by our late Gov. Garcelon.

The people of Maine are of one whole country have cause for holiday your services in grateful remembrance.

Republicans are often strangely oblivious of their obligation, and allow political partisanship to rule the town.

I hope we shall learn to act before it is too late.

I write in part to ask your favor so far as you may think proper in behalf of a friend of mine, a brother of Mrs. Allen.

Mr. Henry Sturdivant of Freeport desires employment under Mr. Richardson Supervisor of Census for several counties in Maine.

I suppose Mr. Richardson is a personal friend of yours, and perhaps a word from you may secure to Mr. Sturdivant a place in this service.

Mr. S. is an intelligent and active businessman honest and competent.

He can obtain abundant testimonials in Portland.

If you can committedly say to word in his favor to Mr. Richardson I shall deem it a personal favor.

I include a recommendation for Mr. S.

Please give such indorsement to it as you please and forward it to Mr. Sturdivant

Freeport Me
Yours truly
Stephen Allen

⌒

James S. Berry to JLC, 1/23/1880
A former Mainer inquires about Chamberlain's relationship with James G. Blaine.

Manchester N H
Jan 23rd 1880
Gen Chamberlain

Dear Sir
I take the liberty to write you a line to ascertain the truth of an assertion that has been made to me a number of times within a few days that is I have been told that you and J[ames] G. Blaine were not on speaking terms had not spoken to each other for 5 or 6 years and would not and would like to know whether it is so or not simply to satisfy myself and reply truthfully to such assertions. You may think me inquisitive the only apology I have to make is I am a Maine man born and lived there 40 years had the privalage of voting for you 4 times I think for Governor I have been here 10 years but have lost none of my interest in my native state I am proud of her and of her people but am sorrow and ashamed of the fusionists from the last 4 or 6 weeks.

If you will answer by return of mail you will oblig I [know] many thought at the time you ought to have been sent to the U.S. senate I was one of that number.

very respectfully yours
Jas S. Berry
Manchester N H

⌐⌐⌐⌐

John Pike to JLC, 1/23/1880
John Pike was Bowdoin, Class of 1836, Doctor of Divinity, 1866, and an overseer from 1863 to 1887.

Rowley [Mass.], Jan 23, 1880

My dear President—

I suppose you are now enjoying the quiet of your Brunswick home. I have followed your late course with great constancy and have much admired the management of your difficult position and the great success with which your efforts have been crowned. It seems to me that the well digested thought and the happy language of your State papers, the care to keep your own counsel, the discretion which anticipated every emergency, the freedom from party and feeling, the extreme courtesy to every man however unreasonable his opinions, the courage that could rise above the most embarrassing circumstances, the utter forgetfulness of yourself in your desire for the public good, and the willingness to retire from the public gaze, when the necessity for your presence was no longer felt, have gone beyond what your most appreciative friends could have expected of you, and will give you an enviable name in the roll of your country's history. The gratitude of the people of Maine and the sense of justice to their deliverer may say to you "go up higher" but the love and interest of those who have welcomed you to the college, and struggled to make your position there comfortable will be greatly increased to detain you as long as possible for the institution, which will gather to itself much honor from the various situations which you have thus far held so honorably to yourself and so safely and happily to others. Accept these, my sincere congratulations, and believe them to be the outflow of the suggestions to which your course has reasonably given rise and of the feelings which have a deep place in my heart.

I thank you for the catalogue you have sent me. Everything that concerns the college is a matter of great interest to me, and whatever I can do for the comfort of its officers, and the good of its students will be cheerfully done as long as I live.

I shall be glad to hear often of your welfare, and to welcome you to my own home, and hope for pleasant intercourse each year on the sacred spot of my youth, which loses more of its charms as my age increases.

Very truly yours,
John Pike

P.S. Since the above was written matters seem to have greatly changed, and I presume you are called again to a scene of confusion, and anticipated conflict. May God bless and keep you, and bring yourself and your associates safely and honorably through a scene so perplexing and dangerous.

J. P.

~

N. F. Maynard to JLC, 1/23/1880

Gen. Chamberlain
Brunswick Maine

Please reserve the congratulation of every honest Republican in KS for your Jackson firmness in standing by the right.

N. F. Maynard
Seneca
Nemahaw Co,
Kansas
Jan 23rd 1880

~

John Jay Pomeroy to JLC, 1/23/1880[15]
Pomeroy, the chaplain of one of the regiments under Chamberlain's command during the Civil War, sent Chamberlain his congratulations.

---

15 Harrisburg 1995.459.5.80

Rahway N. J.
Jan 23d 1880
Gen'l J. L. Chamberlain,

My dear General,
I can assure you your former chaplain has watched your recent course at your state capitol, with more than ordinary solicitude. I can assure you also, that you were remembered at the throne of grace. I had an appreciating sense of the difficult and delicate position you occupied, being in command of the military and at the same time being the practical expositor of Civil and judiciary law.

I feel profoundly thankful that you had wisdom and grace given you, to tide through those ugly days of attempted fraud the sacred rights of the people without an instance of violence or the shedding of a drop of blood. It is humiliating to state and national pride to have as a fact such an imbroglio in one of our New England states. It is a red light of warning that will be of benefit to us in the future. Maine has been in the eye of the nation for a few days. I hope the outcome of it will be to teach a lesson of righteousness to all people. Permit me to congratulate you on the wise, faithful discharge of the duties devolving on you in this emergency.

I have been pastor of the 1st Presbyterian Ch[urch]. of Rahway, N.J. for five years—I am but 19 miles fr. New York City by Penna. C.R.R. leading to Philad. When in New York I would be glad to have you come out and spend the night with me. My wife and children would be glad to form your acquaintance—I inclose you my photograph. If you have one of your own that you could send I would be obliged.

Fraternally yours,
John Jay Pomeroy
Late Chap. 198th Regt Pa. Vols.

~

Herbert Hill to JLC, 1/26/1880
Hill was secretary of the Middlesex Club, a social club for Republicans in Boston, Massachusetts.

Boston, Jan 26/80

My dear General:

We are all happy this morning. I send you 20 copies of the Herald containing a/c [account of] your splendid reception on Saturday in this city by the Middlesex Club. At your reception there were over one hundred gentlemen present of high social and business standing in Massachusetts. The governor of R. I. and N. H. honored you with their presence.

Governor Long of Mass sent a beautiful letter speaking in the highest terms of praise of Genl Chamberlain. The Gov. was called away to attend the funeral of one of our Mass Senators. Gen Rich and congressman Claffin sent very pretty letters indeed all of which I enclose to you with my best wishes. The Herald sent special train and distributed over 4000 of their papers through Maine. My sincerely

Herbert E. Hill
Sec. Mid[dlesex] Club
Maine
General Joshua L. Chamberlain

~~~

Robert Ellis to JLC, 1/26/1880
A native of Topsham, Maine, Ellis (Bowdoin, Class of 1879) was the county clerk and later district attorney of Oconto, Wisconsin.

Oconto, Wisconsin
Jan 26 1880
Joshua L. Chamberlain
Pres. Bowd. College
Brunswick, Me

Dear Sir;

Feeling, as I do, a deep interest in my native state, and in all connected with old Bowdoin, I trust you will pardon me if I take the liberty to express my earnest appreciation of your recent management of affairs of state and apply to you the words which once I had the pleasure to read under your instruction.

"Justum et tenacem propositi virum
Non civium ardor pravu jubentium,
Non vultus instantis tyranni

Mente quatif solida, regue Auster
Dux inquiti turbidus Hadrie
Nec fulmentis magna manus fovis."

Respectfully from
Robert Ellis

~~~~

Hiram K. Morrell to JLC, 1/27/1880[16]

Gardiner, Me., Jan 27 1880

Gen. Chamberlain—
Your note came to hand, and has done me a lot of good and I will give "50 for the privilege of using it with some of the bull-dozers that have almost torn the heart out of me, for the past week.

I do wish you could come up Thursday evening on the 8 o'clock train, if you could not on the 3 o'clock, and stay all night. I want you to give the editors of Maine a chance to see you personally and I think it would do you no harm; and as certain bloody shirt politicians are crowding me rather hard it would be a great pleasure to me.

It shall cost you nothing financially to come as I will most cheerfully pay your expenses,

Yours truly
H. K. Morrell

I have directed or requested Payson Lucker to send you a pass and he will doubtless do so; as he passes our members and ladies.

~~~~

George E. B. Jackson to JLC, 1/27/1880

George E. B. Jackson was president of the Maine Central Railroad (see letter of 1/20/1880).

---

16 Harrisburg 1995.459.5.79

Portland, Me., Jan 27 1880

My dear sir,
My friend E. B. Phillips, President of the Eastern R. R. has sent me the
enclosed, in reply to my suggestion to him that you would be glad to know
that railroads are not ungrateful even if Republicans are.

I have no doubt that you will find it useful.

I am,
yours truly
Jackson
Gen. J. L. Chamberlain
Brunswick

~⟩

H. K. Morrell to JLC, 1/28/1880

Gardiner, Me., Jan 28 1880
Gen. J. L. Chamberlain—
Brunswick

Dear Sir—After I went to bed last night, Mrs. Morrell called my attention
to your letter, in which you say you would be happy to come to our house,
but it is impossible. I had not noticed that. I remembered that in a former
letter you said you must be in New York, but as you had been away and got
home, I concluded you had mistaken the date of our meeting in your first
letter and had been to New York and back.

I write this lest you may think it strange that I should have written you
as I did last night. If anything should happen so you can come it will give
us the quoted pleasure.

~⟩

M. S. Cummings to JLC, 1/29/1880

177 Calumet Dr. Jan 29/80

My Dear Cousin

I feel greatly interested in the recent outbreak in the political circles of Maine and am so proud of and thankful for the stand you have taken that I cannot remain silent to you personally. I want to express to you the thanks of thousands of Chicago citizens. Your name is not only in the public press but in social circles. The good and the true are thanking God for your integrity to the right. My daughter now living in Detroit Mich. writes me "I like the ring of that man (Gen Chamberlain) he has the character Heroes are made of."

I do not hear from my friend in Boston had hoped to see Lydia and Aunt Nancy this month as she wrote me in the fall she was going to Washington this winter. Neither do I hear from my friends in Maine but I have a picture on my table of your mother. It speaks to me and brings up old associations that no other picture does.

I look and say to myself shall I ever see her again in this world—I fear not, but in that Mansion our savior went to prepare for those no care him I do hope to meet her. With much love to yourself and family I remain your friend.

M. S. Cummings

~

Wellington Newell to JLC, 1/29/1880
Rev. Wellington Newell, a Methodist Episcopal minister, was a classmate of Chamberlain at the Bangor Theological Seminary (Class of 1855), though twelve years his senior. He was a minister in Brewer, Maine, from 1862–69 and in Greenfield, Massachusetts, from 1877–86.

Greenfield, Mass.
Jan. 29th 1880
To Gen. J. L. Chamberlain:

My Dear Brother,
Not being present at Augusta, to join in three hearty cheers for you, please permit me, in this more quiet manner, to express my admiration for the coolness, fairness, wisdom, and urbanity with which, so successfully, the duties of your most trying position at the capitol of the state were performed.

Yours Truly—
W. NewellCummings

~~~

Isaac Holden Stearns to JLC, 1/30/1880
Stearns was chaplain of the 22nd Massachusetts Regiment, which was part of a different brigade but the same division of the 5th Corps as the 20th Maine.

Jan 30th 1880
J. L. Chamberlain

My Dear General,
Enclosed I hand you a scrap I furnished A. H. Paul Paper.
I hope the people of Maine will have the good sense and <u>patriotism</u> to send you to the U.S. Senate when Mr. Hamlin's term expires.

Yours truly
I. H. Stearns
Late surgeon 22d Mass and National Home

~~~

Sam S. Gardner to JLC, 1/30/1880
Samuel Spring Gardiner was Bowdoin, Class of 1858, and a close friend of the Chamberlain family.

Washington, D.C.
Jan. 30. 1880

Dear Friend,
Please accept my congratulations upon the grand chorus of approbation which your conduct of affairs at Augusta has evoked, and I am most cordially one of it.

With the old esteem and affection
Sam S. Gardner
Hon J. L. Chamberlain
Brunswick, Me

~~~⌒

Maud to JLC, 2/nd/1880
A postcard sent to Chamberlain signed only by "Maud."

God bless you! He <u>has;</u> since he has blessed Our Country <u>in</u> you and restored all men's faith in our Republic!
"Oh for a <u>Man</u> with heart head, hand;
One still, strong will in a blatant land, that <u>can rule</u> and <u>does not Lie</u>!"

Jan 1880
<u>Maud.</u>

~~~⌒

Dr. Ferris Jacobs to JLC, 2/1/1880
Jacobs was a lieutenant colonel of the 26th New York Cavalry during the Civil War and brevet brigadier general. He was a delegate to the Republican National Convention in 1880 and was elected to the U.S. Congress in 1881.

<u>Delhi.</u> [New York] <u>Feb 1st 80</u>

Please excuse the card? Would like—Back.<u>th</u> last one Catg—[catalogue] or any other thing of your college sermons or what-not? We know some of you. Have him Blaine-Chamberlain-Davis etc—
We love that brave corps—that stood for the right—on the day of trial—success to you—send me Maine papers.

Address
Dr. F. Jacobs M. D.
Delhi, N.Y.
<u>ansd</u>

~~~⌒

Brig. Gen. Milo S. Sherman to JLC, 2/2/1880
Milo was a brigadier general of the Iowa National Guard.

Fredericksburg, Chickasaw Co., Iowa, Feb 2nd 1880
Maj. Gen. J. L. Chamberlain
Augusta Me.

Dear Gen:
Excuse my cunning boldness on my part in addressing you on a matter which is watched with eager interest by all our people and especially by all old soldiers throughout the country.

We, as soldiers, feel that you and your men have proved yourself more than a match for those who have attempted to plunge your state into ruin and trample underfoot the choicest liberties of a free people.

Allow us as Iowa soldiers, to congratulate you heartily on the result of your efforts in bringing order out of confusion and in so curiously protecting the property and interests of your people at so critical a period in the history of your Commonwealth

Cordially Your Comrade
Milo S. Sherman
Brig. Gen. comd 2nd Brig I. N. G.

James T. Davidson to JLC, 2/8/1880
James Thomas Davidson, was born in Oxford, Ohio, attended Wabash College for two years, and graduated from Bowdoin College in the Class of 1878. In fall 1880, he was elected county attorney for Tippecanoe County, Indiana.

ansd
Lafayette, Ind Feb 8th '80

The action of Gen J. L. C. in the "Maine Embroilment" is not only endorsed but warmly affirmed by the people at large throughout this section of the country. Resp'ly etc

Jas. T. Davidson

~~~)

Mark T. Berry to JLC, 2/16/1880
Berry was a cavalry veteran from the Civil War and in the lumber business in Minnesota.

Minneapolis Minn. Feb 16th 1880
Gen J. L. Chamberlain

Dear Genl
It gave me great hopes on the 1st of Jan when the dispatch came that you had qualified as Maj[or] Gen[eral] for I could see that there was hopes of your being able to hold in check the movements and orders of Gov Garcelon before the 7th and of Smith and the rest of the villains after that and you proved to be the right man in the right place, and I feel that the <u>white</u> people of Maine should ever feel grateful to you for the course that you pursued and thereby delivered them from the handle of the communist.

And I a Mainite thank you and the officers and men under your command for your faithfulness to the cause of liberty and right, and I hope that Maine will inscribe it upon her banner with the part you took in receiving the surrender of Gen Lee.

Fraternally yours
Mark T. Berry

~~~)

JLC to John L. M. Willis, 12/18/1882
Chamberlain was frequently invited to speak to groups of all types during his postwar years. This letter to the United Order of the Golden Cross sheds some light on the arrangements made for these speeches. The order was founded by Dr. J. H. Morgan in New England in 1876 as a temperance organization. Willis was a prominent physician who served as an assistant surgeon in the Maine State Militia under Chamberlain.

Brunswick, Dec. 18th, 1882.
John L. M. Willis, K.R., U.O.G.C.

My dear sir;—

Just as it happens now, I could come to Eliot either on the 26th, or 28th. December.

And if I could take that time, I could better afford a less pecuniary return than if I had to make a journey expressly for that lecture.

I am to be in York the 27th.

Perhaps $25. would do in these circumstances.

There might be some other time later when I could come for the same, but I can't be sure of it now.

Respectfully yours,
Joshua L. Chamberlain

~

John W. Burnett to JLC, 1/21/1895

A former sergeant in one of the Pennsylvania regiments that had been under Chamberlain's command in the Civil War wrote of his desire to see him again.

73 Maple St. Waltham, Mass. Jan 21 1895
Major General, Joshua L. Chamberlain
Brunswick Me.

Esteemed Commander:

I trust you may forgive me for this intrusion on your valuable time if such it proves to be, and also overlook what might by some be construed as nothing but vanity.

I have been a house-bound invalid approximately four years, ever since we had hoped to be enabled to look once more on your dear, patient, suffering face, i.e. when arrangements had been perfected for the delivery by you, dear Comrade, of a lecture under the auspices of Post 29, G.A.R. Dec 13. 1890. When the time and place had been settled upon, the impression was strongly made on my mind, "that I would never have the pleasure of beholding your dear face again." I was laid low by a terrible attack of pleura pneumonia, in the early part of Dec '90 but before the arrival of the date of your proposed lecture, my physician Dr. J.Q. A. McCollester tried to rouse me for my condition, by the promise that he would endeavor to effect a meeting on the Sabbath succeeding the proposed lecture; He knew how I yearned to behold you once more and perhaps he only tried to keep me alive by the bright prospect held out. The night of the proposed lecture arrived, and the Sabbath succeeding passed with no allusion to the matter and later I learned that your cup of suffering was also increased, and that you were the victim of pneumonia. How my heart went out to you in sympathy then, although so low with the same disease. I have never rallied much since that dread winter, I see few visitors, get comparatively few letters from old comrades, but very few hours of any day pass by that my mind does not go out toward you, knowing that you must be occupied with business cares and more congenial occupations. I have until now refrained from wearying you with the perusal of such letters, as I inflict on those whom "memory holds dear." Should you have the time, and feel the desire, I would esteem it a great favor to have just a line at your convenience. I would like to ask dear Sir, if you were in command of the 1st Brigade, 1st Div, 5th Corps on February 6th and 7th 1865 at Dabneys Mill on Hatchers Run, Va? An affirmative reply will induce further particulars, which otherwise I will not intrude on you. With hope that you are as comfortable as possible, and then wish that you may be spared to us many long years. I remain as ever your faithful friend.

John W. Burnett.
Serg't Co "M" 198th Pa. vol
Inf 3d Lient 4th Regt Penna Reserves

The Twilight Years

Despite the effects of his Petersburg wound and recurring bouts of malaria, Chamberlain survived well into the twentieth century. This was not the case with all of those closest to him. In August 1896, his brother Tom, the last surviving sibling, died of heart and lung failure complicated by a history of alcohol abuse. Then on October 18, 1905, Fannie passed away after a long illness that had taken her eyesight. In the spring of 1900, Chamberlain accepted an appointment as the Surveyor of the Port of Portland. He bought a home there and commuted the twenty-odd miles back to Brunswick when he could.

JLC typed letter, nd/1905

Chamberlain wrote this letter to an unknown recipient shortly after the death of his wife, Fannie. Mrs. Farrington was his sister, Sae. In 1901, Chamberlain visited Greece and Rome and took ill, retreating to Egypt under a doctor's advice in hopes that the dry climate would aid in his recovery.

I was much moved in hearing through my sister that on the news of the death of Mrs. Chamberlain, Mary Dunn, an Irish girl, neighbor of Mrs. Farrington, an earnest Catholic, ran in to her house strongly expressing her sorrow and sympathy, saying that she would go at once to the church and set up a candle, that all might pray for the rest of the soul of the departed one.

She added that while I was reported seriously ill in Egypt four years ago, candles were burning for me and prayers sent up in her church all the time until they knew I was out of danger.

I was much touched at this. Surely there is some efficacy in such prayers and some good in such religion. At all events, the incident will make me very friendly to those people, and value their prayers.

MS clip attached:

+ bring some of the dear little ones.

Your dearest letter from Upper Egypt yesterday.

The Passing of a Hero

During the last decade of his life, Chamberlain continued to oblige the many groups and publications that invited him to speak or write about wartime experiences. With other veterans he made pilgrimages to the old battlefields to recall the scenes of wartime sadness and triumphs. In May 1913, he traveled to Gettysburg to attend the last major planning meeting for the Fiftieth Anniversary of the battle. The trip greatly taxed his health, so much so that he had not recovered by July and was unable to attend the reunion. His health, in fact, never returned, and he slowly declined until he finally passed in late February 1914. Technically it was pneumonia that caused his death, but his trip to Gettysburg, coupled with yet another infection resulting from the old Petersburg wound fifty years earlier, likely contributed as well.

An elaborate funeral procession passed through Portland, then traveled by train to Brunswick, where he was laid to rest in the family plot at the Pine Grove Cemetery, adjacent to the Bowdoin campus.

~~~~~

Unk. to Daisy, 3/24/1914
Letter to Daisy from an admirer of her father. It reveals that she had plans to publish his biography.

Brewer, Maine, March 24, 1914

Dear Mrs. Allen:

I am returning the letter promptly, having seen nothing to suppress and only some minor points to alter. You will hardly notice the differences. Use any part of it you wish, and in any way you wish. I remembered nothing of it save that I wrote it on the gallop. At such times my machine skips letters and makes me guilty of atrocious blunders in spelling. It was that and possible grammatical errors, (one of which I found), which made me think it wise to look over the original.

I have copied off, rather than corrected, the letter you returned, that you might have a clean copy from which to take whatever you wished. This will insure the printer or copyist understanding any marks you put on it.

I see now that this letter, wholly spontaneous and by me forgotten, must have pleased your father. Considering the outcomes, I am glad it was possible for me to offer this little tribute to him, though in my own mind at the time there was nothing beyond encouraging him, so soon as he should be able to, take up the easy part of this task and carry on a little nearer to completion the work which I so greatly desired that he should finish himself.

I understood Mrs. Farrington, speaking over the phone, that General Schaff was to go on with the work. I may have misunderstood her; but I hope not, for no one so well qualified could have been found. It would be a labor of love to him I am sure. Your father was so pleased by General Schaff's tribute in the Atlantic some two years ago. I remember that I carried it up to Mrs. F's to show it to him and he read it aloud to the family assembled.

I am so glad to know that you are prepared to push this matter of the biography. It was not my place to offer advice, but I feared it might be delayed. Time counts for much now, and you are fortunate in having a publisher already committed to the work and anxious to forward it.

Please tell the biographer of your father one important thing; that your father's name was not originally Joshua Lawrence, but Lawrence (whether with or without the J I do not recollect). Once he got down the old family bible at Mrs. F's, and showed me the entry, telling me, in answer to my question, that his father so much admired Capt. Lawrence of the Chesapeake that he wished to name a son for the man who said "Don't give up the ship!" Little did Capt. Lawrence dream that his dying words just half an hundred years after were to save the nation at Little Round Top, when, but for the memory of them ingrained into the boy who bore his name, (humanly speaking) the nation would have been lost. This is one of the coincidences which any biographer would be glad to have shown him.

Another most important matter is that it be shown how that great fight at Little Round Top turned almost more upon your father's character than upon his generalship. I had the facts from himself, not in casual conversation, but in the course of a full half day of study of his Gettysburg manuscripts a year ago last January. I asked questions and he answered, and I know that I am speaking correctly. He won his position at Little Round Top by using mutineers. And he used them because he was a just man, who understood men and whom men could trust. He told me himself that he was guarding a hundred and fifty mutineers and that he gave them arms and told them that if they would fight, he would do what he could for them later. I can give the details if they are desired. But what no biographers is likely to be able to know, as I know it, is that he kept his word and to an extent which astonished me.

I think I wrote you that I was due to speak at a mass meeting in City Hall,— if I could hold my head up long enough to do it,— the day I wrote it. After a very ill day, in which I was unable to taste anything or to sit up, I went to the Hall, as I said, and spoke upon the Library matter and upon changing its name to the Joshua Lawrence Chamberlain Memorial. And I told them this story of the mutineers—news to them, unless the older ones, and dramatically interesting, for the men were from Bangor, and not so very much to blame. But we reached the climax when I told them how the promise was kept. I had with me the Maine Adjutant General's report for 1863, and read them the official account of the engagement, and then I told them that he never told me the name of the regiment and, not being quite sure of the number, whether it was 150 or 120 men he had to guard, I turned to that book to look up the records of the Maine regiments that 1863 year. I was quite sure that I should find against every man's name his record and that ugly mark holding there for fifty years. But though I looked it through page by page, from one end to the other, I found no Maine Regiment of mutineers. Your father had not only "done what he could", but what seemed almost impossible,— he had prevented it ever becoming a matter of record, so that there must be many families in this vicinity who have great cause to be grateful to him.

It is big, the biggest story on record— with 358 men, almost half of them mutineers, to fight back a whole brigade and then, with the last round of cartridges gone, to overcome the enemy and take twice their own numbers in prisoners (after the dead and wounded were counted out); to save the whole wing of the union Army from being crumpled up and its flank turned, with such a little handful of unarmed men, it stands out alone in history. Others fought great odds; but they died on the field—Thermopylae, the Alamo, Sir Richard Grenville, many more. Only John Paul Jones and your father stand for winning splendid victory out of a foregone defeat.

Acknowledgements

The National Civil War Museum would like to thank the City of Harrisburg and Former Mayor Stephen Reed for his vision in creating the NCWM and his efforts in acquiring an outstanding collection, which will benefit generations to come. Without his dedication and enthusiasm for preserving history, the NCWM would not be able to provide access to such rich material.

The NCWM would like to thank all of those involved in making this project a reality, most notably the NCWM Publishing Committee, with particular thanks to Dr. Mary A. DeCredico of the U.S. Naval Academy; Randall Grespin and J. Robert Hanlon, Jr., Esq., of the Board of Trustees; and Wayne Motts of the Adams County Historical Society. Special thanks also are offered to editor Tom Desjardin for his willingness to utilize his knowledge and expertise in editing this publication, and to esteemed historian James McPherson for composing the foreword and lending his support to this project.

Appreciation is extended to the following institutions for providing supporting images and materials: Bowdoin College; Brewer Historical Society; Pejepscot Historical Society; and Radcliffe Institute for Advanced Study at Harvard University.

Finally, the NCWM acknowledges Kelli Christiansen, John Tintera, and the team at Osprey Publishing for their unflagging support and management of this project.

Index

INDEX

INDEX